Violence in Homes and Communities

D1056278

Issues in Children's and Families' Lives

AN ANNUAL BOOK SERIES

Senior Series Editor

Thomas P. Gullotta, *Child and Family Agency of Southeastern Connecticut*

Editors

Gerald R. Adams, *University of Guelph, Ontario, Canada*

Bruce A. Ryan, *University of Guelph, Ontario, Canada*

Robert L. Hampton, *University of Maryland, College Park*

Roger P. Weissberg, *University of Illinois at Chicago, Illinois*

Drawing upon the resources of the Child and Family Agency of Southeastern Connecticut, one of this nation's leading family service agencies, **Issues in Children's and Families' Lives** is designed to focus attention on the pressing social problems facing children and their families today. Each volume in this series will analyze, integrate, and critique the clinical and research literature on children and their families as it relates to a particular theme. Believing that integrated multidisciplinary approaches offer greater opportunities for program success, volume contributors will reflect the research and clinical knowledge base of the many different disciplines that are committed to enhancing the physical, social, and emotional health of children and their families. Intended for graduate and professional audiences, chapters will be written by scholars and practitioners who will encourage readers to apply their practice skills and intellect to reducing the suffering of children and their families in the society in which those families live and work.

Violence in Homes and Communities

Prevention, Intervention, and Treatment

Editors
Thomas P. Gullotta
Sandra J. McElhaney

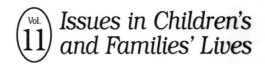

Vol. 11 *Issues in Children's and Families' Lives*

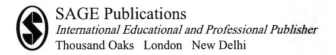

SAGE Publications
International Educational and Professional Publisher
Thousand Oaks   London   New Delhi

For information:

SAGE Publications, Inc.
2455 Teller Road
Thousand Oaks, California 91320
E-mail: order@sagepub.com

SAGE Publications Ltd.
6 Bonhill Street
London EC2A 4PU
United Kingdom

SAGE Publications India Pvt. Ltd.
M-32 Market
Greater Kailash I
New Delhi 110 048 India

Printed in the United States of America

Library of Congress Cataloging-in-Publication Data

Main entry under title:

Violence in homes and communities: Prevention, intervention, and treatment / edited by Thomas P. Gullotta and Sandra J. McElhaney.
    p. cm.— (Issues in children's and families' lives ; v. 11)
    Includes bibliographical references and index.
    ISBN 0-7619-1003-4 (cloth : acid-free paper)
    ISBN 0-7619-1004-2 (pbk. : acid-free paper)
    1. Family violence—United States—Prevention. 2. Spouse abuse—United States—Prevention. 3. Child abuse—United States—Prevention.
4. Violence—United States—Prevention. 5. Abused wives—Services for—United States. 6. Abused children—Services for—United States.
I. Gullotta, Thomas P. II. McElhaney, Sandra J. III. Series.
    HV6626.2 .V57 1999
    362.82′927′0973—dc21   98-51237

    01 02 03 04 05 7 6 5 4 3 2

Acquiring Editor: C. Deborah Laughton
Editorial Assistant: Eileen Carr
Production Editor: Astrid Virding
Editorial Assistant: Nevair Kabakian
Typesetter: Marion Warren

Contents

Violence: Understandings and Preventive Interventions

For nearly one hundred years the *National Mental Health Association* has served as a vehicle for bringing together scholars, practitioners, and consumers to address those problems that cause individuals and families emotional pain and suffering. Thus, it is appropriate that this volume addresses the subject of community violence. Across the 11 chapters that make up this volume, the reader will be introduced to the principal understandings and research that try to make sense of child abuse, domestic violence, and community violence. Further, the reader will explore, with the talented authors who wrote this book, methods to reduce the incidence of violent behavior toward children, spouses, in the workplace, and in our communities.

Acts of violence are not uncommon. While, as a society, we espouse peaceful solutions to disagreements, tolerance to those unlike ourselves, and kindness to loved ones and others, these words are but whispers in the night. Much louder and more shrill are the disturbing sounds of children crying, fists upon the flesh of spouses, gunfire in the workplace and in our neighborhoods. To gain a better appreciation of this subject, this book is organized into three sections.

The first section provides a foundational overview of child, spousal, workplace, and community violence. In the first chapter, Kotch, Muller, and Blakely examine child abuse and neglect from an ecological perspective. They discuss the individual, family, community, and cultural factors that contribute to child abuse. Significantly, the authors give attention to those qualities that place some children at higher risk of abuse. The chapter concludes with an examination of prevention and treatment interventions. Next, Hampton, Vandergriff-Avery, and Kim explore the causes of spousal violence from a historical time when wife beating was acceptable in North America to the present. Using several different theoretical perspectives, the authors provide an overview of the origins, consequences, and interventions possible to reduce the incidence of this behavior. The third chapter in this section focuses on violence in the workplace. McClure's overview covers definitional, demographic, and theoretical perspectives. The chapter concludes with a discussion of the approaches currently in use to reduce workplace violence. This section concludes with a discussion of violence in the community. Potter uses the public health model to define the problem, identify its causes, and describe promising interventions for reducing violent behavior.

With this background, the second section examines three special topics. In Chapter 5, Jason, Hanaway, and Brackshaw review the long-standing research on the powerful influence television exerts on youth and then discuss approaches to moderating this influence. Chapter 6, by Winborne and Cohen, discusses stereotypes and their relationship to racial, ethnic, and religious hatred and violence. In Chapter 7, the issue of stereotypes is revisited. This time the subject matter is mental illness and violence. Faenza, Glover, Hutchings, and Radack challenge understandings that the mentally ill are inevitably violent. Rather, their search of the literature reveals that the mentally ill are more often victims than aggressors.

The third section of this volume discusses efforts to reduce violent behavior in families, among youth, and in communities. Flannery and Williams review the literature identifying the most promising approaches for reducing youth violence. In Chapter 9, Jenkins and Davidson search the domestic violence program literature to form recommendations for policy and model programs. McElhaney and Effley follow this discussion with an examination of community-based approaches to violence prevention. In addition to identifying three promising approaches, these authors provide a useful framework for the design of community interventions. In the epilogue, Faenza and McElhaney identify reoccurring themes and make several recommendations for reducing violence in families, the workplace, and in communities.

This *National Mental Health Association* sponsored book is intended for graduate students and practitioners wanting a comprehensive overview of the origins of violent behavior. It is for program developers wishing to identify programs that appear to reduce violence in families, among youth, in the workplace, and in the community. Finally, it can be used by policymakers to craft new legislation to reduce the incidence of violent behavior, for the editors of this book long for the day when peaceful solutions to disagreements, tolerance for those unlike ourselves, and kindness to all are no longer whispers in the night.

Acknowledgments

We would like to acknowledge Kathi Barr-Chapa, Clare Miller, and Gwen Dixon for their help with the index and the continued support of Mike Faenza, President of the National Mental Health Association.

—THOMAS P. GULLOTTA
Child and Family Agency

—SANDRA J. MCELHANEY
National Mental Health Association

*To my two beautiful sons, Ian Joseph
and Logan Griffith with the hopes that the
information contained in the book will make
a difference and that they can grow up
in a nation of peace.*

Your mother,

Sandy McElhaney

CHAPTER 1

Understanding the Origins and Incidence of Child Maltreatment

JONATHAN B. KOTCH

GREG O. MULLER

CRAIG H. BLAKELY

Over the past generation there has been increasing interest among social scientists and public health practitioners with regard to family violence generally, and child maltreatment in particular. We have witnessed an increasing interest in identifying the factors associated with child maltreatment. In this chapter we review the literature on maltreating families from an ecological perspective. The first section of the chapter focuses on the etiology of maltreatment, while the latter section focuses on the incidence, consequences, and prevention of maltreatment and maltreatment interventions.

Definition

One of the difficulties in reviewing the etiology of child abuse and neglect lies in the wide variation in the way these terms are used. Throughout the literature, the terms researchers use to refer to specific types of maltreatment (sexual abuse, physical abuse, psychological abuse, emotional abuse, neglect, dependency, etc.) are often used interchangeably. This creates conceptual challenges in the collection of data and analysis and interpretation of findings.

This lack of conceptual precision is not simply the result of researchers' different theoretical backgrounds, but is a product of the complex nature of the phenomenon under study. Behavior that constitutes maltreatment for some (e.g., researchers and practitioners) may not for others (e.g., judges and laypersons). Similarly, the context within which the specified behavior is performed often determines whether the behavior is maltreatment or not.

Child abuse and neglect may be defined within the legal sphere as acts of omission or commission resulting in physical or mental harm (i.e., injury) to a child less than 18 years of age. Less narrow definitions have been adopted by researchers of child abuse and neglect, defining it as "any act of omission or commission which deprives a child of equal rights, liberty, or interferes with his/her development" (Gil, 1975). "Sexual abuse involves any sexual activity with a child where consent is not or cannot be given (Finkelhor, 1979). This includes sexual contact that is accomplished by force or threat of force, regardless of the age of the participants, and all sexual contact between an adult and a child, regardless of whether there is deception or the child understands the sexual nature of the activity" (Berliner & Elliot, 1996).

In this chapter we shall broadly consider the literature on child maltreatment. Where possible, we will draw implications from the literature separately for different types of child abuse and neglect.

The problem of definition is not limited to the concepts of child abuse and neglect. While mention is often made of the challenges of defining child abuse and neglect, equally important and daunting is the task of defining the hypothesized correlates of maltreatment. For example, low self-esteem has been found in some studies, though not others, to be a significant predictor of maltreatment. Within the field of social psychology there has been much concern about how to conceptualize self-esteem (Smelser, 1989; Wylie, 1979). Some argue that it is a global aspect of the self, while others argue that it is a multidimensional construct. It could be that the inconsistencies of findings on the link between self-esteem and maltreatment are due in part to discrepancies in how this variable is defined and measured. Family provides another example. There are many ways family can be conceptualized (Weis, 1989). Accurately defining the family and relationships within the family has become all the more important to consider and clarify given recent social trends affecting family patterns, such as divorce, remarriage, and cohabitation.

In addition to problems of definition, there are a host of methodological problems associated with many of the studies of child abuse and neglect. Most have been of small clinical samples that have not been randomly selected from the population, and have lacked adequate control groups necessary to make valid comparisons between abused/abusers and nonabused/nonabusers. Similarly, there have been a limited number of longitudinal prospective studies. While our review of the literature will consider retrospective studies, where we can, we will focus on longitudinal research.

Etiology

The etiology of child maltreatment has been approached through diverse theoretical frameworks that have employed a broad range of methodological orientations. Explanations of child maltreatment have included theories relating to biology, environmental conditions, stress, patterns of deviance, family violence, social learning, and attachment. While it is generally acknowledged that different types of maltreatment have different explanatory factors, there is also general agreement that there is much overlap. Different theories address different questions (e.g., why individuals initiate child maltreatment vs. why individuals continue to maltreat) or focus on different explanatory factors (child development vs. neighborhood breakdown). It is generally accepted that these widely varying theories, rather than competing, contribute to an integrated approach to explaining child maltreatment.

Such a multifocused approach (Bronfenbrenner, 1979) considers how the development of specified characteristics of families and individuals influence and are influenced by broader, macro-level social forces (e.g., neighborhood, community, culture). These ecological influences are often conceptualized in terms of risk and protective factors. This perspective recognizes that some children and adults are at greater risk than others for maltreating, or being maltreated, by virtue of myriad factors at the individual, family, community, and broader environment levels. From this perspective the presence or absence of certain circumstances, traits, and/or behaviors determines the likelihood that an individual will be maltreated or will instigate maltreatment. The cumulative balance of risk and protective factors represents the predictive equation for maltreatment. For example, an infant that would otherwise be at higher risk of being maltreated by her parent as a function of being born prematurely or having a disability, may be at lower risk because her family has a supportive kinship network and neighborhood.

Individual Level

Personality

To the casual observer, the notion that someone would have to be "crazy" to treat a child in the horrific ways reported regularly in the media seems self-evident. Similarly, early research of child abuse and neglect hypothesized that maltreatment was the result of mental illness or personality deficits (Steele & Pollock, 1968). Despite the intuitive appeal of this proposition to laypersons and researchers alike, the research to date has not established a clear causal link between identified psychotic disorders and maltreatment (Melnick & Hurley, 1969; Polansky, Chalmers, Williams, & Buttenweiser, 1981). Among the personality factors that have been hypothesized to contribute to child maltreatment are low self-esteem, poor impulse control, depressive affect, anxiety, and antisocial behavior. While some support is found for the influence of these factors on child maltreatment, there are other studies that find no effects (for reviews see Baumrind, 1992; Belsky, 1993).

Yet, while psychiatric disorders have not been directly and consistently linked to maltreatment, personality and psychiatric disorders may play a role in the onset, continuance, and outcomes of child maltreatment. One way in which personality factors appear to be related to maltreatment is in the disruption of social relations. Depression, anxiety, and antisocial behavior have been shown to be disruptive to social relations, to increase social isolation, and to contribute to social support inadequacies (Crittenden, 1985; Wolfe, 1985). Maltreating parents are more likely to show signs of depression (Lahey, Conger, Atkeson, & Treiber, 1984; Wolfe, 1985), explosiveness, and irritability than nonmaltreating parents (Caspi & Elder, 1988; Patterson, DeBaryshe, & Ramsey, 1989). Although research has not identified the specific mechanisms that link particular psychiatric disorders to maltreatment in various contexts, the association has been observed often enough to merit further research.

Cognitions, Attributions, and Attitudes

The normative expectations of caretakers about child development processes are a factor that has been shown to play a role in child maltreatment (Holden, Willis, & Corcoran, 1992; Zuravin, 1987). Some studies have found that parents with limited understanding of child development are more likely to abuse their child (Disbrow, Doerr, & Caufield, 1977; Spinetta & Rigler, 1972). One recent study employing a longitudinal design looked at the maternal and child factors that place adolescent mothers at risk for abusing their children (Dukewich, Borkowski, & Whitman, 1996). Findings indicate that preparation for parenting (measured as knowledge and attitudes about children's development) was the strongest predictor of abuse potential. This same study found that a mother's psychological predisposition for aggressive coping mediates the effects of knowledge and attitudes about child development on the risks for abuse. However, other studies find no association between knowledge and attitudes about child development and maltreatment (Starr, 1982).

Research exploring the link between attitudes of mothers prior to the birth of their children and subsequent maltreatment indicates that mothers who have negative attitudes about unwanted or unplanned pregnancy are more likely to maltreat their children (Egeland & Brunnquell, 1979; Murphy, Orkow, & Nicola, 1985; Zuravin, 1987). Studies have also shown that maltreating parents sometimes perceive their children as less intelligent, more disobedient, and more aggressive than nonabusing parents, although other research finds no difference between abusing and nonabusing parents on this factor (Mash, Johnston, & Kovitz, 1983; Reid, Kavanaugh, & Baldwin, 1987).

Child Characteristics

The abused child's own characteristics and behavior may be a factor that evokes maltreating responses from parents and other caretakers. For instance, some studies indicate that health problems early in life may predispose certain children to greater risk for maltreatment. Several studies have found that premature and low-birth weight infants, as well as infants that have a handicap or illness, are more likely to be maltreated (Belsky, 1980; Lynch & Roberts, 1982; McCabe, 1984). In addition, it has been suggested that children who have cognitive or psychological deficiencies may also be at greater risk for sexual abuse (Tharinger, Horton, & Millea, 1990). A recent report by the National Center on Child Abuse and Neglect indicated that the incidence of sexual abuse among children who have a disability is nearly double the rate of children who have no disabilities (Panel, 1993).

Some studies, however, have found that children with disabilities are no more likely to be maltreated than those with no disabilities. A recent study by Ammerman and Patz (1996) examined the contributions of child and parental factors related to abuse potential in 132 mothers of young children with and without disabilities. These researchers found that children with disabilities were, once other child and parent variables were accounted for, at no greater risk for maltreatment than children without disabilities (Ammerman & Patz, 1996). These findings are consistent with earlier research that failed to find an association between the child's medical, intellectual, or developmental aberrations and child maltreatment (Ammerman, 1990a, 1990b, 1991).

While health-related problems may not directly influence the risk for child maltreatment, there is good reason to believe that illness and disabilities do influence the contexts and conditions that have been shown to be associated with child abuse and neglect. Health problems may impact the family by increasing the financial and emotional stress associated with caretaking responsibilities, disrupting the family, and interfering with parental monitoring and other family management practices. The proposition that health problems exacerbate the more proximate correlates of child maltreatment gains some support in research findings that suggest that mothers with low-birth weight infants were more likely to report higher levels of anxiety and other stress-related phenomena.

The debate about whether child factors are most accurately thought of as antecedents or consequences of child maltreatment continues. Explanations stressing the former have been characterized as victim blaming. Disagreements over this issue will likely continue until further research can disentangle the myriad relationships associated with child characteristics. Some research indicates that child characteristics may be less important in the initiation of child maltreatment and more important in explaining the continuation of abuse (Ammerman, 1991; Wolfe, 1985). A number of studies indicate that the maltreated child is more likely to be physically and verbally aggressive (Starr, 1988), exhibiting behavior that could explain the continuance of maltreatment.

Children with difficult temperaments (e.g., irritability and fussiness), aggressive behavior, and otherwise deviant behaviors and emotions have been thought to be at greater risk for maltreatment (Belsky & Vondra, 1989; Gil, 1970; Parke & Collmer, 1975). The stress caused by a child with a difficult temperament can interfere with the development and maintenance of secure attachments between child and parent, and may impact negatively on the effectiveness of parenting practices and more generally disrupt parent-child relations (Cicchetti, 1990; Webster-Stratton, 1990). Yet studies that have considered the influence of temperament on child maltreatment have largely relied on retrospective designs based on parent reports of child behavior. As a result, it is unclear whether difficult temperament is a cause or a consequence of maltreatment (Ammerman, 1991; Pianta, Egeland, & Erickson, 1989; Vaughn, Deinard, & Egeland, 1980).

Family Level

Families provide the most important and enduring context for individual development. The disruption of various process and structure elements of the family are associated with increased risk for maltreatment. One such aspect of family life that has received considerable attention in the literature has been the way conflict and violence pervade the relationships within abusive homes.

Families at high risk for child maltreatment are often those with recurrent intrafamilial and extrafamilial conflict and violence. At least one observer has characterized the climate of such families as reflecting "a culture of violence" (Eisenberg, 1981). High levels of conflict and a general tolerance for intersibling violence often characterize parent-child relationships within families at high risk for child maltreatment. In these families, abusive parents and their children display violent and coercive behavior toward one another, and there is decreased cohesion (Azar & Wolfe, 1989; Eisenberg,

1981; Patterson et al., 1989; Straus, 1980). Also, maltreating families tend to have increased rates of marital violence and partner abuse (Fantuzzo et al., 1991; Salzinger, Felkman, Hammer, & Rosario, 1991; Straus, 1983; Straus, Gelles, & Steinmetz, 1980).

Family relationships that are violent and rely on a high degree of coercive control can weaken social ties and increase isolation of family members. Family patterns that foster isolation and limited social contacts are also linked to maltreatment (Garbarino, 1987; Garbarino & Eckenrode, 1997; Polansky et al., 1981). Furthermore, the absence of support and contact with other nonabusing families, which may provide a monitoring and modeling function, is thought to be an important risk factor.

Similar family patterns have been observed for families that are at high risk for sexual abuse. Studies indicate that sexual abuse victims are more likely to come from families that are low in cohesion and more highly disorganized than those of nonvictims (Elliot & Briere, 1994; Harter, Alexander, & Neimeyer, 1988; Hoagwood & Stewart, 1989; Madonna, Van Scoyk, & Jones, 1991). Isolation, communication problems, and lack of emotional closeness and flexibility are often present in families with sexual abuse problems (Dadds, Smith, Weber, & Robinson, 1991; Garbarino & Eckenrode, 1997). However, it is not known to what extent these family dysfunctions are a result of sexual abuse and its concomitant impairments to the family environment.

Research suggests that the perpetrators of incest are not limited to the bounds of the family. In a study of incestuous fathers and stepfathers, researchers found that 49% of those who were referred for outpatient treatment abused other children outside the family (Abel, Becker, Cunningham-Rathner, Mittleman, & Rouleau, 1988). Some elements of family structure may be associated with increased risk for sexual abuse. Research findings suggest that boys and girls who have lived without one of their natural parents, have a mother who is unavailable, or perceive their family life as unhappy, are at greater risk for sexual abuse (Finkelhor & Baron, 1986; Finkelhor, Hotaling, Lewis, & Smith, 1990).

Parenting Practices

Maltreating parents are less consistent in their child-rearing practices (Susman, Trickett, Iannotti, Hollenbeck, & Zahn-Waxler,

1985). They tend to be more critical and aggressive in their management styles (Trickett & Kuczynski, 1986), less pleasant in their interactions with their children (Trickett & Susman, 1988), and more hostile (Crittenden, 1981, 1985) than nonabusive parents. Maltreating parents are also less affectionate, playful, responsive, and supportive with their children (Egeland, Breitenbucher, & Rosenberg, 1980; Kavanaugh, Youngblade, Reid, & Fagot, 1988; Reid et al., 1987; Trickett & Susman, 1988; Twentyman & Plotkin, 1982). They may also display a lack of problem-solving skills (Azar, Robinson, Hekimian, & Twentyman, 1984; Hansen, Pallotta, Tishelam, Conaway, & MacMillan, 1988).

Maltreating parents are more likely than nonmaltreating parents to rely on coercion, punishment, power, and threats in their control attempts, and less likely to employ reasoning and affect control strategies with their children (Lorber, Felton, & Reid, 1984; Trickett & Sussman, 1988). The tendency for maltreating parents to use more coercive, punitive disciplinary techniques may be a reflection of their belief that these behaviors are more effective in producing desired outcomes (Milner & Chilamkurti, 1991).

Consistent with this reasoning is the finding that parents who use corporal punishment are more likely to abuse their children than those who rely on other disciplinary measures (Whipple & Richey, 1997). Corporal punishment may increase aggressive behavior among children, which in turn places them at greater risk for maltreatment (Straus, 1994). In a recent study, Straus, Sugarman, and Gilessims (1997) looked at the causal link between corporal punishment and antisocial behavior. Analyzing data from 807 mothers with children aged 6 to 9 years in the National Longitudinal Survey of Youth-Child Supplement, they found that spanking increased antisocial behavior across a 2-year period. They controlled for family socioeconomic status, sex of the child, and the extent to which the home provided emotional support and cognitive stimulation.

Yet for some children, spanking may not lead to increased aggression. A recent study by Gunnoe and Mariner (1997) used survey data from 1,112 children aged 4 to 11 years in the National Survey of Families and Households to analyze the relationship between parental spanking and schoolyard fights and reported antisocial behavior. They found that spanking predicted fewer fights for children aged 4 to 7 years and for children who are black and more fights for children aged 8 to 11 years and for children who are white. The only subgroup within which spanking was associated with increased aggression was 8- to 11-year-old white boys in single-mother families. Future research should seek to replicate this study using a longitudinal design with observational measures of antisocial behavior and further assess moderators of the effects of spanking on children's adjustment. More needs to be known about the environment and the social context within which spanking occurs and its related implications for maltreatment.

Little is known about how factors such as religion may influence the way parents and children ascribe meaning to corporal punishment and what the consequence of particular religious beliefs might be for the risks of maltreatment. However, one recent study suggests that parents affiliated with conservative Protestant denominations were more likely to report using corporal punishment than other parents. It is suggested, though not empirically verified, that these differences may be the result of theological conservatism and a belief in biblical prescriptions for physical punishment (Ellison, Bartkowski, & Segal, 1996). Future research should explore further the role of religious beliefs as they relate to child discipline and maltreatment.

Intergenerational Transmission

An important proposition that has received much attention over the years in the child maltreatment literature suggests that abused children grow up to be abusing parents (Egeland, 1988; Kaufman & Zigler, 1987; Widom, 1989). Early on, empirical research appeared to support the idea that patterns of child maltreatment are passed down from previous generations. As has been extensively discussed by other reviewers (Belsky, 1993; Garbarino & Eckenrode, 1997), however, many of these studies were methodologically flawed. Most of them were based on small case studies or relied on clinical data lacking adequate control groups. Also, most have been retrospective studies that have drawn their samples from individuals who have already established patterns of maltreatment.

Much concern has focused on understanding the extent of intergenerational transmission of child maltreatment. Retrospective studies indicate the rate of intergenerational transmission of child maltreatment to be somewhere between 7% (Gil, 1970) and 70%

(Egeland & Jacobvitz, 1984). In their test of the intergenerational hypothesis, Kaufman and Zigler (1987) analyzed the results of a selection of studies that were among the more methodologically sound. Based on their review, they found that the rate of intergenerational transmission ranged between 18% and 70%. Their best estimate of the rate of intergenerational transmission was 30% (plus or minus 5%).

The few prospective studies that have tested the intergenerational hypotheses have failed to consider adequately how a child's age and development may interact with parent characteristics in predicting maltreatment. The onset of maltreatment may emerge at different times for different individuals depending on a parent's background and a child's age (Belsky, 1993). Also, others have noted that the intergenerational hypothesis has been studied from a limited perspective and that attachment and social learning theories have been overlooked by most research (Belsky, 1993; Panel on Research on Child Abuse and Neglect [Panel], 1993).

However, the fact remains that many, if not most, individuals who were abused as children do not become abusive parents. Studies indicate that one of the most important factors associated with the cessation of the patterns of maltreatment across generations is parents' having relationships of support. Egeland and his associates' prospective study of 160 mothers at high risk for child maltreatment found that 70% of parents who had been abused as children were observed to maltreat their own children (Egeland, Jacobvitz, & Papatola, 1987; Egeland, Jacobvitz, & Sroufe, 1988). Yet the mothers who were able to break the "cycle of violence" had certain characteristics. They were more likely than maltreating mothers to have a stable and supportive relationship with a mate; they were more likely to have had emotional support from nonabusive adults earlier in their lives; and they were more likely to have been involved in therapy at some point in their lives.

Community

Poverty

A consistent finding in the etiological literature of child abuse and neglect is that maltreatment is found disproportionately among the poorer in society (Garbarino & Eckenrode, 1997; Whipple &

Webster-Stratton, 1991). Numerous studies have found a high correlation between physical abuse and neglect and poverty (Baumrind, 1992; Garbarino, 1987; Pelton, 1978; Pelton, 1994). However, the link between poverty and abuse and neglect is not well understood. For instance, it is not known to what extent the relationship between poverty and maltreatment is a reflection of reporting bias. Some have argued that the poor are more likely to be targeted for investigation by public agencies and therefore are more likely to be reported for child abuse and neglect.

Poverty may be one of a constellation of factors that contribute to a parent's increased social isolation and detachment from networks of support and social interaction. These dislocations may, in turn, increase the likelihood that parents will maltreat their children. Studies have shown that parents with limited social ties and parents who are socially isolated are at greater risk for child maltreatment (Garbarino & Eckenrode, 1997).

Other researchers have argued that the association between poverty and maltreatment is best understood as a product of the stresses that accompany poverty that are themselves linked to child abuse and neglect (Garbarino & Kostelny, 1992; Garbarino & Eckenrode, 1997). Gelles (1978) asserted that family stressors mediate the relationship between social class and maltreatment and that "there tends to be an association in cases where people of low socioeconomic status experience a high degree of stress: people in this category tend to exhibit more violent behavior toward their children" (p. 64). This conclusion has been supported by other research (Gelles & Straus, 1988), indicating that although parents of all social classes maltreat their children, violence toward children, especially severe violence, is more common among poor families. Furthermore, while it is difficult to separate the effects of family structure from poverty, some studies have indicated that single mothers with young children are at greater risk for maltreating their children (Connelly & Straus, 1992; Gelles, 1992). Research should explore further the particular elements of family life among the poor that make maltreatment more likely.

Poverty appears to be associated with sexual abuse; however, the relationship is not well understood (Drake & Pandey, 1996; Gillham et al., 1998). Poverty, within some contexts, may provide stresses associated with increased risk for sexual abuse. In many communities, wealth protects families from certain types of crimes.

In a similar way, wealth may be a protective factor that serves to shield a child from neighborhoods where nonfamilial abuse may be more likely to occur. Currently, however, there is no empirical evidence to substantiate this idea.

Poverty is often inextricably linked with the loss of employment. Various studies have shown a consistent association between unemployment and child abuse and neglect (Gabinet, 1983; Gelles & Hargreaves, 1981; Gil, 1970; Krugman, Lenherr, Betz, & Fryer, 1986; Steinberg, 1981). The relationship between unemployment and maltreatment can be understood from the ecological framework as a result of the stresses, anger, and frustration precipitated by unemployment that heightens the risk for abusive and neglectful behaviors (Garbarino & Eckenrode, 1997; Gil, 1970; Pelton, 1989).

Neighborhood

Neighborhoods play an important role in the availability of support and resources that may ameliorate the lack of personal and psychological resources available to families and individuals. The impact of poverty, unemployment, and other environmental factors on individual and family risk for child maltreatment greatly depends on the neighborhood within which a family resides. A neighborhood is defined not only by its geographic location, but also as a type of "social environment" that is characterized by the quality of relationships that are maintained among individuals and families (Garbarino & Eckenrode, 1997; Kromkowski, 1976). Unlike a community, a neighborhood "constitutes a geographic area within which people feel physically (if not always socially) close to each other" (Barry, 1994, p. 19).

A recent study by Deccio, Horner, and Wilson (1994) demonstrates the way in which the social and physical makeup of neighborhoods can vary widely in their ability to influence specific risks for maltreatment (e.g., unemployment, violence), and how weaker neighborhoods can add to the feelings of isolation and helplessness that increase the likelihood of maltreatment. These researchers replicated Garbarino and Sherman's (1980) high-risk neighborhood study. They compared economically similar neighborhoods that differed according to the risk for child maltreatment. They found that parents' social integration (community membership and belonging) had a significant impact on the risks for maltreatment. The "high risk," or weak, neighborhood reported rates of child maltreatment more than twice the rate reported by the "low-risk," or strong, neighborhood. Among the differences between maltreating and nonmaltreating neighborhoods were stability of residence, possession of a telephone, and housing vacancy rates.

Little is known about the mechanisms by which neighborhood conditions and organizational factors influence, or are influenced by, family structure and process variables. Nor has sufficient attention been directed to the way in which particular family structures and processes may act to buffer, or moderate, the relationship between neighborhood risk factors and maltreatment outcomes. Within the developmental ecological literature there has been little research focused on the influence of peer groups and the ways in which they may influence maltreatment rates.

Culture and Society

The collectively shared norms, attitudes, beliefs, and practices of society influence individual, family, community and neighborhood maltreatment risk factors. Relatively little is known about how culture and society affect child maltreatment. Much of our understanding is informed by little more than speculation. However, often mentioned among the more salient influences are societal attitudes toward violence, values of privacy and individualism, racism, and the status of children in social policy and practice.

Many observers suggest that tolerance of, and fascination with, violence in American society is an important risk factor in the etiology of maltreatment (Garbarino & Eckenrode, 1997; Gelles & Straus, 1988; Gil, 1970). One way the penchant for violence is manifested is through the parental practice of physical punishment to control children's behavior. This widely accepted cultural practice may give rise to other types of violence and maltreatment within families (Garbarino & Eckenrode, 1997; Kaufman & Zigler, 1989; Straus, 1994). Corporal punishment is an example of a behavior that may lead to a maltreatment incident that arises as an extension of a socially sanctioned child-rearing practice and norm. Researchers have yet to determine under what conditions other maltreating behavior may originate from parents' and others' attempts to approximate the behavioral prescriptions and proscriptions of a designated social (e.g., ethnic/cultural) group.

Some have argued that the value Americans place on individuality and personal privacy establishes conditions that increase the possibility of child maltreatment. For instance, Garbarino and Eckenrode (1997) suggest that appropriate and healthy parent-child relationships depend on information flow to and from the family. Those who are effectively engaged in the neighborhood and community tap community information resources in the form of professional expertise, folk wisdom, and regular observation of parent-child relationships. The values of autonomy, privacy, and independence may increase our sense of freedom, but such freedom comes at the price of increased isolation of parents (especially single parents) and children from the important flows of information, nurturance, and support from neighborhoods and communities.

Socioeconomic constraints to resource access may be an important factor in explaining the differences among ethnic/cultural groups' risk for maltreatment. A consistent finding in the literature suggests that African Americans are more likely to maltreat their children than whites (Connelly & Straus, 1992; Hampton & Newberger, 1985). However, some researchers have indicated that the difference may be due, all or in part, to reporting bias among blacks (Ards, Chung, & Myers, 1998). Racism may put ethnic minorities at greater risk for maltreatment. Strong, low-risk neighborhoods are dependent on activities in the American culture that are often less available to blacks and other minorities (e.g., transportation, municipal, and protective services). Limited access to essential community resources, particularly in the job market and educational system, and the lack of access to quality health care facilities and health insurance coverage increase the cumulative stress associated with maltreatment and negatively influences the capacity of a minority group's members' rendering effective support and adequate care for their children, especially in the inner city (see McGowan & Kohn, 1990).

The status that children have in society is also an important maltreatment risk factor. The values that guide the tradeoffs that are made in society and public policy often do not reflect the rhetoric about the care we have for children. Child day care and other care is often of negligible quality, especially for the poor. Care that may border on maltreatment (particularly neglect) within many care facilities may give rise to more serious forms of maltreatment by parents and others as a result of a child's deviant adaptations to the realities of deleterious child care environment.

A balanced consideration of American cultural values should also consider the ways in which the culture ameliorates factors associated with child maltreatment. Unfortunately, at this time there are virtually no cross-cultural studies that can inform us about the differences between American and other societies' cultural and social practices and their association with maltreatment.

Incidence

The problems with definitions of child abuse and neglect, noted above, confound attempts to measure its incidence and prevalence. As the numbers of child maltreatment victims continue to grow, legitimate questions have been raised about whether the increase is more apparent than real, that is, whether the numbers reflect increasing reporting rather than increasing incidence. Although there has certainly been more reporting, there has just as certainly been real increases in the number of incidents. With respect to official reports, the U.S. Department of Health and Human Services, National Center on Child Abuse and Neglect (USDHHS, NCCAN, 1997) reported that official child protective service (CPS) agencies investigated a total of nearly 2 million reports involving an estimated 3 million children in 1995. Although up from the 2.9 million of 1994 (USDHHS, 1996), the rate, 43 per 1,000, was the same.

Of 3 million children reported for maltreatment, 36%, or over 1 million, were substantiated, yielding an incidence rate of 15 per 1,000 children under the age of 18 years. Twice as many (52%) substantiated reports were for neglect, 25% were for physical abuse, and 13% were for sexual abuse. The majority of victims were 7 years of age or younger, and 21% were teenagers. Most victims of physical and medical neglect were younger than 8 years old, whereas most victims of abuse and other forms of maltreatment were older.

Because maltreatment is known to be underreported, Congress has mandated periodic surveys of representative samples of professionals and agencies across the country to get closer to the true incidence of child maltreatment in the United States. The Third National Incidence Study of Child Abuse and Neglect (NIS-3), reporting for calendar year 1993, was published in 1996 (Sedlak & Broadhurst, 1996). The survey, like the two before it, used a "community sentinel" approach, identifying professional staff in 42 counties of the United States likely to come into contact with maltreated children. A total of 5,612 such professionals in 800 non-CPS agencies were included. In addition, cases reported to participating CPS agencies were analyzed.

The study used two sets of definitions of maltreatment: endangerment and harm. The "Harm Standard" requires "an act of omission or commission resulting in a demonstrable harm" (Sedlak & Broadhurst, 1996, p. 3) and is the more stringent standard. The "Endangerment Standard" is more lenient, allowing children not yet harmed to be counted as abused or neglected "if a non-CPS sentinel considered them to be endangered by maltreatment or if their maltreatment was substantiated or indicated in a CPS investigation" (Sedlak & Broadhurst, 1996, p. 3).

The survey found "a sharp increase in the scope of the problem, whether the maltreatment is defined using the Harm Standard or the Endangerment Standard" (Sedlak & Broadhurst, 1996, p. 3). Even using the stricter Harm Standard, NIS-3 found that more than 1.5 million children in the United States had been abused or neglected in 1993, a 67% increase over the 1986 Second National Incidence Survey (NIS-2), and a 149% increase since the 1980 First National Incidence Survey. As was the case with official reports, neglect (879,000 children) was more common than abuse (743,200 children). Within this overall increase, the number of children who were seriously harmed by their maltreatment nearly quadrupled.

Using the Endangerment Standard, the increase in the total estimated number of abused and neglected children in the United States increased even more, from 1,424,400 in 1986 to 2,815,600 in 1993, a 98% increase. In every category of maltreatment except educational neglect, the increase between 1986 and 1993 in the number of cases was substantial and statistically significant.

Girls were more likely to have been reported as sexually abused than boys in the NIS-3, whereas boys were more likely to have been emotionally neglected and more likely to have been seriously injured or killed. In fact, in contrast with boys, fatal maltreatment decreased slightly for girls. The rates of physical neglect and emotional abuse of boys increased more than those of girls since the NIS-2. With respect to age, there were disproportionate increases in maltreatment rates during the younger (under 12 years old) and middle-childhood (ages 6-11) years, possibly reflecting an artifact of the survey design. Children under school age were less observable to community sentinels (Sedlak & Broadhurst, 1996). There were no significant race differences in maltreatment incidence observed.

The sociodemographic risks associated with child maltreatment in the NIS-3 parallel those in the theoretical constructs discussed above. For example, children in single-parent households, and in households with greater numbers of children, were at greater risk. Although less frequent, children living only with their fathers are at statistically greater risk of physical abuse than those living only with their mothers. Not surprisingly, family income was significantly related to incidence rates in nearly every category of maltreatment, and the increased risks are substantial. Children in families with gross incomes less than $15,000 per year, compared (according to the Harm Standard) with those in families with annual gross incomes of $30,000 or more, experienced 40 times the incidence of physical neglect, 16 times the incidence of physical abuse, 18 times the incidence of sexual abuse, and were 60 times more likely to die of some form of maltreatment (Sedlak & Broadhurst, 1996). Such sociodemographic differences have been attributed in the past to differential exposure to observation and reporting among low-income families. Undoubtedly, a higher proportion of maltreatment among upper-income families goes undetected, yet the differences in incidence are too great to be explained by differential exposure alone. According to Sedlak and Broadhurst (1996), "it appears more plausible to assume that the income-related differences in incidence found in the NIS reflect real difference in the extent to which children in different income levels are being abused or neglected" (p. 13).

Given the fact that, for most types of maltreatment in most states, the perpetrator must by definition be a caretaker, it is not surprising that 80% of perpetrators are parents (USDHHS, NCCAN, 1997). Since children are exposed to female caretakers more often than to male, females are more likely to be perpetrators of child abuse and neglect than are males. The average age of perpetrators is mid-30s: 37 for females and 34 for males.

Child fatality presents special problems for measurement. Forty-five states reported an estimated 996 fatalities in 1995 attributable to child maltreatment among children under 18 years of age, a rate of 2 per 100,000 (USDHHS, NCCAN, 1997). Most of these deaths occurred among the youngest victims of abuse and neglect. Although infant and childhood deaths are very accurately reported, the causes of such deaths may not be. Medical examiners have very strict criteria for determining child maltreatment as a cause of death, yet many deaths due to homicide, for example, may not be classified as a maltreatment death by the pathologist or coroner even though the same case might have been substantiated had it first come to the attention of CPS (Herman-Giddens, 1991). Most states, recognizing this discrepancy, have established Child Fatality Teams or Task Forces to bring medical examiners, health providers, social service workers, and others together to investigate the circumstances of infant and child deaths. Should subsequent investigations find child maltreatment behind a suspicious child death, it might be too late for state vital records offices and the National Child Abuse and Neglect Data System to update their reports. It is therefore likely that official statistics seriously underestimate the rates of child fatality due to maltreatment.

The situation with regard to the reporting of child abuse and neglect is different in Canada. The definition of what constitutes "a child in need of protection," who would be counted as an investigated case of maltreatment, varies across political jurisdictions. Similarly, each province and territory has distinct laws addressing mandatory reporting, investigating, and serving cases of child maltreatment. Not all provinces and territories have central registries of child abuse and neglect. For these reasons, the Federal-Provincial Working Group on Child and Family Services Information specifically advises that its Provincial Child Welfare Systems data for a specific province or territory "cannot and should not be compared with data from other jurisdictions" (Federal-Provincial

Working Group, 1994, p. 6). Even the age below which children may be eligible for child protective services varies from jurisdiction to jurisdiction. Therefore, "it [is] not possible to identify common data elements on child abuse and neglect which would permit the generation of national estimates" (Federal-Provincial Working Group, 1994, p. 6).

At the provincial level, the most extensive, province-wide surveys are from Ontario. Ontario has mandatory reporting of child abuse and neglect, and the cases are investigated by the province's 54 children's aid societies. According to Trocme, McPhee, Tam, and Hay (1994), there were 46,683 child maltreatment investigations in Ontario in 1993, a rate of 21 per 1,000 children. Unfortunately, these investigations were classified as substantiated, suspected, or unfounded, not simply substantiated or unsubstantiated as in the United States. Some states in the United States do have a third category, "indicated," between substantiated and unsubstantiated. When aggregated into two categories, substantiated and indicated are usually combined. Applying this strategy to the Ontario data would yield a rate of 12 per 1,000, which is close to the rate of 15 per 1,000 for the United States in 1995. But these rates are really not comparable, since the U.S. data are for children under 18, but in Ontario reported children are under 16. There is also a marked difference in the distribution of reports by type. In Ontario, 41% of the investigations were for physical abuse and 30% for neglect, whereas in the United States, neglect was more common. It is impossible to know whether this difference is due to underreporting in the Ontario survey or to a lower incidence of neglect.

Another source of child abuse incidence in Ontario is the Ontario Health Supplement (MacMillan et al., 1997), which in 1990 included a self-administered questionnaire about a history of physical and sexual abuse among respondents 15 years of age and older. The rates of respondents' reporting physical abuse when they were growing up were 31.2% for males and 21.1% for females. The numbers for sexual abuse were 4.3% and 12.8%, respectively. The numbers for severe physical abuse were 10.7% for males and 9.2% for females, whereas for severe sexual abuse the numbers were 3.9% and 11.1%, respectively. Since these numbers are lifetime prevalence rates, they cannot be compared with the incidence rates for abuse in the United States mentioned above.

Finally, a discussion in the Child Maltreatment Research Listserve about the observed decline in child sexual abuse (CSA) rates in Quebec epitomizes all the problems and pitfalls in estimating the incidence of child maltreatment. On June 23, 1997, one of the coauthors of a paper later delivered at the Fifth International Family Violence Research Conference (Wright, Boucher, Frappier, Lebeau, & Sabourin, 1997) invited subscribers to speculate about why the incidence of confirmed cases of CSA had apparently declined from a high of 1.37 per 1,000 in 1992-1993 to 0.87 in 1995-1996. Among the explanations offered were that:

- The lower rates represented catching up with a backlog of reports that, once cleared, declined to baseline
- A backlash among professionals reporting or investigating CSA, the result of cynicism about the handling of reported and substantiated cases, and dissatisfaction with the judicial response to CSA, contributed to the decline
- Improving socioeconomic circumstances resulted in less unemployment and consequently less CSA
- Improving socioeconomic circumstances propelled many families out of the low income categories most exposed to social work and, specifically, CPS activity
- An artifact introduced by administrative data systems that characterizes maltreatment in terms of the omissions and commissions of adult caretakers resulted in CSA perpetrated by nonadults and non-caregivers being classified as neglect on the part of a caregiver
- Increasing public awareness of CSA, combined with greater sophistication on the part of investigating agencies, resulted in more questionable cases being reported and fewer being substantiated
- Increasing "screen-outs" of less serious reports resulted in lower substantiation rates

Needless to say, no consensus was reached. Probably a combination of some or all of the above is at play. The authors of the paper concluded that tighter criteria for accepting cases for investigation, along with fewer referrals from professionals lacking confidence in CPS and judicial services, combined to reduce the incidence rates, and that there is no support for the hypothesis that there were reduced rates of CSA in Quebec during this period (Wright et al., 1997).

Consequences

Although "conventional wisdom" and "professional opinion" have had a lot to say about the consequences of child maltreatment, in fact we know very little. The Panel on Research on Child Abuse and Neglect (1993) stated, "The scientific study of child maltreatment and its consequences is in its infancy. Until recently, research on the consequences of physical and sexual child abuse and neglect has been based primarily on retrospective studies of children or adults that are subject to clinical bias and inaccurate recall" (pp. 208-209). In the following brief review of the consequences of maltreatment, those child outcomes that can reasonably be attributed to maltreatment based on what is known from longitudinal studies will be emphasized.

By definition, substantiated physical abuse will involve demonstrable harm. These physical findings may vary from the minor (superficial abrasions, bruises, and lacerations) to the major (fractures, intra-abdominal hemorrhage, and intracranial hemorrhage). The former are unlikely to result in any long-term consequences. The latter, however, may be the cause of long-term disability or death. Unfortunately, our knowledge of the frequency with which maltreated children suffer long-term impairment of their physical health is "based primarily on speculation" due to the "paucity of longitudinal research in this area" (Dubowitz, 1991), but it may safely be assumed that child victims of inflicted injury are more likely to experience delay in obtaining medical attention due to caretaker-perpetrator fear, guilt, or denial. In this case, mandatory reporting may have the unintended consequence of exacerbating the severity of a maltreated child's injuries.

Child sexual abuse rarely results in long-term physical injury, and the more superficial injuries, such as redness, bruising, or abrasions, usually heal completely (Dubowitz, 1991). On the other hand, sexual abuse may result in sexually transmitted infection in the child. These diseases may be symptomatic and are diagnostic of sexual abuse in the prepubescent child. Again, long-term serious consequences are infrequent, with one major exception. There have been documented cases of HIV infection in children that were the result of child sexual abuse, and HIV remains invariably fatal.

Child neglect poses a challenge to the researcher attempting to attribute poor health outcomes to parental behavior. Children who are neglected are known to experience delays in growth and development, a condition called "failure to thrive." But the risk factors for delayed growth, mediated by undernutrition, may be the same as the risk factors for maltreatment, so it is difficult to distinguish the contribution of parental neglect alone from the contribution of poverty. Nevertheless, Sturm and Drotar (1989) have demonstrated in a longitudinal study that failure-to-thrive children with no organic explanation for their delay do not reach expected norms for height and weight for their age.

Child neglect may have cognitive consequences as well. In a longitudinal study, Egeland (1991) demonstrated that neglected children showed a 40-point decline in the Bayley Scales of Infant Development by the age of 24 months, and by early school age they were lower than matched controls on the Wechsler Preschool and Primary Scale of Intelligence (WPPSI) and the Wechsler Intelligence Scale for Children (WISC). Similarly, physically abused children scored lower on the WPPSI and the WISC. Egeland also found behavioral consequences of abuse and neglect in his cohort. By 24 months the neglected children were angry, frustrated, and noncompliant in a problem-solving task, compared with controls. At 42 months, they showed poor impulse control, inflexibility, dependence, and incompetence. By early school age, they were aggressive, highly dependent, and depressed. Physically abused children showed some of the same characteristics, such as anger and noncompliance, at preschool age and aggression and lack of self-control at early school age. In addition, the teachers of the physically abused children reported them to be inattentive, unpopular, self-destructive, and obsessive-compulsive (Egeland, 1991).

In their summary of the Lehigh Longitudinal Study, Herrenkohl, Herrenkohl, Egolf, and Wu (1991) describe the results of their meticulous (if small) follow-up study of a cohort of preschool children whose maltreatment status and parental disciplinary practices were assessed in the 1970s. By the time the children were school age, the researchers were able to test their developmental status using interviews, observation, analysis of school records, cognitive testing, and completion of behavioral inventories by parents and teachers. The use of structural equation modeling made it possible to test constructs for emotional health and social functioning while controlling for confounders such as socioeconomic status (SES). The investigators found that SES overwhelmed many of the two-way relationships between maltreatment and the developmental constructs. There remained a significant relationship between emotional maltreatment and social competence, and between the father's negative interaction with the child and the child's being angry/negative. There was also a relationship between negative/neglectful parenting and academic performance. Finally, whereas negative/neglectful parenting was associated with teacher ratings of emotional difficulties, mothers' ratings of emotional difficulties were more closely associated with severity of physical punishment. The bias in this last relationship is discussed by the authors: "Perhaps this perception [that the mothers perceive the children they discipline more harshly as emotionally more difficult] serves as a rationalization for harsh discipline" (Herrenkohl et al., 1991, p. 72).

Much concern focuses on the relationship between child maltreatment and aggression and antisocial behavior in children. Again, prospective studies are rare, and the results of the many clinical, case control, and cross-sectional studies are inconsistent and contradictory (Panel, 1993). One longitudinal study found that school-aged children who were physically harmed were rated as more aggressive than unharmed children by teachers and peers (Dodge, Bates, & Pettit, 1990). The work of one of us (JBK) with a multisite, longitudinal study of children at risk of abuse or neglect found that maltreatment prior to 4 years of age was significantly associated with parent reports of more aggressive behavior at ages 6 and 8 years (Kotch, Dufort, Ruina, Winsor, & Catellier, 1997).

Follow-up studies that continued into adolescence have found that, "Although the majority of abused children do not become delinquent, and the majority of delinquents are not abused as children . . . abused and neglected children are at increased risk for juvenile delinquency" (Panel, p. 217). Whereas delinquency does not necessarily involve violence, violent delinquents may be more likely to have experienced severe abuse. Widom (1989), in her longitudinal study of children with substantiated physical abuse, sexual abuse, and/or neglect prior to age 12 years, found that abused or neglected children had higher arrest rates for violent crime than did the controls.

One final consequence of abuse and neglect that may be the most tragic of all involves child victims doomed to repeat their experience by in turn victimizing their own children. The argument about whether intergenerational transmission of maltreatment is a major etiologic factor continues to wax and wane. The definitive study to address this issue, which ideally would require selecting a representative sample of newborns and following them into their child-bearing years, has never been done, and probably will never be done. Most of the literature is based on self-reports of parents of abused and neglected children (and, it is hoped, parents of a matched control group) of their own upbringing. Such data, weak as they are, give mixed results, but the conclusion remains that the majority of maltreating parents were not necessarily maltreated themselves, and that the majority of maltreated children do not go on to become maltreating parents. In the words of Starr, MacLean, and Keating (1991), "Research findings lead to the conclusion that statements concerning the high probability of the transmission of child maltreatment across generations are unwarranted" (p. 8). The observation of intergenerational transmission may be an artifact of the same convergence of ecological factors in two consecutive generations.

The consequences of sexual abuse in childhood are even more complicated. Most of the early studies purporting to document the lurid behavioral consequences of sexual abuse were retrospective, relying on the recall of adults who reported having been victimized many years before. "The methodological weaknesses of these studies do not provide empirical support for a causal relationship between sexual abuse, sexual dysfunction, and promiscuity" (Panel, 1993, p. 220). The same study by Widom (above) has led to more valid findings that do not completely support the claims of the clinical literature. Widom and Kuhns (1996) found no difference between their maltreated group ($n = 676$) and a neighborhood control group ($n = 520$) in either sexual promiscuity or teenage pregnancy. There was, however, a significant difference ($p < .05$) between the two groups in prostitution. The authors speculated that running away from home, another outcome that significantly differentiated the maltreated group from the controls, might explain some of the difference in rates of prostitution.

Prevention

Public health definitions of prevention include three levels: primary, secondary, and tertiary. Primary prevention includes programs and services offered to the general population to prevent a condition from occurring in the first place. Childhood immunization against infectious disease is a good example. Secondary prevention includes programs and services that are implemented in at-risk populations to prevent a condition in the earliest stages from expressing itself as frank disease. Medical treatment of high blood pressure before the development of symptoms is an example. Finally, tertiary prevention includes those programs and services whose goal is to prevent the progression or consequences of a condition after it has occurred. Treatment of diabetes with medication and dietary intervention is an example of an attempt to prevent the disease from causing blindness and loss of limbs, kidney function, and so on. Such treatment may at the same time be considered tertiary prevention.

Nowhere is the confusion over the differences between prevention and treatment more obvious than in the case of child maltreatment. For example, in 1989 Congress passed legislation authorizing the Emergency Child Abuse and Neglect Prevention Services (ES) program. Even the title is a nonsequitor, for the emergency services authorized follow upon the heels of a serious child abuse or neglect event, making the idea that there is any room left for prevention ludicrous. In addition, the act provides for "primary" services, including child care, respite care, and transportation, for "participants" (read "parents") who are substance abusers. Even when one grants that such services may be considered secondary prevention, it is difficult to find any data supporting the hypothesis that the ES program actually reduced the incidence of abuse or neglect in this at-risk population (Tyler, Fairchild, & Lichtenstein, 1995).

Reviews of primary and secondary prevention of child abuse and neglect programs have pointed out the many difficulties and methodological weaknesses of previous evaluations.

Fink and McCloskey (1990) identified the following shortcomings: inadequate definition of child abuse and neglect; paucity of valid measurements; lack of specification of the characteristics of families who benefit the most from programs; and omission of important topics, such as consequences and costs of medical neglect and cost-benefit analysis. (CSR, 1996, p. 9)

In 1992, the General Accounting Office (GAO, 1992) reviewed studies of primary and secondary prevention programs. According to an evaluation of nine comprehensive, community-based child abuse and neglect prevention programs, the GAO found "positive gains in parental . . . knowledge and attitude [and] . . . improvements in observed parental behavior and, *to a lesser extent* [emphasis added], in indicators of child maltreatment (e.g., child abuse reports)" (CSR, 1996, p. 8). Many evaluations, of both primary and secondary programs, are limited by an unwillingness or inability to collect primary data on the outcome most of interest, child maltreatment. Even the cross-site evaluation of the nine community-based prevention programs rarely monitored or analyzed rates of child abuse and neglect. Instead, the programs examined intermediate outcomes, such as parents' social support, knowledge of child development, and attitudes toward disciplining children. Whether improvements in any of these were accompanied by reduced child abuse or neglect is left to the reader's imagination.

In 1989, Dubowitz reviewed the professional literature for evaluation reports of child abuse and neglect prevention programs. He concluded, "And the majority of evaluation studies have serious methodological shortcomings that limit an assessment of their effectiveness" (p. 576). Similarly, the National Research Council (NRC) report states, "Many community-based intervention programs have demonstrated some impact on knowledge and attitudes, but their impact on abusive behavior toward children remains uncertain. While such programs may offer many advantages, little evidence currently exists that such interventions directly reduce child maltreatment" (Panel, 1993). Nevertheless, there is one example of a community-based secondary prevention program that is promising, namely, home visiting. In a 15-year follow-up of nurse home-visiting for at-risk families, Olds, Eckenrode, Henderson, et al. (1997) have demonstrated reduced child abuse and neglect rates in a controlled intervention trial. Their work conforms with the recommendation of the NRC Panel (Panel, 1993) that prevention programs need to be comprehensive and intensive, incorporate a theoretical framework, and identify multiple pathways to child maltreatment. Furthermore, their work addresses the many functions of social support prescribed by Ross Thompson (1994) for preventing child maltreatment, namely, emotional sustenance; counseling, advice, or guidance; access to information, services, and material resources and assistance; and skills acquisition.

Intervention

Modern concern with child maltreatment began in 1874 in this country with the case of Mary Ellen, an emaciated school-age girl found beaten, stabbed, and chained to her bed in a tenement in New York City. In the absence of public social service agencies, the New York Society for the Prevention of Cruelty to Animals (NYSPCA) took up the case and won. The NYSPCA evolved into the New York Society for the Prevention of Cruelty to Children, ultimately becoming the American Humane Association. Child abuse and neglect services remained the province of voluntary agencies until the publication of Kempe and colleagues' landmark "The Battered Child Syndrome" (Kempe, Silverman, Steele, Droegemueller, & Silver, 1962) led to a U.S. Children's Bureau conference on battered children and the first model child abuse reporting statute (USDHHS, Children's Bureau, 1997).

In 1973, Congress passed the Child Abuse Prevention and Treatment Act (CAPTA, P.L. 93-247), which required mandatory reporting of child abuse and neglect in order for states to qualify for federal child protective service money. By 1989, Child Protective Services (CPS) emerged as the dominant service offered by local social service agencies, and being abused or neglected became the only way to get help (Kamerman & Kahn, 1989, quoted in USDHHS, Children's Bureau, 1997). "Between 1977 and 1994 there has been a dramatic decline in the number of children receiving child welfare services. This decline reflects a child welfare system that has evolved from a broader based social service system into a system primarily serving abused and neglected children and their families" (USDHHS, Children's Bureau, 1997, p. ix).

Despite the growth of both the problem of abuse and neglect and the bureaucracy created to deal with it, outcome evaluations of treatment interventions are few. In 1987, Cohn and Daro published a review of four studies of multisite programs involving 89 different demonstrations over a 10-year period. They concluded that treatment efforts in general were "not very successful. . . . Treatment programs have been relatively ineffective in initially halting abusive and neglectful behavior or in reducing the future likelihood of maltreatment in most cases of physical abuse" (Cohn & Daro, 1987, quoted in Panel, 1993, p. 255).

The U.S. Advisory Board on Child Abuse and Neglect stated that "the [CPS services] *system* the nation has devised to respond to child abuse and neglect is *failing*" (U.S. Advisory Board, 1990, quoted in Melton & Barry, 1994, p. 3, emphasis in the original). The Advisory Board cited numerous problems with the prevailing child protection system, beginning with the explicit reporting requirements of CAPTA, which were not matched by equally explicit requirements for prevention and treatment. The system focused on identifying individual miscreants rather than on the underlying social causes of maltreatment. Despite, or perhaps because of, the huge number of cases reported, fewer than half are substantiated (USDHHS, NCCAN, 1997), and barely more than half of the substantiated are served (Melton & Barry, 1994). Fundamentally, CPS seeks to find "limits for justifiable coercive intervention in family life" rather than develop "effective plans to prevent initial or further harm" to children (Melton & Barry, 1994, p. 5). "Put succinctly, the system is not child centered" (Melton & Barry, 1994, p. 5).

The solution of Congress, the Family Preservation and Support Act of 1993, may have made matters worse. Social service agencies remain torn between the need to protect children, in many cases requiring removing the child from the family, on the one hand, and the legislative language requiring "reasonable efforts to prevent child placement" (USDHHS, Children's Bureau, 1997, p. 1-12) on the other. Unfortunately, "reasonable efforts" were nowhere clearly defined (Gelles, 1996). In the absence of guidelines, CPS agencies took advantage of an opportunity to avoid foster care placement even for children in substantial danger of reinjury. Newspaper accounts of the deaths of children in foster care were replaced with newspaper accounts of the deaths of children who had been inappropriately returned to their abusive parents (Gelles, 1996). Recently, a judge in Maryland said, "it is usually not in the best interest of a child to be separated from the biological mother," when he returned a 2-year-old to his mother despite the fact that she had admitted killing her infant daughter (Janofsky, 1998).

Any social policy that truly has the best interests of children at heart must first be "based on respect for the inherent dignity and inalienable rights of children as members of the human community" (Advisory Board, quoted in Melton & Barry, 1994, p. 5). Child protection, according to the U.S. Advisory Board on Child Abuse and Neglect, requires that government "facilitate comprehensive community efforts to ensure the safe and healthy development of children" (Advisory Board, quoted in Melton & Barry, 1994, p. 6). A cornerstone of this approach, according to Barry (1994), is a neighborhood focus. This neighborhood-based approach seeks both to improve the viability of the neighborhood and to organize services for individuals within the neighborhood. Theoretically, by strengthening the quality of neighborliness—essentially, "neighbor helping neighbor" (Barry, 1994, p. 37) through direct services and the improvement of the physical and social environment where people live—child abuse and neglect may be reduced. Although neighborhood interventions have been reported to have improved parenting, their impact on child maltreatment remains to be determined.

References

Abel, G. G., Becker, J., Cunningham-Rathner, J., Mittleman, M., & Rouleau, J. L. (1988). Multiple paraphiliac diagnosis among sex offenders. *Bulletin of the American Academy of Psychiatry and the Law, 16*(2), 153-168.

Ammerman, R. T. (1990a). Etiological models of child maltreatment. A behavioral perspective. *Behavior Modification, 14,* 230-254.

Ammerman, R. T. (1990b). Predisposing child factors. In R. T. Ammerman & M. Hersen (Eds.), *Children at risk: An evaluation of factors contributing to child abuse and neglect* (pp. 199-221). New York: Plenum.

Ammerman, R. T. (1991). The role of the child in physical abuse: A reappraisal. *Violence and Victims, 6*(2), 87-100.

Ammerman, R. T., & Patz, R. J. (1996). Determinants of child abuse potential— Contribution of parent and child factors. *Journal of Clinical Child Psychology, 25*(3), 300-307.

Ards, S., Chung, C. J., & Myers, S. L. (1998). The effects of sample selection bias on racial differences in child abuse reporting. *Child Abuse & Neglect, 22*(2), 103-115.

Azar, S. T., Robinson, D. R., Hekimian, E., & Twentyman, C. T. (1984). Unrealistic expectations and problem-solving ability in maltreating and comparison mothers. *Journal of Consulting and Clinical Psychology, 52*(4), 687-691.

Azar, S. T., & Wolfe, D. A. (1989). Child abuse and neglect. In E. J. Mash & R. A. Barkley (Eds.), *Treatment of childhood disorders* (pp. 451-489). New York: Guilford.

Barry, F. D. (1994). A neighborhood-based approach: What is it? In G. B. Melton & F. D. Barry (Eds.), *Protecting children from abuse and neglect* (pp. 15-39). New York: Guilford.

Baumrind, D. (1992). *Family factors applied to child maltreatment* (Background paper prepared for the Panel on Research on Child Abuse and Neglect). Washington, DC: National Research Council.

Belsky, J. (1980). Child maltreatment: An ecological integration. *American Psychologist, 35,* 320-335.

Belsky, J. (1993). Etiology of child maltreatment: A developmental-ecological analysis. *Psychological Bulletin, 114*(3), 413-434.

Belsky, J., & Vondra, J. (1989). Lessons from child abuse: The determinants of parenting. In D. Cicchetti & V. Carlson (Eds.), *Current research and theoretical advances in child maltreatment* (pp. 153-202). Cambridge, UK: Cambridge University Press.

Berliner, L., & Elliot, D. M. (1996). Sexual abuse of children. In J. Briere, L. Berliner, J. A. Bulkley, C. Jenny, & T. Reid (Eds.), *The APSAC handbook on child maltreatment*. Thousand Oaks, CA: Sage.

Bronfenbrenner, U. (1979). *The ecology of human development*. Cambridge, MA: Harvard University Press.

Caspi, A., & Elder, G. H. (1988). Emergent family patterns: The intergenerational construction of problem behavior and relationships. In R. A. Hinde & J. Stevenson-Hinde (Eds.), *Relationships with families: Mutual influences* (pp. 218-240). Oxford, UK: Clarendon.

Cicchetti, D. (1990). The organization and coherence of socioemotional, cognitive, and representational development: Illustrations through a developmental psychopathology perspective on Down syndrome and child maltreatment. In R. Thompson (Ed.), *Nebraska Symposium on Motivation* (Vol. 36, pp. 259-366). Lincoln: University of Nebraska Press.

Cohn, A. H., & Daro, D. (1987). Is treatment too late: What ten years of evaluative research tell us. *Child Abuse & Neglect, 11,* 433-442.

Connelly, C., & Straus, M. (1992). Mother's age and risk for physical abuse. *Child Abuse & Neglect, 16,* 709-718.

Crittenden, P. M. (1981). Abusing, neglecting problematic, and adequate dyads: Differentiating by patterns of interaction. *Merrill-Palmer Quarterly 27,* 201-208.

Crittenden, P. M. (1985). Social networks, quality of child rearing, and child development. *Child Development, 56,* 1299-1313.

CSR, Incorporated. (1996). *Cross-site evaluation report. Evaluation of nine comprehensive, community-based child abuse and neglect prevention programs*. Washington, DC: Author.

Dadds, M., Smith, M., Weber, Y., & Robinson, A. (1991). An exploration of family and individual profiles following father daughter incest. *Child Abuse & Neglect, 5,* 575-586.

Deccio, G., Horner, W., & Wilson, D. (1994). High risk neighborhoods and high risk families: Replication research related to the human ecology of child maltreatment. *Journal of Social Service Research, 18*(3-4), 123-137.

Disbrow, M. A., Doerr, H., & Caufield, C. (1977). Measuring the components of parents' potential for child abuse and neglect. *International Journal of Child Abuse & Neglect, 1,* 279-296.

Dodge, K. A., Bates, J. E., & Pettit, G. S. (1990). Mechanisms in the cycle of violence. *Science, 250,* 1678-1683.

Drake, B., & Pandey, S. (1996). Understanding the relationship between neighborhood poverty and specific types of child maltreatment. *Child Abuse & Neglect, 20*(11), 1003-1018.

Dubowitz, H. (1989). Prevention of child maltreatment: What is known. *Pediatrics, 83,* 570-577.

Dubowitz, H. (1991). The impact of child maltreatment on health. In R. H. Starr, Jr., & D. A. Wolfe (Eds.), *The effects of abuse and neglect* (pp. 278-294). New York: Guilford.

Dukewich, T. L., Borkowski, J. G., & Whitman, T. L. (1996). Adolescent mothers and child abuse potential—An evaluation of risk factors. *Child Abuse & Neglect, 20*(11), 1031-1047.

Egeland, B. (1988). Breaking the cycle of abuse: Implications for prediction and intervention. In K. D. Browne, C. Davies, & P. Stratton (Eds.), *Early prediction and prevention of child abuse* (pp. 87-99). New York: John Wiley.

Egeland, B. (1991). A longitudinal study of high-risk families. In R. H. Starr, Jr., & D. A. Wolfe (Eds.), *The effects of abuse and neglect* (pp. 33-56). New York: Guilford.

Egeland, B., Breitenbucher, M., & Rosenberg, D. (1980). Prospective study of the significance of life stress in the etiology of child abuse. *Journal of Consulting and Clinical Psychology, 48,* 195-205.

Egeland, B., & Brunnquell, D. (1979). An at-risk approach to the study of child abuse: Some preliminary findings. *Journal of the American Academy of Child Psychiatry, 18,* 219-235.

Egeland, B., & Jacobvitz, D. (1984, April). *Intergenerational continuity in parental abuse: Causes and consequences.* Paper presented at the Conference on Biosocial Perspectives in Abuse and Neglect, York, ME.

Egeland, B., Jacobvitz, D., & Papatola, K. (1987). Intergenerational continuity of abuse. In R. Gelles & J. Lancaster (Eds.), *Child abuse and neglect: Biosocial dimensions* (pp. 255-276). Chicago: Aldine.

Egeland, B., Jacobvitz, D., & Sroufe, L. A. (1988). Breaking the cycle of abuse. *Child Development, 59,* 1080-1088.

Eisenberg, L. (1981). Cross-cultural and historical perspectives on child abuse and neglect. *Child Abuse & Neglect, 5*(3), 299-308.

Elliot, D. M., & Briere, J. (1994). Forensic sexual abuse evaluations: Disclosures and symptomatology. *Behavioral Sciences and the Law, 12,* 261-277.

Ellison, C. G., Bartkowski, J. P., & Segal, M. L. (1996). Do conservative Protestant parents spank more often? Further evidence from the National Survey of Families and Households. *Social Science Quarterly, 77,* 663-673.

Fantuzzo, J. W., DePaola, L. M., Lambert, L., Martino, T., Anderson, G., & Sutton, S. (1991). Effects of interparental violence on the psychological adjustment and competencies of young children. *Journal of Consulting and Clinical Psychology, 59,* 34-39.

Federal-Provincial Working Group on Child and Family Services Information. (1994). *Child welfare in Canada: The role of provincial and territorial authorities in cases of child abuse.* Ottawa: Minister of Supply Services Canada.

Fink, A., & McCloskey, L. (1990). Moving child abuse and neglect prevention programs forward: Improving program evaluations. *Child Abuse & Neglect, 14,* 187-206.

Finkelhor, D. (1979). What's wrong with sex between adults and children? Ethics and the problem of sexual abuse. *American Journal of Orthopsychiatry, 49,* 692-697.

Finkelhor, D., & Baron, L. (1986). High-risk children. In D. Finkelhor (Ed.), *A sourcebook on sexual abuse* (pp. 60-88). Newbury Park, CA: Sage.

Finkelhor, D., Hotaling, G., Lewis, I. A., & Smith, C. (1990). Sexual abuse in a national survey of adult men and women: Prevalence, characteristics, and risk factors. *Child Abuse & Neglect, 14,* 19-28.

Gabinet, L. (1983). Child abuse treatment failures reveal need for redefinition of the problem. *Child Abuse & Neglect, 7,* 395-402.

Garbarino, J. (1987). Family support and the prevention of child maltreatment. In S. Kagan, R. Powell, B. Weissbourd, & E. Zigler (Eds.), *America's family support programs.* New Haven, CT: Yale University Press.

Garbarino, J., & Eckenrode, J. (1997). *Understanding abusive families.* San Francisco: Jossey-Bass.

Garbarino, J., & Kostelny, K. (1992). Child maltreatment as a community problem. *Child Abuse & Neglect, 16,* 455-64.

Garbarino, J., & Sherman, D. (1980). High risk families: The human ecology of child maltreatment. *Child Development, 51,* 188-198.

Gelles, R. J. (1978). Etiology of violence: Overcoming fallacious reasoning in understanding family violence and child abuse. *Conference proceedings: Children's Hospital National Medical Center.* The University of Rhode Island Family Violence Research Project.

Gelles, R. J. (1992). Poverty and violence toward children. *American Behavioral Scientist, 35*(3), 258-274.

Gelles, R. J. (1996). *The book of David: How preserving families can cost children's lives.* New York: Basic Books.

Gelles, R. J., & Hargreaves, E. F. (1981). Maternal employment and violence toward children. *Journal of Family Issues, 2,* 509-530.

Gelles, R. J., & Straus M. A. (1988). *Intimate violence.* New York: Simon & Schuster.

General Accounting Office. (1992). *Child abuse prevention programs need greater emphasis.* Washington, DC: Author.

Gil, D. (1970). *Violence against children: Physical child abuse in the United States.* Cambridge, MA: Harvard University Press.

Gil, D. (1975). Unraveling child abuse. *American Journal of Orthopsychiatry, 45*(3), 346-356.

Gillham, B., Tanner, G., Cheyne, B., Freeman, I., Rooney, M., & Lambie, A. (1998). Unemployment rates, single parent density, and indices of child poverty—Their relationship to different categories of child abuse and neglect. *Child Abuse & Neglect, 22*(2), 79-90.

Gunnoe, M. L., & Mariner, C. L. (1997). Toward a developmental-contextual model of the effects of parental spanking on children's aggression. *Archives of Pediatrics & Adolescent Medicine, 151*(8), 768-775.

Hampton, R. L., & Newberger, E. H. (1985). Child abuse incidence and reporting by hospitals: Significance of severity, class, and race. *American Journal of Public Health, 75*, 56-60.

Hansen, D. J., Pallotta, G. M., Tishelam, A. C., Conaway, L. P., & MacMillan, V. M. (1988). Parental problem-solving skills and child behavior problems: A comparison of physically abusive, neglectful, clinic, and community families. *Journal of Family Violence, 4*, 353-368.

Harter, S., Alexander, P. C., & Neimeyer, R. A. (1988). Long-term effects of incestuous child abuse in college women: Social adjustment, social cognition, and family characteristics. *Journal of Consulting and Clinical Psychology, 56*, 5-8.

Herman-Giddens, M. (1991). Underreporting of child abuse and neglect fatalities in North Carolina. *North Carolina Medical Journal, 52*, 634-639.

Herrenkohl, R. C., Herrenkohl, E. C., Egolf, B. P., & Wu, P. (1991). The developmental consequences of child abuse: The Lehigh Longitudinal Study. In R. H. Starr, Jr., & D. A. Wolfe (Eds.), *The effects of abuse and neglect* (pp. 57-81). New York: Guilford.

Hoagwood, K., & Stewart, J. M. (1989). Sexually abused children's perceptions of family functioning. *Child and Adolescent Social Work, 6*, 139-149.

Holden, E. W., Willis, D. J., & Corcoran, M. (1992). Preventing child maltreatment during the prenatal/perinatal period. In D. J. Willis, E. W. Holden, & M. Rosenberg (Eds.), *Prevention of child maltreatment: Developmental and ecological perspectives* (pp. 17-46). New York: John Wiley.

Janofsky, M. (1998, July 18). Court allows boy, 2, to be returned to mother convicted of murder. *The New York Times* (late edition), section A, p. 7, column 1.

Kamerman, S. B., & Kahn, A. J. (1989). *Social services for children, youth and families in the United States.* Baltimore, MD: The Annie E. Casey Foundation.

Kaufman, J., & Zigler, E. (1987). Do abused children become abusive parents? *American Journal of Orthopsychiatry, 57*, 182-192.

Kaufman, J., & Zigler, E. (1989). The intergenerational transmission of child abuse. In D. Cicchetti & V. Carlson (Eds.), *Child maltreatment: Theory and research on the causes and consequences of child abuse and neglect* (pp. 129-150). Cambridge, MA: Cambridge University Press.

Kavanaugh, K., Youngblade, L., Reid, J., & Fagot, B. (1988). Interactions between children and abusive control parents. *Journal of Clinical Child Psychology, 17*, 137-142.

Kempe, C. H., Silverman, F., Steele, B., Droegemueller, W., & Silver, H. (1962). The battered child syndrome. *Journal of the American Medical Association, 181*, 17-24.

Kotch, J. B., Dufort, V., Ruina, E., Winsor, J., & Catellier, D. (1997, March 19). *Multi-site, longitudinal study of maltreatment and aggression.* Paper presented at Fifth Federal Forum on Child Abuse and Neglect Research, Bethesda, MD.

Kromkowski, J. (1976). *Neighborhood deterioration and juvenile crime.* South Bend, IN: South Bend Urban Observatory.

Krugman, R. D., Lenherr, M., Betz, L., & Fryer, G. E. (1986). The relationship between unemployment and physical abuse of children. *Child Abuse & Neglect, 10,* 415-418.

Lahey, B. B., Conger, R. D., Atkeson, B.M., & Treiber, F. A. (1984). Parenting behavior and emotional status of physically abusive mothers. *Journal of Consulting and Clinical Psychology, 52,* 1062-1071.

Lorber, R., Felton, D. K., & Reid, J. B. (1984). A social learning approach to the reduction of coercive processes in child abusive families: A molecular analysis. *Advances in Behavior Research and Therapy, 6,* 29-45.

Lynch, M. A., & Roberts, J. (1982). *Consequences of child abuse.* San Diego, CA: Academic Press.

MacMillan, H. L., Fleming, J. E., Trocme, N., Boyle, M. H., Wong, M., Racine, Y. A., Beardslee, W. R., & Offord, D. (1997). Prevalence of child physical and sexual abuse in the community: Results from the Ontario Health Supplement. *Journal of the American Medical Association, 278,* 131-135.

Madonna, P. G., Van Scoyk, S., & Jones, D. P. H. (1991). Family interactions within incest and nonincest families. *American Journal of Psychiatry, 148,* 46-49.

Mash, E. J., Johnston, C., & Kovitz, K. (1983). A comparison of the mother-child interactions of physically abused and nonabused children during play and task situations. *Journal of Clinical Child Psychology, 12,* 337-346.

McCabe, V. (1984). Abstract perceptual information for age level: A risk factor for maltreatment? *Child Development, 55,* 267-276.

McGowan, B. G., & Kohn, A. (1990). Social support and teen pregnancy in the inner city. In A. R. Stiffman & L. E. Davis (Eds.), *Ethnic issues in adolescent mental health* (pp. 189-207). London: Sage.

Melnick, B., & Hurley, J. (1969). Distinctive personality attributes of child abusing mothers. *Journal of Consulting and Clinical Psychology, 33,* 746-749.

Melton, G. B., & Barry, F. D. (1994). Neighbors helping neighbors: The vision of the U.S. Advisory Board on Child Abuse and Neglect. In G. B. Melton & F. D. Barry (Eds.), *Protecting children from abuse and neglect* (pp. 1-13). New York: Guilford.

Milner, J. S., & Chilamkurti, C. (1991). Physical child abuse perpetrator characteristics: A review of the literature. *Journal of Interpersonal Violence, 6,* 345-366.

Murphy, S., Orkow, B., & Nicola, R. (1985). Prediction of child abuse and neglect: A prospective study. *Child Abuse & Neglect, 9,* 225-235.

Olds, D. L., Eckenrode, J., Henderson, C. R., Jr., Kitzman, H., Powers, J., et al. (1997). Long-term effects of home visitation on maternal life course and child abuse and neglect. *Journal of the American Medical Association, 278,* 637-643.

Panel on Research on Child Abuse and Neglect, Commission on Behavioral and Social Sciences and Education, National Research Council. (1993). *Understanding child abuse and neglect.* Washington, DC: National Academy Press.

Parke, R., & Collmer, C. W. (1975). Child abuse: An interdisciplinary analysis. In E. M. Hetherington (Ed.), *Review of child development research* (Vol. 5). Chicago: University of Chicago Press.

Patterson, G. R., DeBaryshe, B. D., & Ramsey, E. (1989). A developmental perspective on antisocial behavior. *American Psychologist, 44,* 329-335.

Pelton, L. H. (1978). Child abuse and neglect: The myth of classlessness. *American Journal of Orthopsychiatry, 48,* 608-617.

Pelton, L. H. (1989). *For reasons of poverty.* New York: Praeger.

Pelton, L. (1994). The role of material factors on child abuse and neglect. In G. Melton & F. Barry (Eds.), *Protecting children from abuse and neglect* (pp. 131-181). New York: Guilford.

Pianta, R., Egeland, B., & Erickson, M. F. (1989). *The antecedents of maltreatment: Results of the Mother-Child Interaction Research Project.* New York: Cambridge University Press.

Polansky, N. A., Chalmers, M. A., Williams, D. P., & Buttenweiser, E. W. (1981). *Damaged parents.* Chicago: University of Chicago Press.

Reid, J. B., Kavanaugh, K., & Baldwin, D. V. (1987). Abusive parents' perceptions of child problem behaviors: An example of parental bias. *Journal of Abnormal Child Psychology, 15,* 457-466.

Salzinger, S., Felkman, R. S., Hammer, M., & Rosario, M. (1991). Risk for physical child abuse and the personal consequences for its victims. *Criminal Justice and Behavior, 18,* 64-81.

Sedlak, A. J., & Broadhurst, D. D. (1996). *Executive summary of the Third National Incidence Study of Child Abuse and Neglect.* Washington, DC: U. S. Department of Health and Human Services, Administration for Children and Families, Administration on Children, Youth and Families, National Center on Child Abuse and Neglect.

Smelser, N. J. (1989). Self-esteem as a social problem. In A. M. Mecca, N. J. Smelser, & J. Vasconcellos (Eds.), *The social importance of self-esteem.* Berkeley: University of California Press.

Spinetta, J. J., & Rigler, D. (1972). The child abusing parent: A psychological review. *Psychological Bulletin, 77,* 296-304.

Starr, R. H., Jr. (1982). A research-based approach to the prediction of child abuse. In *Child abuse prediction: Policy implications.* Cambridge, MA: Ballinger.

Starr, R. H., Jr. (1988). Physical abuse of children. In V. B. Van Hasselt, R. L. Morrison, A. S. Belleck, & M. Hersen (Eds.), *Handbook of family violence* (pp. 119-155). New York: Plenum.

Starr, R. H., Jr., MacLean, D. J., & Keating, D. P. (1991). Life-span developmental outcomes of child maltreatment. In R. H. Starr, Jr., & D. A. Wolfe (Eds.), *The effects of abuse and neglect* (pp. 1-32). New York: Guilford.

Steele, B. F., & Pollock, C. B. (1968). A psychiatric study of parents who abuse infants and small children. In R. E. Helfer & C. H. Kempe (Eds.), *The battered child* (pp. 89-133). Chicago: University of Chicago Press.

Straus, M. (1980). Stress and child abuse. In *The battered child* (pp. 86-103). Chicago: University of Chicago Press.

Straus, M. (1983). Ordinary violence, child abuse, and wife beating: What do they have in common? In D. Finkelhor, R. J. Gelles, G. T. Hotaling, & M. A. Straus

(Eds.), *The dark side of families: Current family violence research* (pp. 213-234). Beverly Hills, CA: Sage.

Straus, M. (1994). *Beating the devil out of them: Corporal punishment in American families.* New York: Free Press.

Straus, M., Gelles, R., & Steinmetz, S. (1980). *Behind closed doors.* Garden City, NY: Doubleday.

Straus, M. A., Sugarman, D. B., & Gilessims, J. (1997). Spanking by parents and subsequent antisocial behavior of children. *Archives of Pediatrics & Adolescent Medicine, 151*(8), 761-767.

Sturm, L., & Drotar, D. (1989). Prediction of weight for height following intervention in three-year-old children with early histories of nonorganic failure to thrive. *Child Abuse & Neglect, 13,* 19-28.

Susman, E. J., Trickett, P. K., Iannotti, R. J., Hollenbeck, B. E., & Zahn-Waxler, C. (1985). Child-rearing patterns in depressed, abusive, and normal mothers. *American Journal of Orthopsychiatry, 55,* 237-251.

Tharinger, D., Horton, C. B., & Millea, S. (1990). Sexual abuse and exploitation of children and adults with mental retardation and other handicaps. *Child Abuse & Neglect, 14,* 301-312.

Thompson, R. A. (1994). Social support. In G. B. Melton & F. D. Barry (Eds.), *Protecting children from abuse and neglect* (pp. 40-130). New York: Guilford.

Trickett, P. K., & Kuczynski, L. (1986). Children's misbehavior and parental discipline strategies in nonabusive families. *Developmental Psychology, 22,* 115-123.

Trickett, P. K., & Susman, E. J. (1988). Parental perceptions of child-rearing practices in physically abusive and nonabusive families. *Developmental Psychology, 24,* 270-276.

Trocme, N., McPhee, D., Tam, K. K., & Hay, T. (1994). *Final report: Ontario Incidence Study of Reported Child Abuse and Neglect.* Toronto: Institute for the Prevention of Child Abuse.

Twentyman, C. T., & Plotkin, R. C. (1982). Unrealistic expectations of parents who maltreat their children: An educational deficit that pertains to child development. *Journal of Clinical Psychology, 38*(3), 497-503.

Tyler, J. A., Fairchild, C., & Lichtenstein, C. (1995). *Executive summary. Evaluation of Emergency Child Abuse and Neglect Prevention Services second program analyses report.* Silver Spring, MD: KRA Corporation.

U.S. Congress. (1973). Child Abuse Prevention and Treatment Act, PL 93-247. 93rd Congress, 31 January 1974.

U.S. Advisory Board on Child Abuse and Neglect. (1990). *Child abuse and neglect: Critical first steps in response to a national emergency* (Stock No. 017-092-00104-5). Washington, DC: Government Printing Office.

U.S. Department of Health and Human Services, Children's Bureau. (1997). *National study of protective, preventive and reunification services delivered to children and their families.* Washington, DC: Government Printing Office.

U.S. Department of Health and Human Services, National Center on Child Abuse and Neglect. (1996). *Child maltreatment 1994: Reports from states to the National Child Abuse and Neglect Data System.* Washington, DC: Government Printing Office.

U.S. Department of Health and Human Services, National Center on Child Abuse and Neglect. (1997). *Child maltreatment 1995: Reports from states to the*

National Child Abuse and Neglect Data System. Washington, DC: Government Printing Office.

Vaughn, B., Deinard, A., & Egeland, B. (1980). Measuring temperament in pediatric practice. *Journal of Pediatrics, 96,* 510-514.

Webster-Stratton, C. (1990). Stress: A potential disruptor of parent perceptions and family interactions. *Journal of Clinical Child Psychology, 19,* 302-312.

Weis, J. G. (1989). Family violence research methodology and design. In L. Ohlin & M. Tonry (Eds.), *Crime and justice: Vol. 11. Family violence* (pp. 117-162). Chicago: University of Chicago Press.

Whipple, E. E., & Richey, C. A. (1997). Crossing the line from physical discipline to child abuse: How much is too much? *Child Abuse & Neglect, 21*(5), 431-444.

Whipple, E. E., & Webster-Stratton, C. (1991). The role of parental stress in physically abusive families. *Child Abuse & Neglect, 15,* 279-291.

Widom, C. S. (1989). The cycle of violence. *Science, 244,* 160-166.

Widom, C. S., & Kuhns, J. B. (1996). Childhood victimization and subsequent risk for promiscuity, prostitution, and teenage pregnancy: A prospective study. *American Journal of Public Health, 86,* 1607-1612.

Wolfe, D. A. (1985). Child-abusive parents: An empirical review and analysis. *Psychological Bulletin, 97,* 462-482.

Wright, J., Boucher, J., Frappier, J.-Y., Lebeau, T., & Sabourin, S. (1997, July). *The incidence of child sexual abuse in Quebec.* Paper presented at the Fifth International Family Violence Research Conference, Durham, NH.

Wylie, R. (1979). *The self-concept* (Vol. 2). Lincoln: University of Nebraska Press.

Zuravin, S. J. (1987). The ecology of child maltreatment: Identifying and characterizing high risk neighborhoods. *Child Welfare League of America, 66*(6), 506.

CHAPTER 2

Understanding the Origins and Incidence of Spousal Violence in North America

ROBERT L. HAMPTON

MARIA VANDERGRIFF-AVERY

JOAN KIM

Over the past 30 years, public and private interest in spousal abuse has dramatically increased. Recently, several highly publicized events involving public figures have heightened the awareness of and the attention given to this type of family violence, perhaps the most prominent being the charges against O. J. Simpson for physically assaulting Nicole Brown Simpson several times before her tragic death. Other celebrities accused of domestic assault include Charlie Sheen, David Soul, Jan-Michael Vincent, Billy Dee Williams, Dudley Moore, and Ike Turner. Unfortunately, this is nowhere near an exhaustive list. Another, more recent, publicized incidence was the arrest in February 1998 of Tommy Lee, drummer for the rock band Motley Crue, for spousal abuse, child abuse, and possession of an illegal weapon. There has also been a rapid increase in television programming surrounding the issue of domestic violence, such as the made-for-TV movie *The Burning Bed* and the public announcement commercials on wife abuse that are run during sports events such as the Super Bowl.

Although some studies have reported that intimate violence between males and females occurs at an equal rate (Stets & Straus,

1990; Straus, Gelles, & Steinmetz, 1980), others have reported that women are more likely than men to be abused by their partner (Bachman & Saltzman, 1995). Regardless, it has been shown that women are more often the victims of severe forms of violence and suffer from more bodily injury than their male counterparts (Stets & Straus, 1990). Therefore, the focus of this chapter is the violence that is perpetrated by men against their female intimate partners. We will begin with a historical analysis of spousal abuse and an examination of incidence and prevalence issues. This will be followed by an exploration of the major theories surrounding wife abuse. Finally, we will end with a discussion of possible intervention and prevention strategies.

Historical Background

The Puritans enacted the first law in America to prohibit wife beating in 1641 in Massachusetts Bay Colony as a "symbolic affirmation" of Biblical values. However, this and other such laws were rarely enforced as a result of the community's strong belief in family privacy and in the authoritative position of the husband within the home. In fact, by 1663 enforcement of these laws had almost completely disappeared (Pleck, 1989, as cited in Fagan & Browne, 1994). In 1672, Plymouth Colony passed the next law against wife abuse, the last major law passed until 1850. In the early 19th century, courts made provisional rulings regarding how the state could legally intervene in situations of domestic violence. During this time, a Mississippi court ruled that husbands had the right, without being prosecuted, to discipline their wives physically as long as they did so in a "moderate manner" (*Bradley v. State*, 1 Miss. 157, as cited in Fagan & Browne, 1994). This ruling was followed in 1866 by the notorious "rule of thumb" motion, which allowed a man to beat his wife without being indicted as long as he did so with something smaller than the width of his thumb (*State v. Rhodes*, 61 N.C. 453, as cited in Fagan & Browne, 1994). Alabama was the first state to abolish the legal right of a husband to abuse his wife physically, but this was not until 1871. In 1874, North Carolina followed Alabama's example with the stipulation that it was best to view such incidences as private family matters unless permanent injury was incurred (*State v. Oliver,* 70 N.C. 60, as cited in Fagan & Browne, 1994).

Public attention by feminists and the Women's Christian Temperance Union (WCTU) led to an increase in the protection of women against wife battering during the last quarter of the 19th century. The WCTU believed that the abuse of wives was directly linked to husbands' use of alcohol. They lobbied for legislation that would increase the legal protection of women who were battered. Twenty states passed legislation that allowed abused women to sue saloon owners and keepers for personal injuries they received from someone who had become intoxicated at their establishment (Dutton, 1995). Yet, even though wife abuse was illegal in many states in the United States and even with the increase in tort protection, violence that took place within the late-19th-century family was often ignored by the criminal justice system in both the United States and Canada unless someone was murdered. Interest in wife abuse, as well as the recognition that it was a serious crime, began to fade by the first quarter of the 20th century (Dutton, 1995).

The "rediscovery" of wife abuse by feminists occurred during the late 1960s and early 1970s. Advocates of the women's movement began to point out the incongruity of the laws against wife abuse and the actual legal policies that surrounded the issue (Dutton, 1995). In response to this inconsistency, feminist grassroots organizations began to develop a variety of services for victims of spouse abuse and began lobbying for change in legislative laws involving protection of victims (Fagan & Browne, 1994). Battered women's shelters were one of the many services developed during this time. The first sanctuary for battered women, Chiswick Women's Aid, was established in 1972 in Britain. In 1973, Women's Advocates in Minnesota was the first shelter to open in the United States, followed by the Transition House in Boston in 1974. An estimated 780 shelters for battered women had opened by 1985 (Carden, 1994). In the past 10 years a variety of domestic violence laws have been passed, including the 1994 Violence Against Women Act. This act, among many other things, bans the possession of firearms by domestic abusers and protects battered women who have moved away from their abuser by penalizing offenders who cross state lines to abuse their spouse or who violate a protection order (U.S. Department of Justice, 1998). This law has also allocated several million dollars to states during the past few years to increase the enforcement of laws that protect women from violence, to increase the prosecution of those who commit crimes of violence against women, and to increase the availability of victim resources. Another recent milestone in the fight against wife abuse was the development of the Department of Justice's Violence Against Women Office, which fights domestic violence by combining new federal laws with direct assistance to states and localities (U.S. Department of Justice, 1998).

Frequency of Marital Violence

It is difficult to estimate rates of violence against women, especially sexual assaults and other crimes committed by intimates, because women are commonly inhibited from reporting such crimes to police and interviewers (Bachman & Saltzman, 1995). When compared to those victimized by strangers (3%), women victimized by intimates (18%) are about six times more likely *not* to report their violent victimization to police. This was often because they feared reprisal from the offender (Bachman, 1994).

Thirty-five states collect some statistical information on domestic violence, and 30 states collect statistical information on sexual assaults (Justice Research and Statistics Association, 1996). There is, however, variation across states—in definitions, in types of victims included in reporting requirements, and in other elements—that makes it difficult to compare or aggregate data at a national level. Most of the data collected come from law enforcement agencies.

The two primary sources of epidemiological data on intimate violence are the two waves of the National Family Violence Surveys (NFS; reported in Straus & Gelles, 1990; Straus et al., 1980) and the ongoing National Crime Victimization Survey (NCVS). A number of other studies have addressed intimate violence using a distinct subpopulation or specific topic, while others have added some questions on violence to a survey focused on another topic.

The NFVS and NCVS are based on nationwide probability samples of households with brief interviews of respondents. Although there are fundamental differences in their methodologies, these two instruments have provided important baseline knowledge about national trends in family violence for over two decades. Even with these impressive surveys and other data on violence, the true rates of partner or intimate violence are unknown. Counting the incidents and prevalence is difficult. The variability in reported rates has been the root of heated debate (Dobash, Dobash, Wilson, & Daly, 1992; Dutton, 1994; Miller, 1994; Renzetti, 1994). The methodological problems associated with access, validity, and reliability are enormous (Dobash & Dobash, 1979; Kurz, 1993; Straus, 1993). These problems have sometimes resulted in a contradictory set of "facts." These "facts"—based on how and who gets counted—have serious implications for funding and policy.

Most of the research in this field assumes that self-reports of perpetration or victimization are valid. A recent study conducted in Ontario, however, has raised some fundamental questions about this assumption. This research found that self-reports, even for such salient life events as interpersonal violence, are heavily influenced by other variables in addition to the number of times the events may have actually occurred (Hilton, Harris, & Rice, 1998). For example, several studies have indicated that men consistently report that their use of violence occurs less frequently and is less severe than their female partners report it to be (Crowell & Burgess, 1996; Fagan & Brown, 1994; Hampton & Gelles, 1994; Jouriles & O'Leary, 1985).

The NFVS provides a rich source of data on the nature, type, severity, and correlates of violence in the family. Data from the 1985 survey revealed that 16 out of every 100 married or cohabiting couples reported a violent incident during the year of the survey. This represented a negligible decrease in the proportion of couples experiencing violence in 1985 compared to 1975 (Straus & Gelles, 1986). Applying the rate to the 54 million couples in the United States that year resulted in an estimate of 8.7 million couples who experienced at least one assault during the year.

Straus and Gelles (1986) estimated that husband-to-wife violence decreased by 6.6% between their 1975 and 1985 surveys. The rate of severe violence by husbands also decreased. The rate declined from 38 per 1,000 couples in 1975 to 30 per 1,000 couples in 1985. This 21% decrease is important because it represents a considerable number of couples.

Using the Conflict Tactics Scale (Straus, 1979), the study found that milder forms of violence were more common than more severe forms of violence. The study also found that wife beating was a pattern, not a single event, in most violent homes. On average, a woman who was a victim of wife abuse was abused three times each year. Several additional important findings about the rates of violence from this survey were that rates were:

- higher for young adults ages 18-24
- higher for African American males
- higher for families with incomes less than $20,000 per year
- higher for women in central cities
- highest among couples who had been together for the shortest time (Straus & Gelles, 1990)

The National Crime Victimization Survey is a second major source of data on violence between couples. The NCVS collects information about crimes, including incidents not reported to police, from a continuous nationally representative sample of households in the United States. The survey was redesigned for 1992 and 1993 to produce more accurate reporting of rape, sexual assault, and other crimes committed by intimates and family members. The NCVS did not specifically ask about sexual assaults or violence prior to 1992.

Violence at the hands of an intimate involved about 9.3 women per 1,000 in 1992-1993. This translates into about 1 million women who became the victims of such violence as rape/sexual assault, aggravated or simple assault, or robbery every year (Bachman & Saltzman, 1995). The study also found:

- Women were about six times more likely than men to experience violence committed by an intimate.
- Women of all races and Hispanic and non-Hispanic women were about equally vulnerable to violence by an intimate.
- The highest rates of violence are experienced by younger women. The average annual rate of victimization is 74.6 per 1,000 for women aged between 12 and 18 and 63.7 per 1,000 for women aged 19 to 29; in comparison, the average annual rate for all women is 36.1.
- Women in families with incomes below $10,000 were more likely than other women to be victims of intimate violence.
- Women separated from their partners were at greater risk for victimization than divorced or married women.

There is debate over the actual number of battered women. These numbers range from 9.3 per 1,000 women (Bachman & Saltzman, 1995) to 220 per 1,000 women (Meredith, Abbott, & Adams, 1986). The most commonly cited figures come from the NFVS (Straus & Gelles, 1990) rate of 116 per 1,000 women for a violent act and 34 per 1,000 for "severe" violence (Crowell & Burgess, 1996).

Both lethal and nonlethal injuries fall disproportionately on women. In 1996, 30% (over 1,500) of all female homicide victims in the United States were known to have been killed by a husband, ex-husband, or boyfriend compared to 3% of all men killed by an intimate (Federal Bureau of Investigation, 1997). In 1992-1993, 29% of all violence committed by lone offenders was committed by an intimate, compared to 4% of violence against men. Women were also more likely to sustain injury when victimized by an intimate. Fifty-two percent of violent victimizations by an intimate involved injury (with 41% requiring medical care), compared to only 20% of violent victimizations by a stranger (Bachman & Saltzman, 1995).

Data from the recent Canadian Violence Against Women Survey revealed an overall prevalence rate of violence against women similar to the rate in the United States. Twenty-nine percent of ever-married Canadian women experienced physical or sexual violence at the hands of an intimate partner (compared to 28% of women in the United States; Straus & Gelles, 1990). Nearly 50% of all Canadian women had experienced at least one incident of physical or sexual assault since the age of 16 (Statistics Canada, 1994). The Canadian survey interviewed a random sample of 12,300 women who were 18 or older, and investigated physical and sexual violence as well as emotional abuse (Crowell & Burgess, 1996).

The majority of research on wife abuse is not large national surveys like the NFVS or NCVS. There are a number of studies that rely on samples derived from those who are seeking help in a shelter (Gondolf & Fisher, 1988), in an emergency room or other medical setting (Stark & Flitcraft, 1996), in an outpatient clinic (Jouriles & O'Leary, 1985), and in family court (Joseph, 1997). While these studies provide us with important data, there are some important limitations associated with their methodological factors. There are often disagreements over the operational definitions of violence and over the importance of nonphysical injury or context in defining and studying marital violence (Fagan & Browne, 1994). There is also wide variation in study samples (e.g., ethnicity, locale), data collection methods, question construction, and context that may account for differences in findings (Crowell & Burgess, 1996).

It is clear to most that clinical samples or other samples of women seeking help often represent the most severely assaulted women, and in many respects these women cannot be understood through the lens created by a large-scale survey like the NFVS. Shelter samples average more than one assault per week, compared to the number of abused women in the national survey who average six assaults per year (Straus, 1990, as cited in Margolin & Burman, 1993). These samples also provide us with a wealth of information on some of the psychological and physical health sequelae that are associated with marital violence. The data collected from shelter samples or other clinical samples, however, are not generalizable to the population of couples involved in marital violence (Woffordt, Mihalie, & Menard, 1994).

Differences in study findings are primarily of magnitude rather than substance. Risk characteristics (e.g., being young) and assault characteristics (e.g., by a nonstranger) are fairly consistent across studies. There continue to be disagreements over the number of women who have been victimized during any specific period of time (Crowell & Burgess, 1996).

Origins

Regardless of which surveys are more accurate in determining how many women are actually abused by their intimate partners, the same questions still remain: What kinds of men abuse their female partners, and why do these men abuse? These questions have been examined and explained from several different levels of analyses, including from an individual level, an interactional level, a social-cultural level, and an ecological level. Although these are by no means an exhaustive list of perspectives used to answer these questions, they are the focus of this section. Attention is given primarily to the characteristics of male batterers versus the characteristics of women who are abused, because they have been found more useful in evaluating the risk of husband-to-wife violence (Hotaling & Sugarman, 1986).

Individual

When examining spousal violence from an individual perspective, it is important to point out that male batterers are not a homogeneous group. There is no complete or unitary "profile" of a man who batters his female partner (Gondolf, 1988). In fact, after reviewing several studies that addressed profiles of assaultive men, Fagan and Browne (1994) found what they termed to be a "bewildering array of findings" (p. 186). There are, however, some general characteristics that have been reported. Men who batter are often more hostile than nonbatterers (Bersani, Chen, Pendleton, & Denton, 1992; Gondolf, 1988; Maiuro, Cahn, Vitaliano, Wagner, & Zegree, 1988), suffer from low self-esteem (Gondolf, 1988), and exhibit a high need for control while at the same time often expressing a low level of assertiveness (Hotaling & Sugarman, 1986). Men who batter also tend to be extremely jealous (Dutton, 1995; Stamp & Sabourin, 1995; Walker, 1984), are often abusive toward children (Hotaling & Sugarman, 1986; Straus, 1990), and are also more sexually aggressive toward their partners (Hotaling & Sugarman, 1986). In addition to these, there appears to be an association between marital violence and the abuse of alcohol by the batterer (Coleman & Straus, 1983; Gondolf, 1988; Hotaling & Sugarman, 1986; Kantor & Straus, 1990a). Eighty-six percent of the assailants in female partner abuse interviewed by Brookoff, O'Brien, Cook, Thompson, and Williams (1997) reported using alcohol on the day of the assault.

Batterers often excuse themselves of responsibility by attributing the violence that has occurred on external factors. Blame is placed on the wife's or female partner's behavior or personality, which "caused" the batterer to be jealous or "pushed" him to his limit of personal control. When violence is admitted, males may feel justified in using it or they may downplay their actions by minimizing the quantity of violence in their relationship or by using minimizing language such as "slap" instead of "punch" or "push" instead of "beat" (Stamp & Sabouren, 1995).

Interactional

Other researchers take a different perspective on wife abuse. These "interpersonal explanations focus on interactions of persons involved with each other" (Margolin, Sibner, & Gleberman, 1988). Emphasis is placed on the family unit instead of the individual, circular rather than linear explanations are used to understand problems, and nonverbal communication is taken into consideration (Nichols, 1984, as cited in Margolin & Burman, 1993). An example of the interactional viewpoint is systems theory. Advocates of systems theory view battering as an interactional pattern between the abused and the abuser—one could not exist without the other. Cascardi and Vivian (1995) found some support for this position in their study of 62 couples who reported an active contribution by both partners in the escalation of violence. Ideas linked to the family systems therapy approach contrast with many profeminists who study marital violence and "reject the notion that a wife shares responsibility for her husband's behavior" (Carden, 1994, p. 552).

Other theories that have developed out of the interactional perspective include Walker's (1979) cycle theory of violence. This theory has three distinct phases. Phase One, the tension building stage, is where a gradual escalation of tension occurs and may include minor incidences of battering such as name-calling and some physical abuse. During this phase, the woman usually minimizes the incident and tries to placate her batterer. Phase Two, the acute battering incident, is where the major violent act takes place. The fact that the batterer is out of control is usually accepted at this point by both the batterer and the battered. After the incident, the battered woman may isolate herself to recover from the blow. The third and final phase, kindness and contrite loving behavior, is where the abuser tries to make up for what he has done by begging for forgiveness, promising never to harm his female partner again, buying his partner gifts, and by showing his partner kindness. This phase is also known as the "honeymoon" phase.

Social/Cultural

At the social and cultural level, domestic violence has been examined through many lenses. For the purposes of this chapter, the feminist framework, social learning theory, social exchange theory, and the impact of race will be explored.

Feminist Framework. Feminists have argued that the prevalence and very existence of wife and intimate partner abuse is rooted in our patriarchal society's view of women (Dobash & Dobash, 1979; Hansen & Harway, 1997; Walker, 1979; Yllö, 1993). The abuse of women by their male partners is an outgrowth of this patriarchy and a culture that maintains the domination of men over women through economic inequalities and non-egalitarian portrayals of women that reinforce male attitudes of superiority (Fagan & Browne, 1994). There also appears to be a direct connection between men who batter and non-egalitarian or patriarchal sex-role attitudes (Smith, 1990; Stith & Farley, 1993). Straus et al. (1980) reported a higher level of wife abuse in couples who engaged in husband-dominate decision-making styles.

Wife abuse is not only associated with patriarchal attitudes within the family but also is linked to the larger structural context of patriarchy. Yllö and Straus (1990) found a curvilinear relationship between the status of women across states and wife abuse. In states where structural inequalities were the highest, so were the rates of violence against wives. As the status of women across the states increased, the rate of wife abuse decreased for the most part. However, in states with the highest status of women (lowest structural inequalities), the rate of wife beatings increased. The authors attributed this finding to a backlash against the improved status of women.

Social Learning Theory. Social learning theory posits that we acquire behaviors by observing others and modeling what we see. In relation to marital violence, social learning theory predicts that someone who has witnessed or experienced a great deal of violence will model that type of behavior him- or herself, especially if doing so has positive results. Crowell and Burgess (1996) argued that male violence against women endures because it generally does have positive results: "it releases tension, leaves the perpetrator feeling better, often achieves its ends by cutting off arguments and is rarely associated with punishment for the perpetrator" (p. 60). Several studies have indicated a link between exposure to violence as a child (either as a witness of parental violence or as a victim of parental violence) and the use of violence toward female partners (Browne, 1987; Gwartney-Gibbs, Stockard, & Bohmer, 1987; Hotaling & Sugarman, 1986; Pagelow, 1984).

Social Exchange Theory. Social exchange theory asserts that "individuals trade, as in a marketplace, emotions for other emotions" (Jenkins, Hampton, & Gullotta, 1996). The core assumptions of the exchange framework are in part based upon the nature of humans. According to Sabatelli and Shehan (1993), these are as follows:

- Humans seek rewards and avoid punishments.
- When interacting with others, humans seek to maximize profits for themselves while minimizing costs. Since it is not possible to know the actual rewards and costs involved in interacting with another before interaction occurs, humans use their expectations for rewards and costs to guide their behavior.
- Humans are rational beings and, within the limitations of the information that they possess, they calculate rewards, costs, and consider alternatives before acting. This includes the possibility that when faced with no desirable alternative, humans will choose the least costly alternative.
- The standards that humans use to evaluate rewards and costs differ from person to person and can vary over the course of time.
- The importance that humans attach to the behavior of others in relationships varies from person to person and can vary over the course of time.
- The greater the value of a reward exceeds one's expectations, the less valued the reward will become in the future. (p. 396)

According to social exchange theory, violence in a relationship will continue when the awards drawn from being violent outweigh the costs of not being violent.

Race/Ethnicity. Studies that have examined whether or not race is a "risk marker" of spousal abuse or whether or not it impacts the reporting of spousal abuse have found mixed results. Hotaling and Sugarman (1986) reported that race is an inconsistent risk marker or one that "shows no consistent pattern across studies" (p. 104). Some researchers have found that there is no significant difference between racial groups in relation to how much intimate violence is sustained (Bachman & Saltzman, 1995; Gondolf, 1988), especially when factors such as socioeconomic status are controlled (Koss et al., 1994).

Several national survey studies have indicated that African Americans are more likely to report the occurrence of intimate physical violence than white Americans (Cazenave & Straus, 1990; Hampton & Gelles, 1994; Sorenson, 1996; Straus & Gelles, 1986, as cited in Crowell & Burgess, 1996). Other studies have found no significant differences between racial groups in the reporting of intimate violence (Kantor & Straus, 1990b).

Ecological Framework

Based on the work of Bronfenbrenner (1979) and of Belsky (1980), Dutton (1985) proposed an ecologically nested theory of male violence toward female partners that integrates several of the already described theories. He suggested that this type of violence is determined by an interplay of forces within the nested factors of the macrosystem, the exosystem, the microsystem, and the ontogenic system. In other words, he indicated that it is not one variable that may result in a man battering his female partner, but an interaction among several.

Macrosystem. The macrosystem includes society's formal and informal social rules and norms. The feminists' argument of the link between marital violence and society's overarching patriarchal value system is an example of how the macrosystem, in this case the social rule of patriarchy, can affect wife abuse.

Exosystem. The exosystem is comprised of the community surrounding an individual or family unit. It can include the neighborhood, workplace, peer groups, formal or informal social supports, and/or lack of social support (Dutton, 1985; National Research Council, 1993). An example of a lack in social support that may contribute to male violence against their female partner is socioeconomic status. The socioeconomic status of a man appears to be a "risk marker" of marital violence. Hotaling and Sugarman (1986) described a risk marker as an "attribute or characteristic that is associated with an increased probability to either the use of husband to wife violence, or the risk of being victimized by husband to wife violence" (p. 102). A risk marker is not, however, an indication of causation. When compared to nonbatterers, batterers were more likely to have lower incomes, less education, and lower-status occupations (Smith, 1990). All of these can result in a lack of social support. Women in lower income brackets have also been found to be at a higher risk for intimate violence than women in higher income brackets (Bachman & Saltzman, 1995; Zawitz, 1994).

Microsystem. The microsystem consists of the nuclear and extended family, including the interactions that take place among the members (Dutton, 1985; National Research Council, 1993). Factors that may contribute to spousal abuse at this level are similar to those mentioned in the discussion of social learning theory, such as witnessing violence between one's parents (Carden, 1994). The factors are also similar to those mentioned in the discussion of interactional causes of wife abuse, such as both partners contributing to the escalation of violence.

Ontogenic System. The ontogenic system involves individual development. Many of the examples discussed in the "individual" section of this chapter apply to this level of the ecological system.

Consequences of Partner Violence

The response to partner violence on the part of individuals who are battered is negative and extensive. Research in recent years has brought an increased understanding of the impact of trauma, in general, and of violence against women, in particular. Some of the early literature on women assaulted by male partners was based on the assumption that some specific traits might predispose them to abuse. Research has failed to show that women assaulted by their male partners have distinct psychological characteristics, suggesting that most of these characteristics appear to be sequelae of partner assaults, rather than antecedents (Koss et al., 1994; Stark & Flitcraft, 1996).

Physical Injuries

About half of all female victims of intimate violence report an injury of some type, and about 20% of these seek medical assistance (Greenfield et al., 1998). A woman is more likely to be injured if she is victimized by an intimate than by a stranger (Bachman & Saltzman, 1995). In a recent study, women accounted for 39% of the hospital emergency department visits for violence-related injuries in 1994 but 84% of the persons treated for injuries inflicted by intimates (Greenfield et al., 1998). These injuries range from bruises to scratches, and from cuts to stab wounds or internal injuries. Some injuries cause permanent impairment and are life threatening.

Psychological Injuries

The literature on abused women reports negative psychological and emotional well-being among battered women who have sought help or refuge in a shelter or agency. These studies have shown that battered women frequently suffer from low self-esteem (Rieker & Carmen, 1986; Roark & Vlahos, 1983) and suffer from feelings of loss and inadequacy (Turner & Shapiro, 1986), depression (Dutton, 1995) and learned helplessness (Walker, 1979).

Several psychological distress items were included in the Second National Family Violence Survey with the intent of measuring the three aspects of mental health that have been mentioned as being related to experiencing violence: depression, stress, and somatic symptoms. Women who reported experiencing violence and abuse also reported higher levels of moderate and severe psychological distress. The multivariate analysis indicated that violence made an independent and nonspurious contribution to the psychological distress experienced by women (Gelles & Harrop, 1989). On further examination of these data for a subsample of African American women, Hampton and Gelles (1994) found a statistically significant relationship between the highest level of reported violence in the past year and 9 of the 10 psychological distress items. At times, the psychological consequences of partner violence and battering may be as serious as the physical consequences (Gelles & Harrop, 1989).

Women's reactions to violence by male partners closely parallel reactions of survivors across a variety of traumatic events (Koss, et al., 1994). Although a single assault may lead to permanent emotional scars, the severity and repetition of violence is clearly deleterious to psychological adjustment (Follingstad, Brennan, Hause, Polek, & Rutledge, 1991). Battering is often seen as a major determinant of female suicide attempts (Stark, 1995) and of post traumatic stress disorder (PTSD; Browne, 1992; Herman, 1992; Walker, 1979).

Battered Women as Survivors

The response of the social system to the battered woman's cry for help has been historically insufficient. It is the writers' view that the battered woman's cry for help should mobilize an entire system of supports required to ameliorate her situation. Contrary to this occurring, there are serious barriers and deficiencies in the help sources that must be addressed to support the help-seeking efforts of the battered woman.

Two views emanate from the literature on the consequences of violence on battered women. The first view sees the battered woman as an active survivor of an abusive situation. The second view categorizes the battered woman as a "helpless and passive victim" (Gondolf & Fisher, 1988). Following is a discussion of the battered woman as a helpless and passive victim. The concept of "learned helplessness" is used to illustrate the victimization process. Walker (1979) suggested that repeated battering diminishes the woman's motivation to respond. As a result, women show a tendency to be submissive in the face of intermittent punishments or abuse. As the abuse continues, the battered woman becomes immobilized, feels a loss of emotion over the battering experience, and begins to blame herself for the abuse inflicted upon her by another. In Walker's conceptualization, learned helplessness is a core feature of battered woman syndrome. It is often the loss of the ability to predict whether behavior will have any effect on an outcome and a corresponding restriction of behaviors (Walker, 1979).

Contrary to learned helplessness theory is the "survivor hypothesis." Gondolf and Fisher (1988) see battered women as "active survivors." Their research found that women respond to abuse with help-seeking efforts that are largely unmet. Other critics have suggested that what we sometimes perceive as helplessness for some victims of partner assault may simply reflect the reality of inadequate resources, such as police responsiveness, child care, education and employment opportunities, and community services that are already overwhelmed. Many battered women remain in abusive situations not due to passivity but due to repeated unsuccessful attempts to escape. These women increase their help-seeking efforts in the face of increased violence. They try in a logical, consistent way to assure themselves and their children protection and survival. Such efforts supersede fear, giving up, depression, or the passivity of the learned helplessness state. There is a growing body of research that supports the argument that women in assaultive relationships show a high degree of resourcefulness in response to their violent situations (Browne, 1987, 1997; Gondolf & Fisher, 1988; Jones 1994).

Ola Barnett and Alyce LaViolette (1993) take a different approach to the critique of learned helplessness. Taking a broader sociocultural perspective, they argue that women have been socialized into a belief system that devalues women, especially unmarried women, and creates in women a higher sense of responsibility for the maintenance of the family unit. Therefore a woman is blamed for the failure of a relationship or marriage even when there are severe assaults and other violence. According to Barnett and LaViolette, relationship hope seems to be an internalized and reinforced concept for women in general. Learned hopefulness is a battered woman's ongoing belief that her partner will change his abusive behavior or that he will change his personality. Learned hopefulness is often an explanation for why some abused women remain with their abusers or why the women Gondolf and Fisher studied were more likely to return to their abusive partners if the men were enrolled in counseling programs for batterers.

Interventions

Interventions to aid physically abused children have the oldest history and originated in the medical community in the 1950s. Formal programs for victims of marital violence began almost two decades later. These programs assumed, in most cases, that survivors of wife assault are adults and that they are able to make their own decisions. There are a number of ways to define and characterize interventions. One way is to describe the larger conceptual framework that underlies an approach and another is to focus on several specific crisis intervention services. We shall do both.

Feminist approaches focus attention on the women victims rather than the family unit as a whole. These gender-based approaches to partner violence provide a theory to explain the experience of females' being victimized by all types of male violence, and, indeed, illuminate male violence in general (Garske, 1996). They emphasize protecting women from harm and empowering them to end the abuse. The approach is often expressed through political and legal activism and in shelters, grassroots organizations, and crisis intervention programs (Fagan & Browne, 1994). One aspect of this approach is to work at both the macro and micro levels to transform sociocultural norms and behaviors in order to prevent partner violence and promote safety, equality, and justice for women (Garske, 1996).

Social control approaches emphasize the family unit, with a focus on family integrity. These approaches may underestimate the severity of risk to victims. The theoretical position of programs with this approach is often a family systems model where all family members are seen as part of a "system" of violence (Fagan & Browne, 1994).

Legalistic approaches focus on victim and assailant in the context of laws that have been broken; they are rooted in assumptions of specific deterrence (Fagan & Browne, 1994). These approaches emphasize that deviant behavior is controlled when punishment is both certain and severe. Individuals are in effect coerced, threatened, and sanctioned into conformity by the threat of legal sanctions ranging from arrest and prosecution to civil and criminal penalties. The threat of arrest and public exposure as a wife beater might deter potentially violent men from abusing their wives (Mederer & Gelles, 1989). Mandatory arrest and prosecution statutes reflect this approach.

As one can easily detect, each of these approaches is informed and conditioned by different assumptions about, and perhaps definitions of, partner violence. These approaches are often operationalized in several crisis intervention services that victims of abuse can turn to and some treatment programs available for abused women and their abusers. We shall briefly discuss four types of intervention that have received considerable attention in the past decade: shelters, including counseling and peer support; hospitals; police interventions; and treatment programs for male batterers.

Shelters

Services available to victims of partner violence vary from community to community. One of the more important developments in the past two decades has been the establishment of safe houses or shelters for battered women. The first facilities to house abused women were established between 1974 and 1976. In 1976, there were probably no more than 5 or 6 shelters in the United States. By 1996, out of 1,800 programs for battered women in the United States, 1,200 were shelters (Plichta, 1995, cited in Crowell & Burgess, 1996). Hotlines, temporary shelter services, group and individual counseling, legal advocacy, social service referral and advocacy, services for children of abused women, transitional housing, child care, and job training are among the services that may be available. Few organizations are able to provide the full array of services that may be needed. Most women who use shelter services tend to be low socioeconomic status. For example, in one study (O'Sullivan, Wise, & Douglas, 1995) more than three fourths of the women who sought shelter were on public assistance. Gondolf and Fisher (1988) found that a substantial portion lived in poverty. The women who sought nonresident services tended to be from higher socioeconomic groups than those who sought resident shelter services.

Shelters provide more than temporary refuge. Individual counseling and peer support are probably the most commonly used services by battered women (Crowell & Burgess, 1996) and may be found at most shelters. They also provide long-term support for victims of partner violence and community education. Shelters can play a pivotal role in facilitating help seeking.

Hospitals

Hospitals and medical personnel play important roles in recognizing, reporting, and treating victims. Frequently, the only, or the first, practitioners who come in contact with victims are medical professionals. There is also evidence that health care workers frequently ignore the initial signs of battering. Flitcraft, Frazier, and Stark (1980) found through their examination of emergency department records that many women seen initially for inflicted injuries subsequently return with inflicted injuries. Stark and Flitcraft (1985) found that only 1 in 25 battered women was identified as battered in the emergency department they studied.

The available data suggest that health care professionals treat a large number of women for injuries that result from interpersonal violence. A study of a representative sample of 1,793 women in Kentucky (Shulman, 1979) found that 1 out of 10 had been physically assaulted by her partner during the year, and 79 of the assaults were serious enough to require medical attention. Forty-three percent of the injured women required treatment, and 44% of these needed two or more treatments. Fifty-nine percent sought treatment in a hospital emergency department.

Two hospital-based studies also concluded that battered women are seen frequently in emergency rooms. In a study conducted at a large general hospital emergency department in Detroit, 25% of the women examined were known victims of domestic violence (Goldberg & Tomlanovich, 1984). Similar results were reported by researchers in San Francisco, who concluded that 36% of admissions to the county trauma center resulted from interpersonal violence (Sumner, Mintz, & Brown, 1986).

McLeer and Anwar (1989) found that when a protocol to identify battered women was introduced to an emergency department, in which they asked female trauma patients if they had been injured by someone, almost 30% of all female trauma patients were battered women.

There is much variability in staff responses to victims, based on their medical specialty, their perception of the victim, and their training. Many medical personnel tend to focus on the injury itself while ignoring the process and circumstances of the incident that produced it. Health care advocates for victims of wife abuse have proposed that health care personnel learn to identify battered women and do interventions of their behalf (Hampton, 1988). The response of the health care community to partner violence has been slow and inconsistent (Stark, 1993). Former Surgeon General C. Everett Koop's (1991) message helped guide the response of health professionals by targeting violence as a priority for the public health and medical care systems:

Identifying violence as a public health issue is a relatively new idea. Traditionally, when confronted by the circumstances of violence, the health professionals have deferred to the criminal justice system. . . . Today the professional of medicine, nursing, and the health related social services must come forward and recognize violence is their issue. (p. v)

Since January 1992, the joint Commission on Accreditation of Healthcare Organizations has recommended that all accredited hospitals implement policies and procedures in their emergency departments and ambulatory care facilities for identifying, treating, and referring victims of domestic abuse. Several frameworks have been developed to assist physicians and other health care providers to recognize victims and provide effective medical intervention ranging from secondary and tertiary prevention to discharge planning.

Police Intervention

Police officers are more likely to come into contact with spousal abuse than any other agency, institution, or form of intervention. They are not only the ones most likely to be called during an incidence of wife abuse, but they also are more likely than other institutions to receive public funding (Sherman, 1992). As a result of this, it is usually the police who must determine what sort of action needs to be taken in response to calls of domestic disputes, whether it be to do nothing, to try to mediate the dispute, to have the perpetrator leave, or to arrest the perpetrator (Dutton, 1995). The actual reaction of police officers to wife abuse has changed dramatically in the past 15 years: "As recently as 1984, police almost never made arrests in domestic violence cases with no visible injury, and 22 states barred police from making warrantless arrests in cases they had not witnessed" (Sherman, 1992). In 1986, many states began to change the way they viewed and treated domestic violence—it was seen as a crime against the state versus a private argument to be taken care of exclusively by the family. "By 1988, 90% of police agencies either 'encouraged' or 'required' arrest in such cases [domestic violence]" (Sherman, 1992, p. 14). This change may have been in part due to the results of the Minneapolis experiment (which will be described in detail). Most likely, this change is a direct result of the *Thurman v. Torrington* suit. This suit awarded Tracey Thurman 2.5 million dollars as a result of the Torrington police department's neglect in arresting her abusive husband. Whether or not arrest is the most effective way for police officers to handle perpetrators of domestic violence usually dominates police intervention discussions (Crowell & Burgess, 1996). Many researchers have examined this very issue (Berk, Campbell, Klap, & Western, 1992; Dunford, Huizinga, & Elliott, 1990; Hirschel, Hutchinson, Dean, Kelley, & Pesackis, 1991; Pate, Hamilton, & Annan, 1991; Sherman, 1992).

In 1980, the Minneapolis Police Department, using a grant from the National Institute of Justice, "carried out the first controlled, randomized experiment in history in the use of arrest for any offense" (Sherman, 1992, p. 2). The main question of this experiment was determining which procedure was most effective in deterring spousal abuse: trying to mediate the conflict, sending the abusing spouse away, or arresting the abuser. Arresting the abuser was found to be the most effective method in preventing a repeat offense by the abuser when following up on both official police records and interviews with the victims. According to police records, mediating between the involved parties proved to be the second best way to handle partner abuse. However, it was found to be the least effective method according to the victims' reports. These results led to a change in the way the Minneapolis Police Department handled reports of domestic violence, by making arrest the preferred policy for dealing with domestic violence cases unless there were obvious reasons to do something else. In instances where they did not arrest a suspect, officers became required to file special reports indicating why they did not arrest.

The Minneapolis experiment results also led to several similar studies in other cities/counties, including Charlotte, Omaha, Milwaukee, Metro-Dade, and Colorado Springs. The results of these studies varied. As in Minneapolis, arrest seemed to have a deterrent effect in Colorado Springs (Berk et al., 1992) and in Metro-Dade (Pate et al., 1991). However, in Charlotte (Hirschel et al., 1991), Milwaukee (Sherman, 1992), and Omaha (Dunford et al., 1990), arrest was not found to have a deterrent effect over time. The Omaha study did find, however, that issuing an arrest warrant for suspects who left the scene of the incident had a strong deterrent effect. Some researchers (e.g., studies by original authors and

Sherman, 1992) have interpreted the results of these last three studies as an indication that arrest, in some cases, actually increases the frequency of future domestic assaults. This increase has been linked to marital status, employment status, and race. In Milwaukee, for instance, arrests were found to increase the chance of repeat spousal assault among those who were unmarried and unemployed (Sherman, 1992). Sherman (1992) also pointed out that in the cities where arrest was found to be a deterrent, the concentration of Caucasians was higher and the concentration of African Americans was lower than in the cities where arrests did not deter future episodes of domestic assault. Dutton (1995) explained these phenomena by pointing out that perhaps arrest works as deterrent only for those men "who have something to lose by being arrested" (p. 240).

It is important to point out that these interpretations have not gone without criticism. Other researchers have explained the results of these studies differently. After reexamining the data gathered in all of the cities, Garner, Fagan, and Maxwell (1995) have argued that a "definitive statement" about the studies' results is impossible because "the available information is inadequate and incomplete" (p. 3). Dutton (1995) has advocated the use of arrest. After comparing all types of groups, he has concluded that the losses of arrests are outweighed by the gains of arrests. He goes on to argue, however, that arrests in and of themselves should not and cannot serve as a panacea.

Men's Treatment Programs

Over the past two decades as awareness and concern about partner abuse has increased, the information about men who batter has also grown. A substantial portion of research has attempted to establish a profile of batterers. Research in this area was in many respects comparable to psychological studies in the related fields of criminology, substance abuse, and child abuse. This research focused on developing a list of traits or characteristics that would help identify potential batterers (Gondolf, 1988; Saunders, 1992). Contradictions and inconclusiveness in the profile research have prompted a turn toward more diverse representations of men who abuse their partners. As already indicated, several studies have substantiated the presence of different types of batterers, suggesting several different profiles (Gondolf, 1993).

Counseling for men who batter began slowly and cautiously in the late 1970s. Beginning with EMERGE in Boston in 1977, Brother to Brother in Providence, Rhode Island, and Amend in Denver, hundreds of additional programs in the United States and Canada have established services for men who batter. The late 1980s saw a surge in batterer programs as court-mandated counseling was encouraged by battered women's advocates. The courts, in lieu of open probation, have increasingly been diverting or sentencing men who batter into counseling (Gondolf, 1993).

Although intervention with men takes place in a variety of ways, the field has adopted small group treatment as the primary modality. The underlying philosophy, operational characteristics, and length of programs vary, as do the curricula. Most programs have at least one component that addresses anger management, skill building, and resocialization (Gondolf, 1993). Some of the programs are psychoeducational, with many having an underlying profeminist orientation to the problem of woman abuse (Edleson & Tolman, 1992). This approach focuses on men holding men accountable for partner abuse and ending the violence (Almeida & Bograd, 1991; Edleson & Tolman, 1992; Garske, 1996; Williams, 1994). Many of these programs have been modified or adapted to a more culturally focused perspective for work with men of color (Williams, 1994, 1998).

Programs vary widely in the sessions required of participants. Generally, batterers' groups meet once or twice a week for approximately 2 hours. Most groups are considered short term, ranging in length from 6 to 32 weeks (Edleson & Tolman, 1992).

Two of the most difficult issues that face these programs are resistance and dropout. There is much denial of partner abuse by the perpetrators. These men often enter treatment with an attitude that tends to minimize their abuse, defer responsibility for it, or deny that abuse is occurring. The group and its facilitator must confront the denial, self-pity, evasiveness, and rationalization associated with so many batterers (Gondolf, 1993). With respect to program dropouts, according to a survey of program directors, nearly half of the programs faced dropout rates of 50% of the men accepted at intake. One program documented that less than 5% of

200 men who contacted a batterer program completed the 6-month program (Gondolf, 1997).

There are many questions regarding the effectiveness of batterer programs. When reports of physical abuse based on partner reports are considered, successful outcomes ranged from 53% to 85%. In these studies, follow-up data were collected from 4 months to 26 months post treatment. On the whole, evidence suggests that many batterers are successful in stopping physical partner abuse for a short period of time (Tolman & Edleson, 1995). A majority of program completers do stop their violence for a period, but we do not know exactly why and how (Gondolf, 1997).

Prevention

Prevention programs targeted at reducing rates of spousal and intimate partner abuse have primarily been composed of school-based programs. These programs usually focus on general violence prevention as well as on dating and spousal abuse, conflict mediation skills, and sexual abuse (Crowell & Burgess, 1996). Many feminists have argued that this is not enough and that prevention needs to begin by challenging the root cause of the domestic violence problem—patriarchal attitudes. According to Garske (1996), these attitudes must not only be challenged, but also changed and replaced:

> Given that the problem reflects the deeply rooted sociocultural belief that men are entitled to have authority over women and that our society is replete with individual, interpersonal, and institutional manifestations of this belief, effective change will require not only the elimination of this belief system, but its replacement with a coherent alternative that offers positive benefits to all. (p. 277)

Garske asserted that this social transformation can take place only through a community-based and communitywide approach. Another preventative way of addressing this type of violence is by launching an extensive public education campaign that identifies wife and female partner abuse as an issue that can, and must, be addressed by both communities and individuals. Klein, Campbell,

Soler, and Ghez (1997) argued that this can be accomplished by encouraging people to claim personal responsibility for ending this type of violence, to recognize their personal role in helping women who are battered, and to appreciate the importance of their personal involvement in the matter.

Conclusions

Are we on the verge of a transformation when it comes to violence against women by their male partners? The answer is we hope so, but there is still a long way to go. Although the past two decades have witnessed increased public awareness, sweeping policy changes, and legal innovations to protect women from abuse by their male partners, many public and private responses to victims remain lodged in decades-old preconceptions about the nature of intimate violence. Some of the legislation recently passed, such as the 1994 Violence Against Women Act, may have positive outcomes in relation to violence against women. The effects that other recent legislation will have, such as the Personal Responsibility and Work Opportunity Act of 1996, are yet to be determined and may not be as positive. Recent trends of economic upturn for some and continued poverty for others may continue to place some women at a greater risk than others.

Most violence prevention and intervention strategies are targeted at a micro level. The true effectiveness of this as a sole strategy is questionable. Violence against women will not cease by changing attitudes and behavior only one man at a time. Although this is important and necessary, it is not sufficient. Real change will involve a basic shift in our social structures and values. Institutional sexism and myths revolving around partner violence must be challenged. A shift must also be made in the way our legal systems handle these types of cases. This shift entails moving away from our societal tendencies to blame victims of intimate violence. Although recent efforts to reduce intimate partner violence against women in the public arena are admirable, their attempts will ring hollow unless a transformation is made in the structures, value systems, and institutions that sustain them.

References

Almeida, R. V., & Bograd, M. (1991). Sponsorship: Men holding men accountable for domestic violence. In *Feminist approaches for men in family therapy* (pp. 243-259). New York: Hayworth Press.

Bachman, R. (1994). *Violence against women: A National Crime Victimization Survey report.* Washington, DC: U.S. Department of Justice, Bureau of Justice Statistics.

Bachman, R., & Saltzman, L. E. (1995). *Violence against women: Estimates from the redesigned survey.* Washington, DC: U.S. Department of Justice, Bureau of Justice Statistics.

Barnett, O. W., & LaViolette, A. D. (1993). *It could happen to anyone: Why battered women stay.* Newbury Park, CA: Sage.

Berk, R. A., Campbell, A., Klap, R., & Western, B. (1992). Bayesian analysis of the Colorado Springs Spouse Abuse Experiment. *Journal of Criminal Law & Criminology, 83,* 170-200.

Belsky, J. (1980). Child maltreatment: An ecological integration. *American Psychology, 35*(4), 320-335.

Bersani, C. A., Chen, H. T., Pendleton, B. F., & Denton, R. (1992). Personality traits of convicted male batterers. *Journal of Family Violence, 7*(2), 123-134.

Bronfenbrenner, U. (1979). *Toward an experimental ecology of human development.* Cambridge, MA: Harvard University Press.

Brookoff, D., O'Brien, K. K., Cook, C. S., Thompson, T. D., & Williams, C. (1997). Characteristics of participants in domestic violence: Assessment at the scene of domestic assault. *Journal of the American Medical Association, 277*(17), 1369-1373.

Browne, A. (1987). *When battered women kill.* New York: Free Press.

Browne, A. (1992). Violence against women: Relevance for medical practitioners. *Journal of the American Medical Association, 267,* 3184-3189.

Browne, A. (1997). Violence in marriage: Until death do us part? In A. P. Cardarelli (Ed.), *Violence between intimate partners: Patterns, causes, and effects* (pp. 48-69). Needham Heights, MA: Allyn & Bacon.

Carden, A. D. (1994). Wife abuse and the wife abuser: Review and recommendations. *The Counseling Psychologist, 22*(4), 539-582.

Cascardi, M., & Vivian, D. (1995). Context for specific episodes of marital violence: Gender and severity of violence differences. *Journal of Family Violence, 10*(3), 265-293.

Cazenave, N. A., & Straus, M. A. (1990). Race, class, network embeddedness, and family violence: A search for potent support systems. In M. A. Straus & R. J. Gelles (Eds.), *Physical violence in American families: Risk factors and applications to violence in 8,145 families* (pp. 321-329). New Brunswick, NJ: Transaction Publishers.

Coleman, D. H., & Straus, M. A. (1983). Alcohol abuse and family violence. In E. Gottheil, K. Druly, T. Skolada, & H. Waxman (Eds.), *Alcohol, drug abuse, and aggression* (pp. 104-124). Springfield, IL: Charles C Thomas.

Crowell, N. A., & Burgess, A. W. (1996). *Understanding violence against women.* Washington, DC: National Academy Press.

Dobash, R. E., & Dobash, R. P. (1979). *Violence against wives: A case against patriarchy.* New York: Free Press.

Dobash, R. P., Dobash, R. E., Wilson, M., & Daly, M. (1992). The myth of sexual symmetry in marital violence. *Social Problems, 39,* 71-91.

Dunford, F. W., Huizinga, D., & Elliott, D. S. (1990). The role of arrest in domestic assault: The Omaha experiment. *Criminology, 28,* 186-206.

Dutton, D. G. (1985). An ecologically nested theory of male violence towards intimates. *International Journal of Women's Studies, 8,* 404-413.

Dutton, D. G. (1994). Patriarchy and wife assault: The ecological fallacy. *Violence and Victims, 9,* 167-182.

Dutton, D. G. (1995). *The domestic assault of women: Psychological and criminal justice perspective.* Vancouver, BC: UBC Press.

Edleson, J. L., & Tolman, R. M. (1992). *Intervention for men who batter: An ecological approach.* Newbury Park, CA: Sage.

Fagan, J., & Browne, A. (1994). Violence between spouses and intimates: Physical aggression between women and men in intimate relationships. In A. J. Reiss, Jr., & J. A. Roth (Eds.), *Understanding and preventing violence* (pp. 115-292). Washington, DC: National Academy Press.

Federal Bureau of Investigation. (1997). *Crime in the United States 1996: Uniform crime reports.* Washington, DC: U.S. Department of Justice.

Flitcraft, A., Frazier, W. D., & Stark, E. (1980). *Medical encounters and sequelae of domestic violence.* Final report to the National Institute of Mental Health, Bethesda, MD.

Follingstad, D. R., Brennan, A. F., Hause, E. S., Polek, D. S., & Rutledge, L. L. (1991). Factors moderating physical and psychological symptoms of battered women. *Journal of Family Violence, 6,* 81-95.

Garner, J., Fagan, J., & Maxwell, C. (1995). Published findings from the Spouse Assault Replication Program: A critical review. *Journal of Quantitative Criminology, 11*(1), 3-28.

Garske, D. (1996). Transforming the culture: Creating safety, equality, and justice for women and girls. In R. L. Hampton, P. Jenkins, & T. P. Gullotta (Eds.), *Preventing violence in America* (pp. 263-285). Thousand Oaks, CA: Sage.

Gelles, R. J., & Harrop, J. W. (1989). Violence, battering, and psychological distress among women. *Journal of Interpersonal Violence, 4*(4), 400-420.

Goldberg, W., & Tomlanovich, M. C. (1984). Domestic violence victims in the emergency department. *Journal of the American Medical Association, 251*(25), 3259-3264.

Gondolf, E. W. (1988). Who are those guys? Toward a behavioral typology of batterers. *Violence and Families, 3,* 187-203.

Gondolf, E. W. (1993). Male batterers. In R. L. Hampton, T. P. Gullotta, G. R. Adams, E. H. Potter, III, & R. P. Weissberg (Eds.), *Family violence: Prevention and treatment* (pp. 230-257). Newbury Park, CA: Sage.

Gondolf, E. W. (1997). Expanding batterer program evaluation. In G. K. Kantor & J. L. Jasinski (Eds.), *Out of the darkness: Contemporary perspectives on family violence* (pp. 208-218). Thousand Oaks, CA: Sage.

Gondolf, E. W., & Fisher, E. R. (1988). *Battered women as survivors: An alternative to treating learned helplessness.* Lexington, MA: Lexington Books.

Greenfield, L. A., Rand, M. R., Craven, D., Klaus, P. A., Perkins, C. A., Ringel, C., Warchol, G., Maston, C., & Fox, J. A. (1998). *Violence by intimates: Analysis of data on crimes by current or former spouses, boyfriends, and girlfriends*. Washington, DC: U.S. Department of Justice, Bureau of Justice Statistics.

Gwartney-Gibbs, P. A., Stockard, J., & Bohmer, S. (1987). Learning courtship aggression: The influence of parents, peers, and personal experience. *Family Relations, 36,* 276-282.

Hampton, R. L. (1988). Physical victimization across the lifespan: Recognition, ethnicity, and deterrence. In M. Straus (Ed.), *Abuse and victimization: Across the lifespan* (pp. 203-222). Baltimore, MD: Johns Hopkins University Press.

Hampton, R. L., & Gelles, R. J. (1994). Violence toward black women in a nationally representative sample of black families. *Journal of Comparative Family Studies, 25*(1), 105-119.

Hansen, M., & Harway, M. (1997). Theory and therapy: A feminist perspective on intimate violence. In A. P. Cardarelli (Ed.), *Violence between intimate partners: Patterns, causes, and effects* (pp. 165-176). Needham Heights, MA: Allyn & Bacon.

Herman, J. L. (1992). *Trauma and recovery*. New York: Basic Books.

Hilton, N. Z., Harris, G. T., & Rice, M. E. (1998). On the validity of self-reported rates of interpersonal violence. *Journal of Interpersonal Violence, 13*(1), 58-72.

Hirschel, J. D., Hutchinson, I. W., III, Dean, C. W., Kelley, J. J., & Pesackis, C. E. (1991). *Charlotte Spouse Assault Replication Project: Final report*. Washington, DC: National Institute of Justice.

Hotaling, G. T., & Sugarman, D. B. (1986). An analysis of risk markers in husband to wife violence: The current state of knowledge. *Violence and Victims, 1*(3), 101-124.

Jenkins, P., Hampton, R. L., & Gullotta, T. P. (1996). Understanding the social context of violent behavior in families: Selected perspectives. In R. L. Hampton, P. Jenkins, & T. P. Gullotta (Eds.), *Preventing violence in America* (pp. 13-31). Thousand Oaks, CA: Sage.

Jones, A. (1994). *Next time she'll be dead: Battering and how to stop it*. Boston: Beacon.

Joseph, J. (1997). Woman battering: A comparative analysis of black and white women. In G. C. Kantor & J. L. Jasinski (Eds.), *Out of darkness: Contemporary perspectives on family violence* (pp. 161-169). Thousand Oaks, CA: Sage.

Jouriles, E. N., & O'Leary, K. D. (1985). Interspousal reliability of reports of marital violence. *Journal of Consulting and Clinical Psychology, 53,* 419-421.

Justice Research and Statistics Association. (1996). *Report on state domestic and sexual violence data collection*. Washington, DC: Author.

Kantor, G. K., & Straus, M. A. (1990a). The "drunken bum" theory of wife beating. In M. A. Straus & R. J. Gelles (Eds.), *Physical violence in American families: Risk factors and applications to violence in 8,145 families* (pp. 203-224). New Brunswick, NJ: Transaction Publishers.

Kantor, G. K., & Straus, M. A. (1990b). Response of victims and the police to assaults on wives. In M. A. Straus & R. J. Gelles (Eds.), *Physical violence in American families: Risk factors and applications to violence in 8,145 families* (pp. 473-487). New Brunswick, NJ: Transaction Publishers.

Klein, E., Campbell, J., Soler, E., & Ghez, M. (1997). *Ending domestic violence: Changing public perceptions/Halting the epidemic.* Thousand Oaks, CA: Sage.

Koop, C. E. (1991). Foreword. In M. L. Rosenberg & M. A. Fenley (Eds.), *Violence in America: A public health approach* (pp. v-vi). New York: Oxford University Press.

Koss, M. P., Goodman, L., Browne, A., Fitzgerald, L., Keita, G. P., & Russon, N. F. (1994). *No safe haven: Male violence against women at work, at home, and in the community.* Washington, DC: American Psychological Association.

Kurz, D. (1993). Physical assaults by husbands: A major social problem. In R. J. Gelles & D. R. Loseke (Eds.), *Current controversies on family violence* (pp. 88-103). Newbury Park, CA: Sage.

Maiuro, R. D., Cahn, T. S., Vitaliano, P. P., Wagner, B. C., & Zegree, J. B. (1988). Anger, hostility and depression in domestically violent versus generally assaultive men and nonviolent control subjects. *Journal of Consulting and Clinical Psychology, 56,* 17-23.

Margolin, G., & Burman, B. (1993). Wife abuse versus marital violence: Different terminologies, explanations, and solutions. *Clinical Psychology Review, 13,* 59-73.

Margolin, G., Sibner, L. G., & Gleberman, L. (1988). Wife battering. In V. B. Van Hasselt, R. L. Morrison, A. S. Bellack, & M. Hersen (Eds.), *Handbook of family violence* (pp. 89-117). New York: Plenum.

McLeer, S. V., & Anwar, R. (1989). A study of women presenting in an emergency department. *American Journal of Public Health, 79,* 65-67.

Mederer, H., & Gelles, R. J. (1989). Compassion or control: Intervention in cases of wife abuse. *Journal of Interpersonal Violence, 4*(1), 25-34.

Meredith, W. H., Abbott, D. A., & Adams, S. L. (1986). Family violence: Its relation to marital and parental satisfaction and family strengths. *Journal of Family Violence, 1,* 299-305.

Miller, S. L. (1994). Expanding the boundaries: Toward a more inclusive and integrated study of intimate violence. *Violence and Victims, 9,* 183-200.

National Research Council. (1993). *Understanding child abuse and neglect.* Washington, DC: National Academy Press.

Nichols, M. P. (1984). *Family therapy: Concepts and methods.* New York: Gardner.

O'Sullivan, C., Wise, J., & Douglas, V. (1995). *Domestic violence shelter residents in New York City: Profile, needs, and alternatives to shelter.* Paper presented at the Fourth International Family Violence Research Conference, Durham, NH.

Pagelow, M. D. (1984). *Family violence.* New York: Praeger.

Pate, A., Hamilton, E. E., & Annan, S. (1991). *The Minneapolis Community Crime Prevention Experiment: Draft evaluation report.* Washington, DC: The Police Foundation.

Pleck, E. (1989). Criminal approaches to family violence, 1640-1980. In L. Ohlin & M. Tonry (Eds.), *Crime and justice: An annual review of research: Vol. 2. Family violence.* Chicago: University of Chicago Press.

Plichta, S. B. (1995, September). *Domestic violence: Building paths for women to travel to freedom and safety.* Paper presented at the Symposium on Domestic Violence and Women's Health: Broadening the Conversation, the Commonwealth Fund, College of Health Sciences, Old Dominion University, New York.

Renzetti, C. M. (1994). On dancing with a bear: Reflections on some of the current debates among domestic violence theorists. *Violence and Victims, 9*, 195-200.

Rieker, P. P., & Carmen, E. H. (1986). The victim-to-patient process: The disconfirmation and transformation of abuse. *American Journal of Orthopsychiatry, 56*(3), 360-370.

Roark, M. L., & Vlahos, S. (1983). An analysis of the ego status of battered women. *Transactional Analysis Journal, 13*, 164-167.

Sabatelli, R. M., & Shehan, C. L. (1993). Exchange and resource theories. In P. G. Boss, W. J. Doherty, R. LaRossa, W. R. Schumm, & S. K. Steinmetz (Eds.), *Sourcebook of family theories and methods: A contextual approach* (pp. 385-417). New York: Plenum.

Saunders, D. G. (1992). A typology of men who batter wives: Three types derived from cluster analysis. *American Journal of Orthopsychiatry, 62*, 264-275.

Sherman, L. W. (1992). *Policing domestic violence: Experiments and dilemmas.* New York: Free Press.

Shulman, L. (1979). *The skills of helping individual and groups.* Itaska, IL: F. E. Peacock.

Smith, M. D. (1990). Patriarchal ideology and wife battering: A test of a feminist hypothesis. *Violence and Families, 5*, 257-273.

Sorenson, S. B. (1996). Violence against women: Examining ethnic differences and commonalities. *Evaluation Review, 20*, 123-145.

Stamp, G. H., & Sabourin, T. C. (1995). Accounting for violence: An analysis of male spousal abuse narratives. *Journal of Applied Communication, 23*, 284-307.

Stark, E. (1993). Mandatory arrest of batterers: A reply to its critics. *American Behavior Scientist, 36*, 651-680.

Stark, E. (1995). Killing the beast within: Woman battering and female suicidality. *International Journal of Health Services, 25*, 43-64.

Stark, E., & Flitcraft, A. (1985). Spouse abuse. In *Surgeon General's workshop of violence and public health: A sourcebook* (pp. SA1-SA43). Atlanta, GA: Centers for Disease Control.

Stark, E., & Flitcraft, A. (1996). *Women at risk: Domestic violence and women's health.* Thousand Oaks, CA: Sage.

Statistics Canada. (1994). *Family violence in Canada* (Product No. 89-5410-XPE). Ottawa: Statistics Canada, Canadian Centre for Justice Statistics.

Stets, J. E., & Straus, M. A. (1990). Gender differences in reporting marital violence and its medical and psychological consequences. In M. A. Straus & R. J. Gelles (Eds.), *Physical violence in American families: Risk factors and applications to violence in 8,145 families* (pp. 151-165). New Brunswick, NJ: Transaction Publishers.

Stith, S. M., & Farley, S. C. (1993). A predictive model of male spousal abuse. *Journal of Family Violence, 8*(2), 183-201.

Straus, M. A. (1979). Measuring intrafamily conflict and aggression: The Conflict Tactics Scale. *Journal of Marriage and the Family, 41*, 75-88.

Straus, M. A. (1990). Ordinary violence, child abuse, and wife-beating: What do they have in common? In M. A. Straus & R. J. Gelles (Eds.), *Physical violence in American families: Risk factors and applications to violence in 8,145 families* (pp. 403-424). New Brunswick, NJ: Transaction Publishers.

Straus, M. A. (1993). Physical assault by wives: A major social problem. In R. J. Gelles & D. R. Loseke (Eds.), *Current controversies on family violence* (pp. 67-87). Newbury Park, CA: Sage.

Straus, M. A., & Gelles, R. J. (1986). Societal change in family violence from 1975 to 1985 as revealed by two national surveys. *Journal of Marriage and the Family, 48,* 465-479.

Straus, M. A., & Gelles, R. J. (1990). *Physical violence in American families: Risk factors and adaptions to violence in 8,145 families.* New Brunswick, NJ: Transaction Publishers.

Straus, M. A., Gelles, R. J., & Steinmetz, S. K. (1980). *Behind closed doors: Violence in the American family.* Garden City, NY: Anchor/Doubleday.

Sumner, B. B., Mintz, E. R., & Brown, P. L. (1986). Interviewing persons hospitalized with interpersonal violence-related injuries: A pilot study. In *Homicide, suicide, and unintentional injuries* (U.S. Department of Health and Human Services, Report of the Secretary's Task Force on Black and Minority Health, Vol. 5, pp. 267-317). Washington, DC: Government Printing Office.

Tolman, R. M., & Edleson, J. L. (1995). Intervention for men who batter: A research review. In S. M. Stith & M. A. Straus (Eds.), *Understanding partner violence: Prevalence, causes, consequences, and solutions* (pp. 163-173). Minneapolis, MN: National Council on Family Relations.

Turner, S. F., & Shapiro, C. H. (1986). Battered women: Mourning the death of a relationship. *Social Work, 30,* 372-376.

U.S. Department of Justice. (1998). *Violence against women office* [On-line]. Available: http://www.usdoj.gov/vawo

Walker, L. E. (1979). *The battered woman.* New York: Harper & Row.

Walker, L. E. (1984). *The battered woman syndrome.* New York: Springer.

Williams, O. J. (1994). Group work with African American men who batter: Toward more ethnically sensitive practice. *Journal of Comparative Family Studies, 25*(1), 91-103.

Williams, O. J. (1998). Healing and confronting the African American male who batters. In R. C. Carrillo & J. Tello (Eds.), *Healing the spirit: Men of color and domestic violence* (pp. 74-94). New York: Springer.

Woffordt, S., Mihalie, D. E., & Menard, S. (1994). Continuities in marital violence. *Journal of Family Violence, 9*(3), 195-225.

Yllö, K. A. (1993). Through a feminist lens: Gender, power, and violence. In R. J. Gelles & D. R. Loseke (Eds.), *Current controversies on family violence* (pp. 47-62). Newbury Park, CA: Sage.

Yllö, K. A., & Straus, M. A. (1990). Patriarchy and violence against wives: The impact of structural and normative factors. In M. A. Straus & R. J. Gelles (Eds.), *Physical violence in American families: Risk factors and applications to violence in 8,145 families* (pp. 283-399). New Brunswick, NJ: Transaction Publishers.

Zawitz, M. W. (1994). *Violence between intimates.* Washington, DC: Department of Justice, Bureau of Justice Statistics.

• CHAPTER 3 •

Origins and Incidence of Workplace Violence in North America

LYNNE F. McCLURE

Data Regarding Workplace Violence in the United States and Canada

Workplace violence is not new. Like domestic violence, it has faced a great deal of denial—in this case, primarily on the part of employer organizations. Only relatively recently has workplace violence begun to receive the attention it warrants as an epidemic and as a significant factor in the area of family and community violence. This chapter presents the topic as an emerging field. It explores the origins and incidence of workplace violence in the United States and Canada, from both scholarly and empirical perspectives, and identifies current preventive measures and additional preventive steps that must be taken.

Workplace Violence as a Social Problem

Definitions of "Workplace Violence"

Nearly 1,000 individuals a year are killed at work, and homicide is the number one cause of death for women who die on the job. Although homicide is the most publicized form of violence at work in the United States, "workplace violence" also includes beatings, rape, assault, battery, theft, robbery, threats, harassment, and intimidation. Based on these definitions, from 1992 to 1996, more than 2 million violent incidents were reported in U.S. workplaces *every year*—and experts estimate that fewer than *half* of the actual incidents are even reported. The reported incidents—more than 80% of which were committed by male perpetrators—included a yearly average of 1.5 million simple assaults, 51,000 rapes and sexual assaults, 84,000 robberies while at work, and 1,000 homicides (U.S. Department of Justice, 1998).

Research regarding workplace violence in Canada began even more recently than in the United States, and what was described in 1995 as a "frustrating lack of data" (Pearson, 1995) has improved only slightly as of the printing of this chapter. A survey conducted by Statistics Canada showed that, as in the United States, close to 1 million violent incidents occurred in Canadian workplaces during 1993 (Burroughs & Jones, 1995). Collected—but as of this writing unpublished—data indicate that in 1995, workplace violence caused 10 deaths, or 1.3% of total deaths in the workplace. Also during 1995, workplace violence caused injuries among 2,293 employees (Association of Workers' Compensation Boards of Canada, 1997).

A recent Canadian study (The Research Team, 1997) reports significant impact of domestic violence on the workplace, in terms of absenteeism, stress, productivity, costs, and related issues. Building on results of Canada's first nationwide survey of violence against women (Statistics Canada, 1993), the purpose of the study is to encourage employer organizations in Canada to recognize the seriousness of this impact. Another Canadian study (Boyd, 1995) used the number of claim files of the Workers' Compensation Board to identify the number and types of incidents. Results indicated that nurses and other health care workers faced risks similar to those of police officers.

Another aspect of the definition of workplace violence is the source. Workplace violence may come from two major sources: external and internal (McClure, 1996). This distinction is important because, as described later in this chapter under "Additional Preventive Measures Employer Organizations Can Take," the sources have different implications regarding the types of preventive measures that can be taken.

External Sources. Attackers who are outsiders to the organization include customers, random criminals, and others who have no official association with the organization or any of its employees. Of all violent attacks at work, 75% occur during armed robberies and similar crimes in which the source is external (Phillips, 1996). Because of their randomness, however, these forms of violence are more difficult to predict and prevent than are those from internal sources.

Internal Sources. Current and former employees are the most obvious internal perpetrators in a workplace, but internal sources also include spouses, former spouses, relatives, boyfriends, friends and acquaintances of current and former employees, and others known to employees. As discussed in more detail under "Domestic Violence," workplace violence also may include a spillover of domestic violence. Workplace violence from internal sources is more predictable and preventable than that from external sources, as described below under "Warning Signs" and "Additional Preventive Measures Employer Organizations Can Take."

Other Ways of Describing/Measuring Workplace Violence. Male victims were attacked at work by strangers more than 65% of the time, by acquaintances nearly 30% of the time, by intimates 0.9% of the time, and by other relatives 0.5% of the time. Female victims were attacked at work by strangers 47% of the time, by acquaintances 46% of the time, by intimates 2.2% of the time, and by other relatives 1% of the time (U.S. Department of Justice, 1998).

By all its definitions, and in all its forms, workplace violence clearly is an issue that must be recognized and addressed.

Correlations Between Types of Employer Organizations and Types of Incidents

Workplace homicides accounted for about 17% of all fatal occupational injuries. By occupation, in descending order, homicides victims were retail salespersons, executives or managers, law enforcement officers, security guards, taxi drivers or chauffeurs, and truck drivers. Homicide was the second leading cause of death in the workplace for all workers, and the number one cause of death for women who died on the job. About 75% of workplace homicides each year were related to robberies, 10% came from victims' co-workers or customers, and 5% were due to victims' personal acquaintances. More than 60% of violent workplace incidents took place during daylight hours. The perpetrator had a weapon 20% of the time, and firearms were used in fewer than 10% of all workplace occurrences (U.S. Department of Justice, 1998).

In a broader, more general sense, jobs that involve dealing with the public, exchanging money, working alone or in small groups, working at night, and working in high-crime or isolated areas have the highest risk for workplace violence (U.S. Department of Justice, 1994). However, these patterns reflect only homicides committed by external sources, in situations where the primary motive is robbery.

From 1992 through 1996, by occupation, non-fatal workplace assaults took place, in descending order of frequency, in law enforcement, retail sales, teaching, medical, mental health, and transportation. By nature of employment, 56% of victims worked in the private sector, 33% worked for state or local government, 7% were self-employed, and 3% worked for the federal government. Each year, 330,000 retail sales workers were attacked, including approximately 61,000 convenience store and liquor store clerks and 26,000 bartenders. More than 160,000 medical workers were attacked, including 70,000 nurses, 24,000 medical technicians, and 10,000 physicians annually. Attacks on teachers were estimated at about 149,000 every year, including 33,000 in high schools, 35,000 in elementary schools, and 47,000 in junior high and middle schools. Law enforcement officers were victims of more than 431,000 attacks each year. In the mental health field, more than 102,000 attacks occurred annually (U.S. Department of Justice, 1998).

In addition, in 1996, two thirds of nonfatal assaults in the workplace occurred in hospitals, nursing homes, residential care facilities, and other social service locations (U.S. Department of Labor, 1996). For women, jobs in health care, education, and social services have the highest risk of violence at work. Every year, approximately 260,000 women in all fields of work are victims of rapes, beatings, and other forms of violence (Center for Women in Government, 1996). These patterns reflect both external and internal sources of violence.

Although government employees constituted about 16% of the workforce, they made up 37% of the victims of violence between 1992 and 1996 (U.S. Department of Justice, 1998), perhaps because of public exposure and the nature of specific government occupations (such as public safety). It is possible to speculate, however, that at least three other factors may contribute to this overrepresentation: characteristics of an organization (e.g., autocratic) in which current or former employees become violent; behavior patterns of the individuals currently or formerly hired by these organizations (internal sources); and the use of government agencies as symbols on the part of individuals with strong antigovernment views (external sources) (McClure, 1996). Externally caused workplace violence may be a growing threat to public employees (Nigro & Waugh, 1996).

In Canada, violence patterns are similar to those in the United States: police officers, taxi drivers, bartenders, doormen, gas station attendants, grocery clerks, hotel or motel workers, and hospital employees are at the highest risk of being victims of violence at work (Hales, Seligman, Newman, & Timbrook, 1988). However, nurses' unions are credited with taking the lead in exposing the risk faced by health care workers (Wigmore, 1995). This risk—especially for those working in long-term care institutions—has increased since the mid-1980s and appears to match the risk faced by police officers (Boyd, 1995). Ironically, one study indicated that 24% of nurses who had been assaulted did not report the incident (Liss & McCaskell, 1994). This fact may reflect a "traditional expectation" that violence will occur on the job (J. B. Curtis, Canadian Centre for Occupational Health and Safety, personal communication, July 21, 1997)—an expectation that contributes to denial. It also is important to note that in health care, patients may be at risk of harm from employees, as well as vice versa (Selden & Pace, 1997).

Statistics Regarding Victims, Costs, and Other Outcomes of Workplace Violence

In addition to the immeasurable emotional costs, workplace violence has tremendous negative financial impact on employees and their families, employer organizations, and the community at large.

Medical and Income Costs. At least 750 employees were murdered in the workplace each year between 1980 and 1989, and the annual number of workplace homicides grew to more than 1,000 by 1992. From 1992 through 1996, 17% of all fatal injuries on the job came from workplace homicide, and more than 80% of these victims were killed with firearms (U.S. Department of Justice, 1998).

More than 2 million U.S. workers reported being physically attacked on the job every year, from 1992 through 1996. In 1992, 111,000 "significantly" violent incidents occurred, costing employers about $6.2 billion in lost wages, medical costs, and support costs. On average, workplace violence causes 500,000 employees to miss 1,751,000 workdays, totaling $55,000,000 in lost wages annually (U.S. Department of Justice, 1994; 1998).

Litigation Costs. When violent acts at work result in death or injury, multiple lawsuits have been filed against employers (Johnson & Indvik, 1994). Grounds for litigation have included "negligent hiring" and "negligent retention" (Workplace Violence Research Institute, 1995). Whether cases have been settled in or out of court, they have been extremely costly to employer organizations. For example,

1. For "inadequate security," jury awards average $1.2 million nationwide, and out-of-court settlements average $600,000 (Perry, 1994).
2. A $4.25 million award went to a Michigan postal worker who had been shot by a co-worker (Mattman, 1994).
3. Other awards have exceeded $3 million each (*Workplace Violence: A Survey,* 1995).

In addition, even when an employee is murdered by a co-worker *"away from business premises"* [italics added], the employer has been held responsible for "negligent retention" of an employee "known" as a potential danger (Johnson & Indvik, 1994; Perry, 1994). Employers have also been held responsible for "negligent infliction," which results in the emotional distress suffered by employees who *witness* injury or death, on the job, of a co-worker (Podgers, 1995).

Managers face an ironic dilemma: They are held responsible for identifying and preventing potential violence, but until recently have had no means to do either. As discussed below, new approaches and methods make early identification, early intervention, and prevention possible.

Productivity Costs. Even beyond the tragic incidents themselves, violent acts have negative effects on the productivity of all workers. Following a violent incident at work, organizations experience up to 80% decrease in productivity for about 2 weeks, due to loss of the injured or murdered worker; investigations by police and internal security; employees suffering from post traumatic stress; employees' time in counseling sessions; discussions about the incident; and related causes. In addition, morale often decreases and turnover increases after a violent episode. Costs of hiring and training increase. Much of the problem comes from the fact that workers see their employers as responsible for providing a safe work environment, and when violence occurs, the workers feel betrayed and unsafe (Mattman, 1994). In the United States, the Occupational Safety and Health Administration (OSHA) supports this expectation, saying that employers are responsible for preventing workplace violence. Some experts estimate that the cost to employer organizations of workplace violence is in the billions (Johnson & Indvik, 1994).

The financial costs ultimately get passed on to consumers and to the community at large, along with the emotional costs, which are more difficult to measure but easy to feel. Workplace violence clearly is a social problem, affecting all aspects of society in the United States. Although data regarding the costs of workplace violence in Canada currently are not available, it appears likely that they would be proportionally similar to costs in the United States.

Efforts to Explain Workplace Violence

Separation between "scholarly" and "empirical" research is difficult because of both the emerging nature of this issue as an area of study and the availability of more publicly available tangible data (e.g., real episodes of workplace violence) than may be the case in other topical areas. Even the data used in scholarly research come from actual events, rather than from experiments. "Currently, the management field has neither clear definitions nor any models or theories to structure and guide research on organizational violence" (O'Leary-Kelly, Griffin, & Glew, 1996, p. 226).

Scholarly Theories and Research, and Empirical Research

Two early studies (Baker, Samkoff, & Fisher, 1982; Baker, Teret, & Dretz, 1980) focused on the types of occupations most likely to be vulnerable to violence: law enforcement; retail groceries; gas stations; the alcohol-hospitality industry; and taxi service. Both studies used only homicide as the operational definition of workplace violence.

A more expansive study (Hales et al., 1988) also identified occupations that were most vulnerable to violent episodes: law enforcement; the alcohol-hospitality industry; the hotel industry; and the health care industry. In contrast to the studies by Baker and colleagues, this study broadened the operational definition of workplace violence to include all actions—in addition to homicide—involving either a firearm or a knife, in which the victim received a cut, puncture wound, or multiple injuries.

The research of both Baker et al. and Hales et al. is limited to intentional acts of violence with either a gun or knife. Other studies on workplace violence expanded the definition to include all acts of physical violence, whether the acts were intentional or not and whether or not they included a weapon.

Poyner and Warne (1988) focused on types of interactions (as opposed to occupations) most likely to result in violence: providing a service; caring for the mentally or physically ill; education; money transactions; delivery of goods; and controlling or inspecting traffic, retail stores, or public transportation. Although their focus was not on occupations, Poyner and Warne were, like Hales et al., among the first researchers to identify health care as a field vulnerable to violence.

Lipscomb and Love (1992) identify violence toward health care employees as an emerging issue in the United States. They note that mental health care facilities, emergency rooms, pediatric units, medical-surgical units, and long-term care facilities place health care workers at high risk of assault.

Boyd (1995) identifies similar problems in British Columbia, stating that most of the increase in workplace violence has occurred in the health care industry. Most victims have been health care workers, care aides, and nurses. It is interesting to note that, although these researchers do not identify it as such, the violence they describe in all the occupations except health care comes from external sources (e.g., a police officer injured by someone who was being arrested). In health care, the violence discussed comes from patients, who are internal sources. Although the patients are "customers" rather than employees, are not part of the official health care organization, and typically do not have personal relationships with employees, their inpatient status and their long-term residence make them, in fact, part of the organizational system. This distinction is important because it may mean that potential violence can be identified early and prevented.

Recent research, discussed immediately below, includes both the types of occupations and the kinds of interactions that increase the risk of violence. It also explores possible causes of workplace violence and considers individual, organizational, and social factors.

Individual Factors Contributing to Workplace Violence

One approach to understanding workplace violence is to study factors characteristic of individuals who have committed violent acts.

Domestic Violence. One possible link between domestic and workplace violence comes from a perpetrator's history. An abused child may, as an adult, act out, at work, the rage originally directed toward his abuser—and many perpetrators have histories of being abused as children (Johnson & Indvik, 1994). The cycle of violence—reenactments and repetitions, in the outside world, that occur in consecutive generations within the same family—is well known in the field of domestic violence. Whether the perpetrator is part of the organization or is a stranger, a history of childhood abuse may contribute to violent behavior.

Another possible connection focuses on current situations of domestic violence spilling over into the workplace. Between 1992 and 1996, in approximately 2% of cases where women were attacked at work, the perpetrator was the husband, ex-husband, boyfriend, or ex-boyfriend of the victim. In another 47% of cases where women were victimized at work, the attacker was either a casual acquaintance, a friend, or a relative (U.S. Department of Justice, 1998). Although the details about these relationships are not known, it is significant that nearly 50% of the attacks against women at work—compared to less than 37% of attacks against men—come from personal relationships that may fit a broad definition of domestic violence. Regarding homicides at work, between 1992 and 1994, 17% of women killed at work were killed by their current or former husbands or boyfriends (U.S. Department of Labor, 1996). The perpetrators are examples of internal sources of violence because of their relationships to the female employees.

The spillover creates a complex risk for organizations and all their employees: Even if his intended victim is on the job when the perpetrator looks for her, there is no guarantee that he will focus only on her, and even if he does, there is no guarantee that his aim will be accurate.

Substance Abuse and Mental Illness. Although data regarding employees' psychiatric disorders are limited, several studies indicate that both substance abuse and mental illness may be more prevalent in the workplace than is commonly known. Though mental illness may be a risk factor regarding employee behavior, it is important to note that mentally ill individuals more often are victims, rather than perpetrators, of violence.

Records from a study of one organization's employee assistance program (EAP) indicate frequent employee complaints regarding anxiety disorders, depression, stress, substance abuse, marital problems, family problems, and financial problems (Manuso, Harris, & Dewey, 1984). Another study (Holland, 1988) found a high frequency among employees of affective disorders, anxiety disorders, psychotic disorders, and personality disorders.

High-level positions within organizations do not rule out the occurrence of mental illness or substance abuse. A study of impairment among executives (Bromet, Parkinson, & Curtis, 1990) found that the rates of major depression were 23% for men and 36% for women, and rates of alcoholism were 16% for men and 9% for women. In another study of executives, alcoholism, substance abuse, depression, bipolar disorder, and schizophrenia were found to be significant forms of impairment (Speller, 1989).

Heidel (1993) describes an increase in emotional crises in the workplace and attributes the increase to five sources: layoffs; accidents; several forms of workplace violence (threats, robberies, fights, co-worker's death); substance abuse (leading to an unsafe or disruptive environment); and mental illness (depression leading to an unsafe or disruptive environment, and psychoses leading to dangerous behaviors). According to this view, the traumatic impact of workplace violence can lead to even more workplace violence.

In Canada, where most of the reported workplace violence occurs in the health care field, the poor mental condition of residents institutionalized for long-term care is identified as a contributing factor (Boyd, 1995). Their long-term presence makes dangerous patients an *internal* source of violence. It also is important to recognize that long-term patients in hospitals and nursing homes may become victims of employees, as well as vice versa.

These examples focus on emotional, psychological, and mental characteristics that may be associated with some of the occurrence of workplace violence. A closely related approach looks at neurology, where biological factors may contribute to the emotional, psychological, and mental conditions of a small percentage of perpetrators.

Neurological Factors. Historically, studies of violent behavior have focused on the environment and overlooked neurological, psychiatric, and other biological factors (Bach-y-Rita, Lion, Climent, & Ervin, 1991). However, various studies indicate that a relatively small percentage of the population may commit the largest percentage of violent crimes. For example, a study by Hamparin, Schuster, Dinstz, and Conrad (1978) found that among 627 chronic offender delinquents, from a group of 10,000 males born in 1945, 6% had committed 71% of the homicides, 73% of the rapes, and 69% of the aggravated assaults. These and other findings suggest that biological factors may play a significant role in violent behaviors. Mednick and Christiansen (1977) and Wilson and Herrnstein (1985) see the sociological model being replaced by a view that violence comes from interactions among biological and environmental variables.

Neurological factors—organic bases of what otherwise appear to be strictly psychological or emotional symptoms—also may be part of the work environment (Sperry, Kahn, & Heidel, 1994). Although the distinction often is difficult to make, it is possible, for example, that in the Canadian patients described by Boyd (1995), and in any number of homicides or other incidents of workplace violence, neurological disorders may contribute to the violent behaviors.

Elliott (1992) describes eight studies that show a "much higher prevalence of overt and covert neurologic and neurophysiologic abnormalities in recurrently violent individuals than in nonviolent control subjects or in the population at large" (p. 602). Elliott also notes that the violent subjects' personality changes, immense physical strength, and primitive behaviors were more likely to come from gross lesions of the limbic system and midbrain than from cognitive or other handicaps the subject had.

Too often, however, the connection between neurological factors and violent behavior has been overlooked, because the legal system has only relatively recently begun to consider these factors. Ironically, "the unfortunate reality for those who come into the courts by virtue of their dysfunction, however, is that the underlying causes of their disorder are inaccurately evaluated or simply unattended" (Fishbein, 1990).

The gap between the legal and medical orientations raises two long-standing questions: how much "free will" a violent criminal has; and whether, or to what extent, violent criminals should be "punished" versus "rehabilitated." In addition, research regarding workplace violence may awaken employees, employers, and society in general to the realization that many "functional," and even "successful," employees at work are emotionally, mentally, and/or neurologically ill. The implications may be vast, in terms of what this fact requires of employers, communities, and society. This realization also is likely to be met with even greater denial than that facing workplace violence.

"Profiles" of Perpetrators. Another attempt to understand individual factors contributing to workplace violence is the use of "profiles" that are supposed to identify potential predators. Much-publicized profiles describing traits and characteristics of former predators give accurate descriptions of individuals who have

committed violent crimes at work. However, these profiles are not helpful as preventive tools because of three major flaws:

1. They are too general to make significant distinctions between high-risk employees and others.
2. They are too psychologically oriented for managers to use in ways that are practical and legal.
3. They focus on the time-frame shortly before an employee becomes violent, instead of on the lengthy time period in which the high-risk employee exhibits behaviors that are nonviolent *but indicative of the high potential to become violent* under the "right" conditions.

For example, one profile includes "white males who are poor performers or loners, have a fascination with guns, have threatened to act violently and have been working at a company for about five years" (Berry, 1994). Another uses this list and adds a history of violent behavior, evidence of psychosis or personality disorder, substance abuse, depression, neurological disorder, chronic frustration, strange behavior, and a triggering event (Kelleher, 1997). Another profile lists 10 "warning signs," including "closing out or withdrawing large amounts of money from corporate credit unions," "bragging about owning weapons," and "repeated violations of corporate policy" (Hoffman, 1993). Kurland's (1993) description includes "loner types suffering from low self-esteem" and "paranoid-schizophrenic personality disorder." Mantell (1994) and Baron (1993) describe potentially violent employees in terms that are similarly vague and psychologically oriented. DeBecker (1997) uses the same type of profile, but adds the recommendation that in the prehiring process, employers use open-ended questions as ways to get applicants to reveal more about themselves.

In addition to being too general, too psychological, and too late, these profiles focus on character traits rather than on work behaviors. If managers use these traits to assess an individual's potential for violence, they will find themselves in the precarious position of judging "character"—an act that is both subjective and potentially illegal—instead of objectively evaluating behaviors, which is appropriate for managers to do.

Warning Signs. In contrast to profiles, another approach to assessing employees' potential for violence (McClure, 1996) specifically focuses on internal sources and aims at a much earlier place in the time line than does earlier research. McClure (1996) focuses on eight categories of behaviors—which employees may exhibit every day for years, before showing any direct signs of violence—that are indicative of high-risk employees. Using this approach, managers can prevent violence by intervening when the employee exhibits high-risk—and still nonviolent—behaviors at work. McClure's eight categories of high risk behaviors are:

1. Actor behaviors: the employee acts out what he or she feels, instead of talking about feelings
2. Fragmentor behaviors: the employee sees no connection between what he or she does and what the results or consequences are
3. Me-first behaviors: the employee takes care only of his or her own needs, without taking into account the impact these actions will have on others
4. Wooden-stick behaviors: the employee refuses to adapt to change
5. Mixed-messenger behaviors: the employee's actions contradict his or her words
6. Escape-artist behaviors: the employee avoids reality
7. Shocker behaviors: the employee's behaviors change suddenly and dramatically
8. Stranger behaviors: the employee acts in extremely withdrawn or remote ways

McClure (1996) notes that although many employees exhibit several of these behaviors at various times, the manager can assess the risk according to three criteria: how many of these categories of behaviors an employee exhibits; how often the employee exhibits them; and how intensely the employee carries them out. The higher the employee's behavior scores in each of these categories, the greater the risk. With appropriate organizational support, this approach allows managers to focus on employee behaviors and to intervene when they see behaviors that are high risk but not yet violent. The same principles could apply to identifying high-risk patients in long-term care institutions, discussed by Boyd (1995).

Other Individual Factors. Another contributor to workplace violence may be stress. Stress is such a common factor in U.S. workplaces that it is estimated to cost $200 billion a year for compensation claims, added insurance costs, absenteeism, reduced productivity, and medical treatment. In organizations experiencing downsizing, mergers, and layoffs, the level of stress can become overwhelming (Sperry et al., 1994). This is especially true of individuals whose self-identity depends heavily on their jobs, and becomes even worse if these individuals lose their jobs (Johnson & Indvik, 1994). The identity issue is even more likely to occur today than in the past, because work has become such a major focus of many Americans' lives that love and friendship needs are more likely to be met at work than in personal life (Sperry et al., 1994). Stress also may increase any potential for violence an individual already has (McClure, 1996).

Individual factors contributing to workplace violence may include domestic violence, substance abuse, mental illness, neurological factors, profiles of perpetrators, warning signs, and stress. But in attempting to explain workplace violence, organizational factors must be considered as well.

Organizational Factors Contributing to Workplace Violence

Another approach to understanding workplace violence is to look at common elements among organizations in which violent incidents have occurred.

Management Practices and Behaviors. To date, insufficient data exist to allow for quantitative assessment of risk factors. However, various case studies have identified factors common to businesses and agencies where violent incidents have been reported. While these factors cannot be seen as direct "causes" of workplace violence, they must be considered as pieces of the larger picture. Organizational factors that appear significant include

1. Employers' neglect of physical security issues (e.g., lighting, alarm systems)
2. Heavy workloads and related stress
3. Employees' sense of loss of control over their work
4. Authoritarian and/or punitive management styles
5. Personnel policies that are indifferent to employees' problems
6. Insufficient supervisory support of workers

7. Cultural conflicts (Nigro & Waugh, 1996, p. 329)

The first item, employers' neglect of physical security issues, relates primarily to external sources of violence, although these factors also may be secondary factors in the case of internal sources of violence. All the remaining items relate to internal sources.

Employees also perceive a "psychological contract" between themselves and employers. When employers appear to break the contract—for example, by failing to respond to employee requests in certain ways, or by firing employees—employees may believe the organization has betrayed them. Similar perceptions may come from employers mistreating or ignoring employees (Johnson & Indvik, 1994).

Researchers also have found that many managers allow a "hostile" work environment to exist (Baron, 1993; Hatcher & Mathiason, 1994; Kinney, 1995). In this type of environment, such behaviors as verbal abuse, sexual harassment, and other forms of intimidation have been allowed to take place without reprimand. Managers' refusal to discipline may be part of the broader issue of denial.

Organizational Culture. Denial is a strong organizational factor that contributes to violence (Phillips, 1996). Despite facts and statistics indicating the reality and the risks, many corporations to date have difficulty acknowledging that workplace violence is an issue, that they can and must take steps to prevent it, and that both the acknowledgment and the preventive steps would enhance rather than harm their image (McClure, 1996). Among firms that have established policies and formed committees to address the issue, many resist making either step visible to the public or even to their own employees below management levels. The secrecy only adds to the risk.

In addition, an important shift has occurred since the 1970s, creating a gap between how employees and employer organizations view "work" and "life." Culturally, employer organizations still tend to view work life and personal life as separate domains. Yet work is becoming more central in the lives of many people. For example, in 1991, the average American worked the equivalent of one month longer than his or her counterpart in 1970 (Sperry et al., 1994). The organizational expectation that employees can perform well at work regardless of what is going on in their personal lives may create expectations that employees perceive as unrealistic. Also, the increased amount of time spent at work, and the correspondingly decreased amount of time spent at home, may intensify and/or create personal problems and stress.

Staffing, Hiring, and Retention Practices. As mentioned above under "Litigation Costs," employers have been held responsible for negligent hiring and/or negligent retention when an employee commits violence at work. Hiring can be seen as the one activity that has the greatest impact on employer organizations (Maggio, 1996), yet many employers do not take appropriate precautions.

In lawsuits regarding negligent hiring, the most common circumstance is that an employee who commits violence at work had a prior criminal record, but when the employee applied for the job, the organization failed to check for such records (Selden & Pace, 1997). Ironically, however, there may be restrictions in various regions about using criminal history as the reason for refusing to hire an applicant (Maggio, 1996).

In lawsuits regarding negligent retention, the victims' position is that even if background checks were done and did not indicate histories of criminal convictions, "some behavior on the job should have given an indication that the employee might commit a violent act" (Selden & Pace, 1997, p. 31) and the supervisor failed to discipline or dismiss the perpetrator when previolent but indicative behaviors were exhibited. Employers often are hesitant to act on these indicative behaviors (McClure, 1996).

Another issue regarding staffing involves downsizing, where fewer employees are expected to perform more work. As an example, in Canada's health care industry, violence on the part of institutionalized residents is attributed, in part, to the reduction in the number of staff members working with individual patients and the resultant work overload on individual workers (Boyd, 1995). Comparable problems exist throughout all fields of work.

Changing Demographics in the Workforce. As women become a larger percentage of the workforce, the risk of spillover from domestic violence increases. Every year, about 1 million women are victimized by someone close to them, and women are about six times more likely than men to experience violence from someone who is an intimate (U.S. Department of Labor, Women's Bureau, 1996).

The risk of this spillover may increase as minorities become a larger percentage of the workforce—although 17% of all women killed at work between 1992 and 1994 were victims of current or former boyfriends or husbands, the figure among black women was 28% and among Hispanic women, 20% (U.S. Department of Labor, 1996).

In addition to the spillover of domestic violence, the increase in numbers of employees from various national, religious, ethnic, generational, and other orientations raises the likelihood of conflicts over differences. Although these types of conflicts are not new to the workplace, it is possible that their frequency and intensity may increase.

Organizational Changes. Changes within employer organizations also contribute to the potential for workplace violence.

1. Downsizing. As organizations reorganize and cut back on the number of positions, including midmanagement jobs, remaining workers are expected to "do more with less." The result often is increased stress, along with fear of being laid off during the next downsizing (Johnson & Indvik, 1994). Fear can create a negative atmosphere that, in turn, can lead to greater stress and more fear.

Several well-publicized workplace homicides were committed by employees who had been fired. Although a broad perspective of circumstances would indicate that there is no simple, direct line between downsizing and firing, on the one hand, and homicide, on the other hand, it is clear that firing can be a "last straw" for a high-risk employee who already feels close to the edge.

2. Global competition. As both the markets of, and the resources within, employer organizations expand to cover the world, employees often feel pressured and threatened. Employer expectations and demands increase, and in a number of cases, employees must choose between moving to another country or losing their jobs. Global competition also may threaten the survival of individual companies.

3. Constantly changing technology. In addition to the normal adjustments that are required when dealing with change, ongoing changes in technology increase the difficulty of staying expert in

one's field. Employees may feel that their jobs are threatened, and organizations may increase the pressure to stay "on top" of things.

Job-Related Stressors. Along with these organizational changes, employees also are subject to more job stressors than in the past.

1. Less security than in the past. Jobs are far less secure than the current workforce has experienced in the past. This lack of security has both practical and emotional effects on employees. It is particularly difficult for employees whose identities are centered around their work—especially if these employee lose their jobs (Johnson & Indvik, 1994).

2. Longer shifts. Among many employers, reorganization and downsizing include changing from three 8-hour shifts to two 12-hour shifts. Longer hours, especially with greater workloads and fewer employees, can increase employee stress (Boyd, 1995). Although employers perceive reduced costs, it is possible that in the long term, the stress on employees' work and personal lives may cost more, in terms of lower productivity and increased risk, than what the organizations are saving (McClure, 1996).

3. Other organizational factors. Beyond management practices and behaviors, and unknown to management, organizational norms often contribute to the potential for violence. McClure (1996) identifies eight organizational norms that unintentionally support the eight categories of high-risk behaviors. These norms include avoiding talking about problems at work; failing to confront employees about performance or behavior problems; and valuing "office politics" over productivity.

Organizational factors include management practices and behaviors; organizational culture; staffing, hiring, and retention practices; changing demographics in the workforce; organizational changes; and job-related stressors. Social factors, as well as individual and organizational factors, contribute to workplace violence.

Social Factors Contributing to Workplace Violence

Because employer organizations are part of society as a whole, social problems will be acted out at work. In a number of ways, violence in the workplace reflects the violent nature of our society today.

Cultural Norms, Cultural Values, and Gender Issues. In discussing workplace violence, cultural norms and values cannot be separated from gender issues. The U.S. culture continues to become increasingly violent (Younger, 1994), with men committing 89% of all violent crimes in the United States (Levy, 1991). Every 6 minutes in the United States a woman is raped, and every 18 seconds a woman is beaten (Salholz, 1990). Several theories propose that males are socialized to believe violence against women is an acceptable behavior (Levy, 1991; Younger, 1994). These cultural norms and values spill over into the workplace, as indicated by the fact that homicide is the leading cause of death for women at work (U.S. Department of Justice, 1994).

Relationship violence—including, but not limited to, domestic violence—also spills over into the workplace. Considering all forms of violence, in addition to murder, only 47% of women victims at work were attacked by strangers. Nearly 50% were attacked by someone they knew: more than 2% were attacked by a husband, ex-husband, boyfriend, or ex-boyfriend; 1% were attacked by a relative; 46% were attacked by a friend or acquaintance. In contrast, among male victims at work, nearly 60% were attacked by strangers; 1% by a current or former wife or girlfriend; 0.5% by a relative; and 35% by a friend or acquaintance (U.S. Department of Justice, 1998). The higher percentage of women attacked by someone known to them may suggest that male stereotypes of ownership, control, and dominance versus subservience, compliance, and weakness still may characterize U.S. cultural views of male-female relationships, despite apparent progress—including progress that has been made in the workplace.

A Canadian survey of violence against women (Statistics Canada, 1993) indicates that 50% of women have experienced (in their personal lives) some form of physical violence since the age of 16. Of these women, nearly 50% reported violence by men known to them and 25% reported violence by a current or former partner. Traditional stereotypes of a separation between personal life and work life prevent employer organizations from seeing the relevance of domestic violence to the workplace (Engelken, 1987).

Ironically, it is possible that violence against women at work—at the hands of both strangers and those familiar to the victims— comes, in part, as a reaction to women's progress at work. Faludi

(1991) notes that as women have tried to improve their status in the workplace, men consistently have seen these efforts as direct challenges to their own masculinity. To date, no studies have tested the correlation between men's frustration about losing control of the work environment and violent behavior toward women at work.

Cultural norms, cultural values, and gender issues clearly contribute to the occurrence of workplace violence.

Generational Norms and Values. Although violence and gender issues are not new, there may be differences among age groups regarding assumptions about what is "appropriate," "normal," and "healthy."

For individuals who are now 60 years of age and older, the image of work and relationships may have had the women at home, while the men went out into the world as breadwinners—but this image also assumed that the women at home and the men at work were *safe.* For a 35-year-old single mother whose ex-husband stalks her at work, the image of work and relationships is vastly different; and for 20-year-olds starting in the workforce—or 15-year-olds soon to begin work, or 5-year-olds raised in divorced and/or abusive families—the difference is even greater.

When mass media—television shows, movies, videos, and video games—use violence as a form of entertainment, complete with women-, men-, and children-as-objects, it is not difficult to anticipate the likelihood that violence will worsen in our society. Our technical ability is far greater than our wisdom, and our culture already has produced events that have never happened before in the history of civilization: children killing children.

From the perspective of generational norms and values, it is possible that workplace violence will continue to worsen unless organizations—and the society of which they are part—take preventive actions quickly enough.

Role of Aggression and Envy in Workplace Violence. Noting that surprisingly little research has been done in the management field regarding aggression, O'Leary-Kelly et al. (1996) distinguish between "aggression" and "violence" and point out the need for precision in defining each. Using social learning theory, they emphasize the necessity of considering organizational, as well as individual, factors contributing to workplace violence. Envy is another condition that is overlooked by management research, even though it is "especially common in business" (Bedeian, 1995, p. 49).

Social factors contributing to workplace violence include cultural norms, cultural values, gender issues, generational norms and values, aggression, and envy. Social factors provide the backdrop against which individual and organizational factors interact in the occurrence of workplace violence.

Preventive Measures

Because individual, organizational, and social factors all contribute to workplace violence, one optimistic possibility is that preventive steps within any one of these three areas may lead to prevention in the other two areas. If employer organizations get past their denial, take significant preventive measures—*and* make these measures public knowledge, available both as recognition of the social problem of violence and as examples of possible solutions—they can contribute greatly to the reduction of risk in the individual and social realms. Organizations that require high-risk employees to get help before any crises occur will directly reduce the risk faced by potential victims, potential perpetrators, and families of both groups, and indirectly reduce the risk to society as a whole.

Steps Employer Organizations Have Taken

Among employer organizations that have taken steps to prevent workplace violence, several have publicized their efforts, although most have kept this information in-house.

Employee Assistance Programs (EAPs). Employee Assistance Programs (EAPs) provide in-house counseling for employees, referrals to external counseling resources, or both. EAPs may be either departments within employer organizations or external providers. In all circumstances, confidentiality is essential to the success of EAPs. In addition to serving employees who voluntarily self-refer because of personal issues, EAPs also act as resources for managers when employees exhibit problem behaviors, fail to benefit from training, and refuse to get professional help. If the employer organization has an appropriate system to support managers, employees behaving in problematic ways may be required, by their managers, to go to the EAP for help. EAPs also may train managers and employees about warning signs of a troubled employee.

Security Measures. Security measures are aimed primarily at external sources of violence, although they also may be helpful against internal sources. These measures include better interior and exterior lighting, alarms throughout the premises, interior and exterior surveillance cameras, areas that are restricted, door controls, and security guards (CPCU, 1995). Bullet-proof windows (e.g., for cashiers and bank tellers), metal detectors, and alarm buzzers also are used in some organizations. Having employees park close to the building, minimizing cash on premises, and cooperating with local police are additional effective security steps. Threat-assessment and threat-management teams also increase security.

Policies. Policies aimed at prevention start with an official antiviolence organizational stance, supported by hotlines allowing employees to report suspicious circumstances (Scammell, 1995). Grievance and harassment policies can reduce incidents of violence (Richardson & Gilham, 1994), as long as these policies are enforced by all levels of management and the organizational culture allows employees to speak up (McClure, 1996). Hiring policies that lower the risk include prescreening for behavior problems, calling applicants' references, and doing background checks (de Becker, 1997; Scammell, 1995). Once an employee is hired, an effective preventive policy is to address performance problems immediately. Effective policies for terminating employees include structured and supportive steps (McClure, 1996).

Management Training. In organizations that have gone beyond the denial stage, training helps managers support and implement the preventive policies the organization has established. In addition, managers are better at dealing with a wide variety of employee behaviors when the managers get training in conflict management, stress reduction, change management, and other communication skills. Effective training also includes ways to identify troubled employees, along with specific steps to take regarding the organization's EAP.

Employee Training. Employees at levels below management receive, so far, little training directly related to violence prevention, mostly because of organizational denial. However, many workers have access to training in interpersonal skills, conflict, and related topics. Although these classes are not related directly to violence prevention, employees' use of these skills can help reduce the likelihood of violent incidents (McClure, 1996).

Sharing Information and Training. A number of employers share information, experience, and training to help prevent workplace violence. This sharing may be done on an informal basis or by joining formal groups established to facilitate the sharing. Chambers of Commerce, professional associations, industry associations, and civic groups also offer training and information sharing for their members and guests.

Surveys. Several corporations have conducted surveys to assess employee awareness of such issues as domestic violence, substance abuse, and workplace violence. Although administering these surveys does not relate directly to preventing workplace violence, they indicate the organizations' efforts to identify areas in which employees may benefit from future training.

Recognizing the Relationship Between Domestic and Workplace Violence, and Educating Employees About Related Issues. A number of employer organizations have, as of this writing, begun to recognize the need to educate employees about domestic violence and related issues. These employers offer training in ways to identify women who are being abused, sources of support available to them, and ways of getting them to use the resources.

Although, as of this writing, organizational denial still is strong and employers still prefer to keep any preventive efforts relatively under cover, a number of organizations have found effective ways to lower the risk of workplace violence. Additional steps they may take are described below.

Additional Preventive Measures
Employer Organizations Can Take

With external sources, security is the only area in which employers have room to anticipate. Security steps can be planned in advance, equipment can be installed in advance, and two clerks, instead of one, can be scheduled for night-shift. Still, the identity of an attacker, and the timing of an attack, remain unpredictable. Despite the ability to plan and implement security steps in advance, external sources of violence keep organizations in a reactive mode. Organizations have more opportunity to prevent violence from *internal* sources than from *external* sources, because internal sources are more observable and therefore less random and more likely to be anticipated.

Internal sources are much easier for employers to identify and take proactive steps to prevent, but to do so would require employers to get beyond denial and address the problem at much earlier stages than they currently do. A significant—though seemingly simple—step employers can take is to carry out their written policies and put appropriate consequences on problem behaviors. Ironically, many refuse to act even after a crisis has occurred—which means the violent employee remains within the same organization and even within the same department. Top management, HR (human resources), EAPs, legal counsel, and security must work together to give managers the tools they need to address high-risk behaviors while they remain management and behavior issues—before they become security issues. This proactive change would benefit employers and the society within which they operate (McClure, 1996).

As part of the larger community, employer organizations can begin preventing violence by addressing indicative behaviors immediately, and requiring high-risk employees to get help.

Conclusions

Workplace violence in North America is a traumatic, costly—and growing—issue in the area of family and community violence. Yet because of widespread denial on the part of employer organizations, it is only beginning to emerge as a field of study in both scholarly and empirical research. Its occurrence in Canada is relatively recent, compared to the United States, but data from both countries indicate similar patterns.

Whether from external or internal sources, "workplace violence" includes homicide and many other forms of physical abuse. In U.S. workplaces, an average of more than 2 million victimizations are reported annually, and experts estimate that fewer than half of the actual incidents are even reported. More than 80% of perpetrators are men. Among employees who die at work, homicide is the number one cause for women and the second leading cause for men.

Emotional costs of workplace violence are immeasurable. Financial costs include medical treatment, income loss, litigation fees, loss of productivity, and lawsuit settlements. Some experts estimate that the cost to employer organizations is in the billions.

Individual factors contributing to workplace violence include domestic violence, substance abuse, mental illness, neurological factors, perpetrators' "profiles," behavior patterns that are warning signs, and stress. Organizational factors include management practices and behaviors; organizational culture; staffing, hiring, and retention practices; changing demographics in the workforce; organizational changes; and job-related stressors. Social factors include cultural norms; cultural values; gender issues; generational norms and values; aggression; and envy. Individual and organizational factors interact in the context of social factors when workplace violence occurs.

Most employer organizations that have taken preventive steps keep the information internal. Known preventive steps, however, include Employee Assistance Programs (EAPs), security measures, antiviolence policies, management training, employee training, sharing of information and training, surveys, and recognition of the relationship between domestic and workplace violence.

Because internal sources of violence are easier for managers to observe and anticipate than are external sources, employer organizations could take additional preventive steps regarding internal sources. These steps would begin with getting beyond denial, establishing and carrying out written policies, and putting appropriate consequences on employees' problem behaviors.

Employers' opportunities to lower the risk of violence is an emerging issue. To carry out this role, employers must implement zero-tolerance reactions to high-risk behaviors. By doing so, they can begin the process of reducing violence not only within their own organizations, but also within the families and communities of the United States and Canada.

References

Association of Workers' Compensation Boards of Canada. (1997). *Workplace injury and death due to violence, Canada 1995.* Unpublished report.

Bach-y-Rita, G., Lion, J. R., Climent, C. F., & Ervin, F. R. (1991). Episodic dyscontrol: A study of 130 violent patients. *American Journal of Psychiatry, 127,* 1473-1478.

Baker, S. P., Samkoff, J. S., & Fisher, R. (1982). Fatal occupational injuries. *Journal of the American Medical Association, 248,* 692-697.

Baker, S. P., Teret, S. P., & Dretz, P. E. (1980, August). Firearms and the public health. *Journal of Public Health Policy,* pp. 224-299.

Baron, S. A. (1993). *Violence in the workplace.* Ventura, CA: Pathfinder.

Bedeian, A. (1995, April 1). Workplace envy: Role in workplace violence. *Organizational Dynamics,* pp. 49-55.

Berry, K. M. (1994, March 28). How to protect your company from office violence. *Investor's Business Daily,* p. 4.

Boyd, N. (1995, November). Violence in the workplace in British Columbia: A preliminary investigation. *Canadian Journal of Criminology,* pp. 491-519.

Bromet, E., Parkinson, D., & Curtis, C. (1990). Epidemiology of depression and alcohol abuse/dependence in a managerial and professional workforce. *Journal of Occupational Medicine, 32,* 989-995.

Burroughs, S., & Jones, J. W. (1995, March/April). Looking out for trouble. *OH&S Canada,* pp. 34, 36-37.

CPCU Society's Upstate South Carolina Chapter. (1995). Workplace violence: Analysis of the issues and recommendations to reduce the exposure. *CPCU Journal, 48*(December), 208-215.

Center for Women in Government. (1996). *Domestic violence in the workplace.* Albany: State University of New York, Center for Women in Government.

de Becker, G. (1997). *The gift of fear.* Boston: Little, Brown.

Elliott, F. A. (1992). Violence, the neurological connection: An overview. *Archives of Neurology, 49,* 595-603.

Engelken, C. (1987). Fighting the costs of spouse abuse. *Personnel Journal, 66*(3), 31-34.

Faludi, S. (1991). *Backlash: The undeclared war against American women.* New York: Crown.

Fishbein, D. H. (1990). Biological perspectives in criminology. *Criminology, 28,* 27-72.

Hales, T., Seligman, P. J., Newman, S. C., & Timbrook, C. L. (1988). Occupational injuries due to violence. *Journal of Occupational Medicine, 30,* 483.

Hamparin, D. M., Schuster, R., Dinstz, S., & Conrad, J. P. (1978). *The violent few: A study of violent offenders.* Lexington, MA: Lexington Books.

Hatcher, C., & Mathiason, G. (1994). *Workplace violence: First line of defense.* California: The Kenwood Group.

Heidel, S. (1993). Emotional crises in the workplace. In J. P. Kahn (Ed.), *Mental health in the workplace: A practical psychiatric guide.* New York: Van Nostrand Reinhold.

Holland, P. (1988). Psychiatric aspects of occupational medicine. In R. McKunney (Ed.), *Handbook of occupational medicine.* Boston: Little, Brown.

Hoffman, M. (1993, September 13). Protecting employees from workplace violence. *Business Insurance,* pp. 24-25.

Johnson, E. R., & Indvik, J. (1994, January). Workplace violence: An issue of the nineties. *Public Personnel Management,* p. 23.

Kelleher, M. D. (1997). *Profiling the lethal employee: Case studies of violence in the workplace.* Westport, CT: Praeger.

Kinney, J. A. (1995). *Violence at work.* Englewood Cliffs, NJ: Prentice Hall.

Kurland, O. M. (1993, June). Workplace violence. *Risk Management,* pp. 76-77.

Lawless, P. (1993). *Fear and violence in the workplace.* Minneapolis, MN: Northwest National Life Insurance.

Levy, D. (1991, September 16). Why Johnny might grow up to be sexist. *Time,* pp. 16-19.

Lipscomb, J., & Love, C. (1992). An emerging occupational hazard. *AAOHN Journal, 40,* 219-228.

Liss, G. M., & McCaskell, L. (1994). Injuries due to violence: Workers' compensation claims among nurses in Ontario. *AAOHN Journal, 42*(August), 384-390.

Maggio, M. (1996, March 1). Keeping the workplace safe: A challenge for managers. *Federal Probation, 60,* 67.

Mantell, M. (1994). *Ticking bombs.* New York: Irwin.

Manuso, J., Harris, J., & Dewey, M. (1984). Stress. In M. O'Donnell & L. Ainsworth (Eds.), *Health promotion in the workplace.* New York: John Wiley.

Mattman, J. W. (1994, Spring). Rise in workplace violence expected to increase. *Safe Workplace, 2* (National Council on Compensation Insurance).

McClure, L. F. (1996). *Risky business: Managing employee violence in the workplace.* Binghamton, NY: Haworth.

Mednick, S. A., & Christiansen, K. O. (1977). *Biological bases of criminal behavior.* New York: Gardner.

Nigro, L. G., & Waugh, W. L. (1996). Violence in the American workplace: Challenges to the public employer. *Public Administration Review, 56,* 326-332.

O'Leary-Kelly, A. E., Griffin, R. W., & Glew, D. J. (1996, January). Organization-motivated aggression: A research framework. *Academy of Management Review,* pp. 225-250.

Pearson, G. (1995, August 14). Workplace violence: Incidence rises in health care, social services. *HR Reporter,* pp. 18-20.

Perry, P. (1994). Assault in the workplace: How to cut your legal risk. *Editor & Publisher, 127,* 33.

Phillips, A. E. (1996). Violence in the workplace: Reevaluating the employer's role. *Buffalo Law Review, 44,* 139-195.

Podgers, J. (1995, March). Witnesses to tragedy. *ABA Journal.*

Poyner, B., & Warne, C. (1988). *Preventing violence to staff.* London: Tavistock Institute of Human Relations.

The Research Team on Family Violence and the Workplace. (1997). *Report on an exploratory study of relationships between family violence and the workplace.* Muriel McQueen Fergusson Centre for Family Violence Research, Fredericton, New Brunswick, Canada.

Richardson, S., & Gilham, D. S. (1994, Spring). Texas research mirrors U.S.: Nonfatal violence affects 1 of 4 workers. *Safe Workplace, 2* (National Council on Compensation Insurance).

Salholz, E. (1990, July 23). Women under assault. *Newsweek,* pp. 23-24.

Scammell, S. (1995, January). Violence in the workplace. *Government Risk Management Reports.*

Selden, D. A., & Pace, J. A. (1997, February). *Violence in the workplace.* Paper presented at the meeting of Quarles & Brady, Attorneys at Law on Violence in the Workplace.

Speller, J. (1989). *Executives in crisis: Recognizing and managing the alcohol, drug-addicted or mentally ill executive.* San Francisco: Jossey-Bass.

Sperry, L., Kahn, J. P., & Heidel, S. H. (1994). Workplace mental health consultation: A primer of organizational and occupational psychiatry. *General Hospital Psychiatry, 16,* 103-111.

Statistics Canada. (1993, June). *Canadian crime statistics 1993.* Ottawa: Author.

U.S. Department of Justice. (1994). *Violence and theft in the workplace* (BJS Publication No. NCJ-148199). Washington, DC: Government Printing Office.

U.S. Department of Justice. (1998). *Workplace violence, 1992-1996* (NCJ Publication No. 168634). Washington, DC: Government Printing Office.

U.S. Department of Labor. (1996). *Protecting community workers against violence* (DOL Publication No. 96-53). Washington, DC: Author.

U.S. Department of Labor, Women's Bureau. (1996, October). Domestic violence: A workplace issue. *Facts on Working Women* (Newsletter, entire issue).

Wigmore, D. (1995). Violence in the workplace: It doesn't have to go with the job. *Horizons, 8*(Winter), 26-31.

Wilson, I. Q., & Herrnstein, R. J. (1985). *Crime and nature.* New York: Simon & Schuster.

Workplace violence: A survey of literature and recommendations to reduce exposure. (1995). Chartered Property Casualty Underwriters, May.

Workplace Violence Research Institute. (1995). *Workplace violence* (Report #4/95). Newport Beach, CA.

Younger, B. (1994). Violence against women in the workplace. In M. Lunday & B. Younger (Eds.), *Women in the workplace and employee assistance programs: Perspectives, innovations, and techniques for helping professionals.* Binghamton, NY: Haworth.

CHAPTER 4

Understanding the Incidence and Origins of Community Violence: Toward a Comprehensive Perspective of Violence Prevention

LLOYD B. POTTER

In many of our communities, violence has escalated beyond tolerable levels. We use the phrase *community violence* to describe interpersonal violence that occurs in public places, outside our homes. In reality, the distinction between community violence and violence that occurs in "private" places is difficult to make. Most sources of information on homicide and assault do not distinguish between that which occurs in public and in private places. In addition, much violence that occurs in "public" places evolves from "private" places. In this chapter, we consider the topic of community violence from a public health perspective focused on prevention of injuries resulting from interpersonal violent behavior. This perspective entails four interrelated steps: defining the problem, identifying causes, developing and testing interventions, and implementing effective interventions in affected populations. In describing the problem, we draw on statistics from a variety of sources to examine the magnitude and trends of community violence in the United States. We then discuss issues of taxonomy and an ecological framework for understanding causes of violent behavior. We describe some of the interventions that have been developed and efforts to evaluate them. Finally, we discuss the process of implementation and dissemination of effective preven-

tion strategies through communication strategies, diffusion of in-
novation, and technology transfer approaches.

The Public Health Approach

Public health has always responded to epidemics of infectious
disease with a focus on environmental modification and vaccina-
tion. During the past few decades, public health has incorporated
efforts to modify high-risk behavior, with the goal of preventing
chronic disease and injury. In the 1980s, the Centers for Disease
Control and Prevention (CDC) initiated efforts to prevent injuries
from violence by using a public health approach. These efforts were
prompted by a dramatic rise in homicide rates in the United States,
especially among youths aged 15 to 24, along with increasing
acceptance within the public health community of the importance
of behavioral factors in the etiology of disease and injury (Mercy
& O'Carroll, 1988). In addition, it was becoming increasingly clear
that the nation needed to move beyond relying solely on a criminal
justice approach to prevent violence (Mercy & O'Carroll, 1988).

To understand and prevent violence, a scientific approach is
central to moving efficiently and effectively toward relieving this
public health burden. The science is derived from observation,
study, and experimentation to determine the nature or principles
of what is being studied. The public health approach described in
Figure 4.1 provides a multidisciplinary, scientific approach that is
explicitly directed toward identifying effective approaches to prevention (Mercy, Rosenberg, Powell, Broome, & Roper, 1993). This
approach starts with defining the problem and progresses to identifying associated risk factors and causes, developing and evaluating
interventions, and implementing intervention programs.

Definition of the Problem

The first step in the public health approach, defining the problem, includes delineating incidents of violence and related mortality
and morbidity. This step goes beyond counting cases to include
obtaining, analyzing, and presenting information on characteristics
of violence-related injury, as well as efforts to describe prevalence

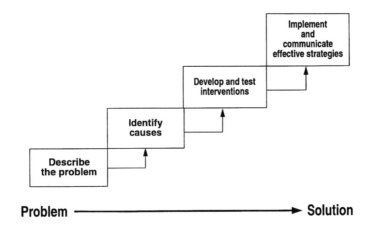

Figure 4.1. The Public Health Approach to Prevention

and trends of risk factors. Information on the demographic characteristics of the persons involved, the temporal and geographic
characteristics of the incident, the victim-perpetrator relationship,
circumstances of the injury, and the severity and cost of the injury
are essential in defining the problem. These variables may be
important in identifying discrete subsets of violence for which
various interventions may be appropriate. Because every community is unique, it is important to collect information that will give
an accurate picture of violence and related problems in specific
communities. Information can be collected from a number of
sources including focus groups, incident reports, and surveys. For
homicide, information about the problem comes primarily from the
vital statistics system and police reports. Little information is collected on nonfatal injuries from violence at the national, state, and
local level. When information on nonfatal injuries is collected, most
of it is derived from acute care settings or from surveys. In this
section, we summarize the magnitude and trends of community
violence.

Magnitude of Community Violence. As the magnitude of interpersonal violence has grown in the United States, so has the social
resolve to address the problem. To approach this problem methodi-

cally, we must first understand who is most affected. The risk of homicide and violent victimization in communities varies drastically by geography, age, and sex. Understanding the details of risk allows us to assess an individual's risk and to identify population segments that should be targeted for prevention efforts.

Homicide rates among young men in the United States are vastly greater than those in other Western industrialized nations (Figure 4.2) (Krug, Dahlberg, & Powell, 1997; World Health Organization, 1995). In 1995, more than 22,000 people in the United States were homicide victims, making homicide the 11th leading cause of death (National Center for Health Statistics, 1997). Adolescents and young adults face an extraordinarily high risk of death and injury from violence. Homicide is the second leading cause of death among 15- to 24-year-olds in the United States (Table 4.1) and the leading cause of death for young African American males and females (National Center for Injury Prevention and Control, 1997). Among persons aged 10 to 14 years, homicide is the third leading cause of death. In addition, 12- to 24-year-olds face the highest risk of nonfatal assault of any age group in our society (U.S. Department of Justice, 1992).

The impact of homicide on young people is further illustrated by years of potential life lost (YPPL), an indicator of the impact that specific causes of death have on the life expectancy of a population (Centers for Disease Control and Prevention, 1993). YPPL emphasizes the causes of death that disproportionately affect younger persons and signifies societal loss in terms of lost productivity and quality of life. YPPL-65 is the number of life-years that persons killed by a particular cause would have contributed to society, had they all lived to age 65. In 1991, homicide was the third leading cause of YPPL-65 for the general population, behind unintentional injury (motor vehicle crashes, falls, etc.) and cancer (Centers for Disease Control and Prevention, 1993). Among African Americans, homicide was the leading cause of YPPL-65.

Homicide data indicate that offenders tend to be demographically similar to their victims. Using data on victim-offender relationships from the Federal Bureau of Investigation-Supplemental Homicide Report (FBI-SHR), we examined the age relationship between young homicide offenders and their victims (Figure 4.3) (Federal Bureau of Investigation, 1995). In 1993, 205 people were killed by offenders who were 10 to 14 years old, 26% of the victims

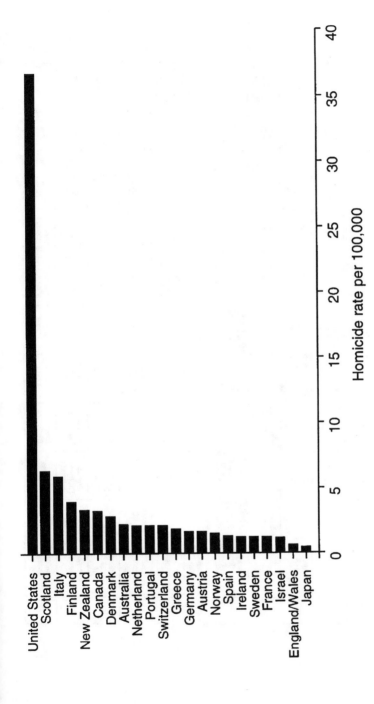

Figure 4.2. International Variation in Male Homicide per 100,000 Males Aged 15-24 Years, 1991-1993

Table 4.1 Ten Leading Causes of Death by Age Group, United States, 1995

Rank	<1	1-4	5-9	10-14	15-24	25-34	35-44	45-54	55-64	65+	Total
					Age Groups						
1	Congenital Anomalies 6,554	Unintentional Injuries 2,280	Unintentional Injuries 1,612	Unintentional Injuries 1,932	Unintentional Injuries 13,842	Unintentional Injuries 13,435	HIV 18,860	Malignant Neoplasms 44,186	Malignant Neoplasms 87,898	Heart Disease 615,426	Heart Disease 737,563
2	Short Gestation 3,933	Congenital Anomalies 695	Malignant Neoplasms 523	Malignant Neoplasms 503	Homicide 7,284	HIV 11,894	Malignant Neoplasms 17,110	Heart Disease 34,498	Heart Disease 68,240	Malignant Neoplasms 381,142	Malignant Neoplasms 538,455
3	SIDS 3,397	Malignant Neoplasms 488	Congenital Anomalies 242	Homicide 405	Suicide 4,784	Suicide 6,292	Unintentional Injuries 14,225	Unintentional Injuries 9,261	Bronchitis Emphysema Asthma 9,988	Cerebro-vascular 138,762	Cerebro-vascular 157,991
4	Respiratory Distress Synd. 1,454	Homicide 452	Homicide 157	Suicide 330	Malignant Neoplasms 1,642	Homicide 6,162	Heart Disease 13,603	HIV 8,179	Cerebro-vascular 9,735	Bronchitis Emphysema Asthma 88,478	Bronchitis Emphysema Asthma 102,899
5	Maternal Complications 1,309	Heart Disease 251	Heart Disease 130	Congenital Anomalies 207	Heart Disease 1,039	Malignant Neoplasms 4,875	Suicide 6,467	Cerebro-vascular 5,473	Diabetes 8,188	Pneumonia & Influenza 74,297	Unintentional Injuries 93,320
6	Placenta Cord Membranes 962	HIV 210	HIV 123	Heart Disease 164	HIV 629	Heart Disease 3,461	Homicide 4,118	Liver Disease 5,247	Unintentional Injuries 6,743	Diabetes 44,452	Pneumonia & Influenza 82,923
7	Perinatal Infections 788	Pneumonia & Influenza 156	Pneumonia & Influenza 73	Bronchitis Emphysema Asthma 105	Congenital Anomalies 452	Cerebro-vascular 720	Liver Disease 3,705	Suicide 4,532	Liver Disease 5,356	Unintentional Injuries 29,099	Diabetes 59,254
8	Unintentional Injuries 787	Perinatal Period 87	Benign Neoplasms 50	HIV 66	Bronchitis Emphysema Asthma 246	Pneumonia & Influenza 622	Cerebro-vascular 2,772	Diabetes 3,996	Pneumonia & Influenza 3,458	Alzheimer's Disease 20,230	HIV 43,115
9	Pneumonia & Influenza 492	Septicemia 80	Bronchitis Emphysema Asthma 38	Benign Neoplasms 55	Pneumonia & Influenza 207	Diabetes 614	Diabetes 1,844	Bronchitis Emphysema Asthma 2,756	Suicide 2,804	Nephritis 20,182	Suicide 31,284
10	Intrauterine Hypoxia 475	Cerebro-vascular 57	Anemias 31	Pneumonia & Influenza 55	Cerebro-vascular 172	Liver Disease 604	Pneumonia & Influenza 1,480	Pneumonia & Influenza 2,079	HIV 2,320	Septicemia 16,899	Liver Disease 25,222

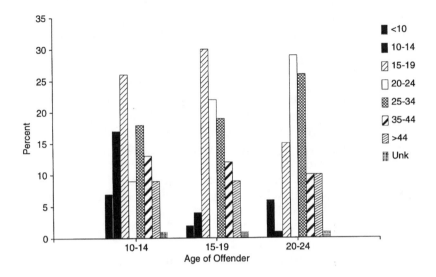

Figure 4.3. Percentage Distribution of Homicide Victims by Age of Offender, United States, 1993

were aged 15 to 19 years, and 17% were aged 10 to 14 years. Of the 3,181 people killed by 15- to 19-year-old offenders, 30% of the victims were aged 15 to 19 years, and approximately 22% were aged 20 to 24 years. Very few victims of 15- to 19-year-old offenders were of younger ages. Of the 3,298 people killed by 20- to 24-year-old offenders, 29% were 20 to 24 years old, 26% were 25 to 34 years old, and 15% were 15 to 19 years old. These data illustrate that homicide offenders and their victims tend to be of similar or proximate ages. Rarely are young homicide offenders much younger or much older than their victims. In addition, homicide victims and offenders tend to be of the same sex and race (Centers for Disease Control, 1986).

Weapon carrying and fighting among youths are important indicators of the potential for injury. Information from CDC's 1995 Youth Risk Behavior Survey asked high school students, "During the past 30 days, how many times have you carried a weapon, such as a gun, knife, or club, for self-protection or because you thought you might need it in a fight?" Results indicate that approximately 31% of males, 8% of females, and 20% of all surveyed students reported carrying a weapon (knife, razor, club, or firearm) at least once during the 30 days preceding the survey (Centers for Disease Control and Prevention, 1994b). Nearly, 8% of high school students reported carrying a firearm in the past 30 days. The percentage of students carrying firearms, combined with other weapon-carrying behavior, suggests the potential for injury is of great concern. In addition to weapon carrying, fighting is common among youths and is obviously a precursor to assault-related injury. In the 1995 Youth Risk Behavior Survey (Centers for Disease Control and Prevention, 1996), students were asked whether they had been in a physical fight or injured in a physical fight during the past 30 days. Of all high school students answering, 39% reported they had been in a physical fight—46% of males and 31% of females. While these large percentages suggest a significant amount of violence, only 4% of the students reported being in a fight in which they sustained injuries requiring treatment from a doctor or nurse. It is important to note that the percentages are for high school students nationwide, and the rates and percentages vary among schools and specific subgroups. Although, violence is very evident in school settings, school-associated violent deaths are relatively rare (Kachur et al., 1996). However, the magnitude of fighting and other indicators of interpersonal violence suggest that violence is a significant problem among youths in the United States.

One of the more important aspects of community violence that has far-reaching consequences is the issue of witnessing violence. It is difficult to measure the magnitude of witnessing violence and the psychological and physical effects on witnesses. Numerous studies attempting to assess the prevalence of exposure to violence have been conducted. In general, these studies found that inner-city youths are both witnesses and victims of violence at very high rates (Bell & Jenkins, 1993; Cooley, Turner, & Beidel, 1995; Fitzpatrick & Boldizar, 1993; Gladstein, Rusonis, & Heald, 1992; Richters & Martinez, 1993a; Schubiner, Scott, & Tzelepis, 1993). Research suggests that witnessing or being victims of community violence has psychological and psychiatric impacts that may severely hinder these youths through life (Fitzpatrick & Boldizar, 1993; Frederick, 1985; Martinez & Richters, 1993a; Pynoos & Nader, 1989; Terr, 1990).

Trends in Community Violence. Since 1933, homicide rates in the United States have varied more than twofold, ranging from a low of 4.5 homicides per 100,000 persons in 1955, 1957, and 1958 to a high of 10.7 homicides per 100,000 persons in 1980. The rate was 9.7 homicides per 100,000 persons in 1933, declined during the 1950s, and then increased substantially during the 1960s and early 1970s. Since the early 1970s, the rate has varied to some extent but has remained within 25% of its historical high in 1980. In the past few years homicide rates appear to be declining slightly, although they remain at near-record levels. The homicide rate and changes over time correspond with the rates of firearm-related homicide.

Rates of nonfatal assaults have been tracked only since 1973, when data from the National Crime Victimization Survey first became available. Overall rates of nonfatal assaults, however, have not exhibited a discernable trend between 1973 and 1992, and have ranged between 28 assaults per 1,000 persons to 35 assaults per 1,000 persons aged 12 years and older (U.S. Department of Justice, 1994).

These overall trends in rates of interpersonal violence obscure some very important changes in the nature and patterns of inter-personal violence in the United States. First, over the past decade, rates of interpersonal violence have increased among young people, and the victims and perpetrators appear to be getting younger and younger. Second, although there has been a recent decline in homicide overall, rates among young males increased rapidly over the past decade. Third, an increasing percentage of the victims of young offenders appear to be strangers and acquaintances. Finally, the lethality of interpersonal violence among young people has increased and appears to be associated with greater access to firearms, greater "firing power," or greater willingness to use firearms.

Young people are disproportionately represented among the per-petrators and victims of interpersonal violence. Arrest rates for homicide, rape, robbery, and aggravated assault in the United States peak among older adolescents and young adults (U.S. Department of Justice, 1993a). Interviews with assault victims indicate that offenders aged 12 to 24 years committed almost 50% of the estimated 6.4 million nonfatal crimes of violence in 1991 (U.S. Department of Justice, 1992).

The disproportionate involvement of youths in committing inter-personal violence has grown over the past few decades. Between 1965 and 1993, arrest rates for murder and non-negligent man-slaughter increased by more than 100% for youths between the ages of 13 and 22 years, while arrest rates for those in every age group from 30 years and older declined (U.S. Department of Justice, 1993a). Arrest rates for the perpetration of nonfatal interpersonal violence has increased among youths as well. Since 1965, arrest rates for violent offenses tripled among youths aged 13 to 18 years, more than doubled for those aged 19 to 39 years, while increasing more modestly among those 40 years of age and older (U.S. Depart-ment of Justice, 1993a).

As with the perpetration of interpersonal violence, the dispro-portionate involvement of youths as victims has increased as well. For example, between 1965 and 1985, homicide rates for 15- to 19-year-old males were one third to one half the rates of persons aged 20 to 34 years. Between 1985 and 1992, however, annual rates for 15- to 19-year-old males increased 154%, surpassing the homi-cide rates for men 25 to 29 and 30 to 34 years old (Centers for Disease Control and Prevention, 1994a). Similarly, victimization rates for nonfatal interpersonal violence have increased among youths. Among teens 12 to 15 and 16 to 19 years old, nonfatal assault rates increased by approximately 30% between 1973 and 1992, with most of this increase occurring since 1985 (U.S. Depart-ment of Justice, 1994). In comparison, nonfatal assault victimiza-tion rates increased only modestly or declined among persons aged 20 years and older. Because of the increasing involvement of youths in interpersonal violence, particularly during the past decade, the average age of both violent offenders and victims has been declining (U.S. Department of Justice, 1993a, 1994).

Another disturbing trend is that young offenders are becoming more likely to kill acquaintances and strangers. FBI-SHR data, which allow us to examine the social relationships between homi-cide victims and offenders, show that many relationships are unde-termined (Federal Bureau of Investigation, 1995). By looking at trends over time, we observe some distinct patterns (Figure 4.4). In general, homicide offenders aged 10 to 24 years are most likely to kill an acquaintance. Very few homicides are committed by children aged 10 to 14 years; however, of those children who did commit murder in 1993, almost 45% killed acquaintances, up from 36% in

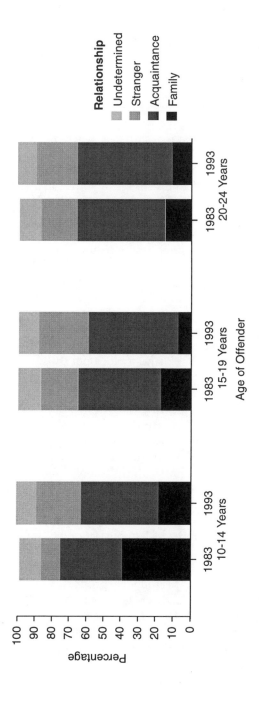

Figure 4.4. Percentage Distribution of Homicide Offenders by Age and Relation to Victim, United States, 1983 and 1993

111

1983. The percentage who killed family members declined dramatically from 39% in 1983 to 18% in 1993, while the percentage of those who killed strangers increased from 11% in 1983 to 26% in 1993. Very little change was observed in the percentage of 10- to 14-year-old homicide offenders whose relationship with the victims could not be identified over the decade.

Perhaps the most striking shifts between 1983 and 1993 were among persons aged 15 to 19 years, with a substantial decline in the percentage of family homicides and an increase in homicides involving strangers. The percentage of youths in this age group who killed family members decreased from 17% to 7%, while the percentage of acquaintance homicides increased, from 48% to 52%, as did homicides involving strangers, from 22% to 29%. The percentage of undetermined relationships between 15- to 19-year-old offenders and their victims remained almost unchanged over the decade. This same pattern of declines and increases was also seen among homicide offenders aged 20 to 24 years, but the shifts were less dramatic.

The lethality of violence among adolescents and young adults also has increased substantially since the mid-1980s, as is suggested by trends in the number of homicides per 100,000 violent events (Figure 4.5) (National Center for Health Statistics, unpublished data; U.S. Department of Justice, 1993b, 1994). Data from the National Center for Health Statistics and the National Crime Victimization Survey indicate that although lethality over the 20-year period varied substantially, after the early 1980s, the rates of lethal assaults increased substantially among each age group between 12 and 24 years, particularly among teens 16 to 19 years old. No clear increase in the lethality of assaults was observed in other age groups, except the 65-years-or-older age group.

Although rates of non-firearm-related homicide have remained fairly flat over time, rates of firearm-related homicide have closely tracked the overall U.S. homicide rate since 1933. Trends in homicide victimization are strongly associated with firearm involvement. During this six-decade period, the proportion of homicides committed with a firearm has varied from a low of 51% in 1951 to a high of 69.8% in 1992. Evidence indicates quite clearly that recent increases in youth homicide are almost entirely attributable to increases in homicides involving firearms (Centers for Disease Control and Prevention, 1994a).

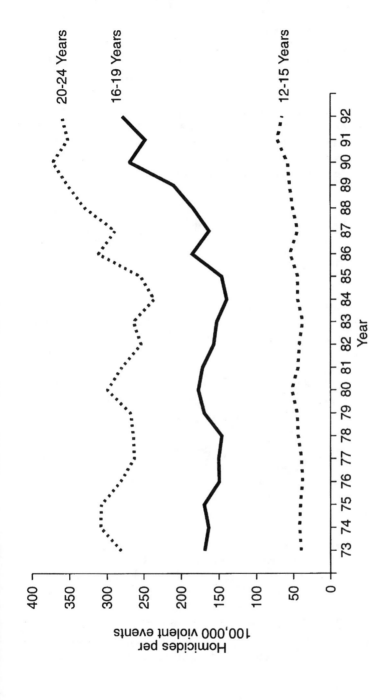

Figure 4.5. Homicides per 100,000 Violent Events Among Persons Aged 12-15, 16-19, and 20-24 Years, United States, 1973-1992

Identifying Causes

The second step in the public health approach involves identifying causes. This process may also be used to define populations at high risk and to suggest specific interventions. Some research into risk factors such as alcohol and drug use, media violence, and social and economic influences have been explored. However, many questions remain regarding the role that these and numerous other possible causes play in producing violent behavior and, more important, how risk factors may be modified to prevent violent behavior.

Definitional Barriers. The lack of definitive answers regarding the causes of violent behavior is probably due to both the infancy of scientific inquiry into the problem and the complexity of the problem. There appear to be many forms of violence with multiple etiologies, which implies there is no simple answer to defining the cause or causes of violent behavior. Furthermore, as the taxonomy of violence develops, it has become clear that thinking and language related to the topic of violence lack specificity.

A fundamental question is whether there are specific subtypes of violent behavior that require multiple theories to explain a variety of etiologies. The alternative is that violence is a homogenous construct requiring one comprehensive theory to explain its etiology. Some of the difficulties in developing a precise taxonomy for violence and its causes result from an undeveloped understanding and agreement around this issue. Many people use the term *violence* to refer to a fairly broad range of behaviors (or potential behaviors, thoughts, or images) without providing much specification of how one behavior may differ from other violent behaviors. Thus the issues of taxonomy and specificity of language are barriers to developing a better understanding of violence. There appear to be subtypes of violence with differing etiologies, and a first step is to begin to describe the various forms (Reiss & Roth, 1993). Although this chapter has attempted to describe the problem, homicide and assault information and information on the circumstances surrounding homicide and assault are inadequate. Therefore it is difficult to describe the violence problem in terms of subtypes of violence, partly because subtypes of violence are poorly articulated and partly because collecting data on circumstance is difficult.

Efforts to specify different forms of interpersonal violence that occur in community settings have been limited and disparate. Generally, investigations have focused on the distinction between emotive ("crimes of passion") and instrumental ("crimes for material gain") forms of violence (Block & Block, 1992; Berkowitz, 1978), but little progress has been made on understanding the similarities and differences between these two forms of violence. For example, it is possible there are subtypes of instrumental violence. Violence in the commission of carjacking may differ in etiology from that in a convenience store robbery, a mugging, a purse snatching, or an armed bank robbery. We are currently unable to state whether or not there is some shared underlying characteristic of individuals who engage in these forms of instrumental violence.

Another characterization of violent types is that of Loeber and Hay who classify violent behavior into authority conflict, covert offending, and aggression (Loeber & Hay, 1997). This typology further develops the concept of more than one causal pathway and provides some basis for delineating different forms of violent behavior. For prevention purposes, however, we still need a better understanding of these issues to specify more clearly forms of violence and their causes.

The developmental sequences leading to violent behavior are uncertain, but several possibilities regarding behavioral indicators and potential interventions have been outlined (Reiss & Roth, 1993, pp. 360). First, different behavioral indicators of violence potential may be manifestations of the same underlying characteristics, regardless of a person's age. From this perspective, early intervention would not break the causal chain leading to development of violence potential. Second, behavioral indicators are part of an underlying characteristic and are sequentially related to an individual's development of violent potential. In this perspective, early intervention may very well disrupt the development of violence potential. Third, a behavioral indicator is part of the interaction of multiple characteristics and is influenced by exposure to developmental effects; thus one characteristic can cause changes in an indicator of another characteristic. None of these three possibilities has been clearly eliminated and each appears to be able to find some support in both commonsense and observational studies. However, given the complexity of human development and behavior, the third option may be the most viable. This perspective suggests myriad interrelated conditions and influences over the life span of an individual that, in sum, are predictive of behavioral tendencies. It may also provide potential for identifying configurations of characteristics, conditions, and influences that may be more or less likely to result in the potential expression of one or more specific forms of violent behavior.

Ecological View of Violence. It is impossible to understand the causes of violence in our communities without considering the interplay between the behavior of individuals, the immediate environments in which they act and are socialized, and social and economic institutions that define behavioral norms and influence the social processes that define environments. Ecological theory has been employed empirically in various forms in several scientific disciplines (e.g., Bronfenbrenner, 1977; Hawley, 1950, 1986). Ecological analysis allows for assessment of relations within systems. In the case of humans and violent behavior, the focus is on the relationship of the individual with the immediate environment, as well as with and between the larger social contexts, both formal and informal. The concept of the ecological environment is topological and involves a nested arrangement of systems, each contained within the next.

An ecological systems model of human development provides a useful framework for understanding the etiology of community violence as well as for identifying opportunities for intervention (Belsky, 1980; Bronfenbrenner, 1977, 1988; Cicchetti & Lynch, 1993). According to this model, intrapersonal, social, cultural, economic, and physical environments influence the development of violent behavior. In Bronfenbrenner's (1977) model, the microsystem includes an individual's interpersonal relationships with family and peers. The next level, the mesosystem, describes interactions among the social systems at the micro level. An example would be relationships between a reference person's family and peer group. Finally, the macrosystem is the overarching institutional patterns of the culture or subculture, such as the economic, social, educational, legal, and political systems, of which micro- and mesosystems are the concrete manifestations. Macrosystems are conceived and examined not only in structural terms but as carriers of information and ideology that, both explicitly and implicitly, endow meaning and motivation to particular agencies, social networks, roles, activities, and their interrelations. Although not specifically described by Bronfenbrenner (1977), the individual's characteristics are important to consider because as the individual interacts with his or her environment over time, these characteristics predispose the person toward certain behaviors. Biological and psychological factors influence the perspective of individuals and their ability to interact with their environment effectively.

There are several implications of this ecological model for understanding community violence. The model accepts that environmental factors (familial, societal, and physical) exert a direct influence on behavior. It also explicitly acknowledges the multilevel determinants of behavior. Thus, it is not just family or neighborhood or impoverished environment but all of these levels that contribute to the development of community violence. Moreover, these levels interact with each other to influence whether or not individuals engage in violence in their communities.

Several studies have attempted to employ an ecological framework to assess the influences of levels on behavior. For example, Brooks-Gunn, Duncan, Klebanov, and Sealand (1993) examined the effects of neighborhood characteristics on individual child outcomes. Richters and Martinez (1993b) explored the effects of violent communities and family characteristics on adaptational failure (measured by school performance and the Child Behavior Checklist) of individual children. Another study combining data at multiple levels of analysis found that collective efficacy of communities was negatively associated with violence (Sampson, Raudenbush, & Earls, 1997).

Most etiologic research into violent behavior occurs at one level of analysis because such studies are easier to conduct, although at higher levels of aggregation, they suffer from potential interpretation problems when attempting to compare across levels (Glick & Roberts, 1984; Iversen, 1991; Richards, Gottfredson, & Gottfredson, 1990). The following discussion utilizes the basic framework of the ecological model (individual, microsystem, mesosystem, macrosystem) as the basis for reviewing research at each level.

Individual-Level Influences. The development and expression of violent behavior among individuals is likely to be partially determined by biological and other predispositional conditions. Although all human behavior has an important environmental component, it is also influenced in some way by genes (Carey & Goldman, 1997). The question emerging in genetic research in relation to antisocial behavior is not, "Is there genetic influence?" but "What are the mechanisms for a genetic effect?" Numerous studies of the heritability and role of genetics in violent and aggressive behavior have been conducted in animal populations (Carey, 1994). In humans, there is some evidence that certain personality traits and cognitive styles have a genetic component that may be associated with tendencies toward aggressive and violent behavior (Carey, 1994). There is also evidence that neurobiology, hormones, neurochemistry, and diet are related to antisocial behavior (Berman, Kavoussi, & Coccaro, 1997; Brain 1994; Brain & Susman, 1997; Ferris & De Vries, 1997; Kanarek, 1994; Miczeck et al., 1994; Mirsky & Siegel, 1994). In addition, prenatal and perinatal factors may have some influence on potential for violence later in life (Lewis, Pincus, Bard, & Richardson, 1979; Litt, 1971; Mednick & Kandel, 1988; Mungas, 1983). Although biological factors may play some role in the development and expression of violent behavior, at present it is unclear how this knowledge can further our understanding of the causes and variation of community violence. It is also unclear how much influence environmental factors may have on biological factors. Thus as biological factors associated with violent behavior are elucidated, we must also learn how we can modify those environmental factors to reduce the risks of developing violent behavior.

There is significant evidence that psychiatric disorders are associated with violent behavior (Beck, 1994; Hodgins, 1995; Monahan, 1997; Mulvey 1994), antisocial personality disorder in particular has been associated with violent behavior (Robins & Regier, 1991). The degree to which alcohol use and abuse contribute to violence perpetration and victimization is a complicated issue, although there are clear associations (White, 1997).

While most research into the causes of violent behavior among individuals has focused on risk factors, there has been some effort to address the issue of resiliency (Garmezy, 1993). Why is it that some children, despite their risk characteristics, become peaceful, productive citizens? Characteristics and experiences related to education, vocation, marriage, children, and social support were found to be associated with resilience (Werner, 1989). It was found that resilient children were those who exhibited good coping strategies when given adult responsibilities (Werner & Smith, 1992). However, the concept of resilience as represented in research and the utility of this concept for violence prevention have been questioned (Tolan, 1996).

Microsystem Influences. The primary socializing agent for most children is the family. Many violent offenders were raised by adults with poor child-rearing skills, were poorly supervised, separated from their parents at a young age (Farrington, 1997), physically and/or sexually abused, or neglected (DiLalla & Gottesman, 1991; Tebbutt, Swanston, Oates, & O'Toole, 1997; Widom, 1989, 1991). It is also becoming more apparent that youths who witness violence within their homes are affected significantly by the experience (David, Steele, Forehand, & Armistead, 1996). Moreover, children's adaptational failure has been found to be related to unstable or unsafe homes (DiLalla, Mitchell, & Arthur, 1988; Richters & Martinez, 1993b).

Research has suggested that aggressive youths are frequently rejected by peers (Coie, Dodge, Terry, & Wright, 1991; Huesmann & Eron, 1986), yet the role played by peer rejection in the development of aggressive behavior is unclear. However, there is evidence that peers have significant influence on the behavior of adolescents and teenagers (Evans, Oates, & Schwab, 1993; Levy, 1992).

School environments appear to be relatively safe places where homicides and victimizations are rare (Kachur et al., 1996). However, many students report being in fights and getting hit while in school (Centers for Disease Control, 1992; Kann et al., 1996; Lowry, Sleet, Duncan, Powell, & Kolbe, 1995). There is also evidence that carrying weapons on school property is fairly common and is even more common among high school youths outside of schools (Kann et al., 1996). Thus, while serious injury and homicide on school property appear to be rare, the realities of violence in the form of fighting and potential violent victimization are significant for many youths. It is unclear how witnessing peers fighting, knowing that peers carry weapons, and being a victim of violence at school influence the violence potential of youths or how these events may influence or be influenced by violence in the community. There are also characteristics of the school environment that appear to be associated with risk for violent behavior, such as school buildings that are in disrepair (Cotten et al., 1994).

Other conditions in the immediate environment may also play a role in the escalation and effects of violent behavior. For example, a 1986 telephone survey found that while 90% of respondents were occasionally annoyed by neighbors, such annoyances rarely (6%) led to more significant situations such as moving or threats of violence (Paquin & Gambrill, 1994). Exposure to violence and victimization among adolescents are associated with frequency of fighting (Durant, Pendergast, & Cadenhead, 1994). Scientific research clearly indicates that the presence of a gun in a violent interaction dramatically increases the likelihood that one or more of the participants will be killed (Cook, 1991). Consequently, one could hypothesize that trends in homicide are associated with access to firearms or a willingness to use firearms on the part of young assailants.

Mesosystem Influences. At a higher level of aggregation, the mesosystem is focused on understanding how the microsystems of an individual's existence interact with each other. There is little published research on these interrelationships as they affect violence in communities. One exception is a study of the relationship between reducing violence and collective efficacy, defined as social cohesion among neighbors and willingness to intervene for the common good (Sampson et al., 1997). Yet it is still largely unclear how home environments influence school environments or how microsystems interface to affect each other and how this interaction may affect a child's potential for violent behavior.

Macrosystem Influences. Social and economic conditions appear to influence development of violent behavior. Several neighborhood or community-based studies have found a number of community dimensions to be associated with violence. Poverty is probably the most commonly studied variable in ecological analyses of violence. In fact, across studies, several indicators of poverty and income inequality have been found to be significant predictors of violence (Beasley & Antunes, 1974; Block, 1979; Harries, 1995; Messner & Tardiff, 1986; Sampson, 1985; Shaw & McKay, 1942; Smith & Jarjoura, 1988; Taylor & Covington, 1988).

Community stability, which is frequently measured as mobility, is another characteristic that is associated with measures of violence (Harries, 1995; Sampson, 1985; Smith & Jarjoura, 1988; Taylor & Covington, 1988). Several studies have also found associations between the racial and ethnic composition of communities and indicators of violence (Block, 1979; Block & Block, 1992; Curry & Spergel, 1992; Messner & Tardiff, 1986). Other associations with community violence include family structure and stability, housing and population density, and social organization (Roneck, 1981; Sampson 1985; Sampson & Groves; 1989; Smith & Jarjoura, 1988).

Another potential causal aspect of community violence includes local economic activities that may support violence. The increase in the rate and lethality of interpersonal violence began at the time that crack cocaine was widely introduced into the inner cities. It has been theorized that the recruitment of adolescents and young adults into the distribution of crack increased their access to guns and accelerated widespread use of guns by more young people (Blumstein, 1995).

There has been lively discussion about the culture of violence in the United States and the role it plays in promoting the acting out of violent behavior in our everyday lives. One important aspect is how the media contribute to both developing and maintaining the culture of violence. There is significant evidence to suggest that exposure to dramatic violence on television is associated with aggressive behavior (Huesmann & Miller, 1994). Although exposure to media violence does appear to be related to aggression, this relationship is mediated by a number of factors such as cultural norms (Landau, 1984), group norms (Huesmann & Bacharach, 1988), and family characteristics (Tangney & Feshbach, 1988). Media may play a significant role in community violence, but some evidence suggests that direct models of interpersonal violence (i.e., witnessing real-life acts of violence) are much more influential than indirect models (i.e., dramatic presentation of violence; Friedlander, 1993).

A number of key concepts at several levels of aggregation appear to be central to understanding the causes of violence in our communities. Unfortunately, research has been unable to link all these levels together simultaneously, to provide an understanding of the causes of violence that would allow us to develop and implement highly effective multisystemic interventions for preventing violent behavior. This brings us back to the issue raised at the start of this section: taxonomy. When it comes to prevention, we must be clear about what is to be prevented. If the goal is to prevent aggressive behavior, our prospects are much more daunting than if our goal is to prevent something like firearm-related homicides in convenience stores in a specific city. In reviewing the literature on violence, very few studies use the same outcome variable. Variables and constructs that we use as predictors occupy a vast range, as do variables and constructs that actually measure some form of violence. Thus we are left with a rapidly developing field of research that is struggling for both a more refined taxonomy and a better developed framework for understanding the causes of violence.

Developing and Testing Interventions

The next step in the public health model is to develop interventions based, in large part, upon information obtained from the previous steps and to test these interventions. This step includes evaluating the efficacy of programs, policies, or interventions already in place. Methods for testing include prospective randomized controlled trials, evaluation of interventions to determine health outcomes in comparison populations, time series analysis of trends in multiple areas, and observational studies, such as case-control studies.

Preventive interventions are usually efforts to break a causal chain between the potential for a negative outcome and actually achieving that outcome. Thus, development of effective interventions is dependent upon the previous step in the public health model, in this case, understanding causes of violent behavior. In practice, however, interventions are often implemented and occasionally evaluated with little or no specification of the causal chain or how the intervention will affect this chain (National Center for Injury Prevention and Control, 1993).

The Institute of Medicine (Mrazek & Haggerty, 1994) report on reducing risks for mental disorders suggests a framework for describing different intervention approaches based on the target of the intervention: indicated, selective, and universal (Gordon, 1983). Indicated interventions are highly targeted interventions that involve identification and treatment of the problem and skill building among individuals and families. Selective interventions target high-risk groups with a focus on screening and group prevention activities. Universal interventions target communities or larger populations and may include media or educational campaigns and other broad population-based prevention strategies. This model appears to have some level of congruence with an ecological model of human development. As we find characteristics of individuals that put them at high risk for perpetration or victimization, we can attempt to develop and evaluate indicated interventions to reduce this risk. Similarly, as we identify characteristics of groups that are indicators of members' potential to perpetrate or to be a victim of violence and as we understand the causal pathways involved, we can develop, test, and deliver selective interventions that may lead to reductions of community violence. Finally, as we understand more of societal influences on development and expression of forms of community violence, we will be able to implement universal interventions (laws, education, media images, etc.).

Although a large number of violence prevention interventions have been developed and implemented, there is very little evaluation information on the fidelity and efficacy of most interventions (Powell et al., 1996). The CDC has mounted an effort to identify potentially effective interventions and to conduct evaluations of these efforts (Mercy & Potter, 1996). Numerous prevention strategies and populations have been targeted for evaluation (Bosworth, Espelage, DuBay, Dahlberg, & Daytner, 1996; De Vos, Stone, Goetz, & Dahlberg, 1996; Embry, Flannery, Vazsonyi, Powell, & Atha, 1996; Farrell, Meyer, & Dahlberg, 1996; Gabriel, Hopson, Haskins, & Powell, 1996; Hudley & Friday, 1996; Huesmann et al., 1996; Kelder et al., 1996). Initial findings suggest that many interventions have moderately positive effects, but eliminating violent behavior among young people will require comprehensive efforts leading to create environments that do not support aggressive and violent behavior.

Several scientific evaluations are being conducted, but only a limited number of prevention strategies have been evaluated and assessed for sustained effects. The Colorado Violence Prevention Center has reviewed prevention strategies, which has resulted in a series of publications titled "Blueprints for Violence Prevention" (Elliot, 1997). This effort identifies and describes effective implementation strategies for 10 scientifically evaluated violence prevention strategies. These include nurse home visitation, mentoring in the form of big brothers and big sisters, social cognitive curriculums, bullying prevention, educational incentives, family interventions, temporary foster care, and drug abuse prevention, among others. The Blueprints project represents a significant step toward identifying effective youth violence prevention strategies.

Implementing Interventions and Measuring Prevention Effectiveness

The final stage in the public health model is to implement interventions that have demonstrated effectiveness. Data collection to evaluate the program is essential, particularly since an intervention that has been found effective in a clinical trial or an academic study may perform differently in other settings. Another important component of this fourth stage is determining the cost effectiveness of such programs. Balancing the costs of a program against the cases prevented by the intervention can be very helpful to policymakers in determining optimal public health practice.

At the implementation phase, it is important to develop guidelines and procedures for putting effective programs in place. Several issues appear to be central to intervention: involving parents and students in programs designed to prevent violence; building effective coalitions across traditionally separate sectors such as criminal justice, education, and public health; and continuously assessing and improving programs. Assessing implementation and developing implementation guidelines are especially important because there is little information on what programs work on a large scale. There is also little information on how interventions can be adapted for particular community values, cultures, and standards and, at the same time, allow for and benefit from racially and culturally diverse participation from all parts of the community.

Application of the public health approach to prevent violence is a new endeavor. We are just now beginning more extensive surveillance efforts to understand the problem better. Very little research has been completed that provides definitive answers regarding causes of violent behavior. Many violence prevention programs are being implemented, but only now are the first comprehensive evaluations of some programs being completed. Essentially, violence prevention, addressed from a scientific perspective, is a young science. We have made some significant progress in recent years in defining the magnitude and trends in violence.

Summary and Conclusion

Using the public health approach as a framework, this chapter describes the problem of community violence and suggests a more comprehensive framework for developing an understanding of the causes of violent behavior in our communities. This chapter also provides a description of the current state of prevention intervention and suggests future directions for the field of violence prevention. Although the spectrum of possible efforts we can direct toward violence is limited, we can begin to take several actions toward prevention. First is to invest in injury surveillance systems that will provide us with meaningful and timely information on the magnitude, circumstances, trends, and affected populations. Second, we must further develop the taxonomy of violence and appropriate theoretical models to begin moving toward a comprehensive and thorough understanding of the causes and methods to prevent community violence. Third, we must take what we learn from conducting surveillance and research and start developing and testing prevention programs. Finally, we must streamline the pathway between science and program implementation by developing systems for rapidly and effectively disseminating information on the practice of violence prevention as interventions are produced.

As people die from violent behavior in our communities, we strive to understand the causes and to develop effective means to reduce the toll. This task is daunting, given the magnitude of the problem and the complexity of the causes. Yet it is encouraging to see the amount of progress that has been made over a short period of time. With continued focus and increased resources, our ability to understand the causes and prevent violent injury in our communities will progress significantly.

References

Beasley, R. W., & Antunes, G. (1974). The etiology of urban crime: An ecological analysis. *Criminology: An Interdisciplinary Journal, 11*(4), 439-461.

Beck, J. (1994). Epidemiology of mental disorders and violence: Beliefs and research findings. *Harvard Review of Psychiatry, 2,* 1-6.

Bell, C. C., & Jenkins, E. (1993). Community violence and children on Chicago's South Side. *Psychiatry, 56,* 46-54

Belsky, J. (1980). Child maltreatment: An ecological integration. *American Psychologist, 35*(4), 320-335

Berkowitz, L. (1978). Is criminal normative behavior? *Journal of Research in Crime and Delinquency, 15,* 148-161.

Berman, M. E., Kavoussi, R. J., & Coccaro, E. F. (1997). Neurotransmitter correlates of human aggression. In D. M. Stoff & J. Breiling (Eds.), *Handbook of antisocial behavior* (pp. 305-313). New York: John Wiley.

Block, R. (1979). Community, environment, and crime. *Criminology, 17,* 46-57.

Block, R., & Block, C. R. (1992). Homicide syndromes and vulnerability: Violence in Chicago community areas over 25 years. *Studies on Crime & Crime Prevention, 1*(1), 61-87.

Blumstein, A. (1995). Youth violence, guns, and the illicit-drug industry. *The Journal of Criminal Law and Criminology, 86*(1), 10-36.

Bosworth, K., Espelage, D., DuBay, T., Dahlberg, L. L., & Daytner, G. (1996). Using multimedia to teach conflict-resolution skills to young adolescents. *American Journal of Preventive Medicine, 12*(Suppl.), 65-74.

Brain, P. F. (1994). Hormonal aspects of aggression and violence. In A. J. Reiss & K. A. Miczek (Eds.), *Understanding and preventing violence: Vol. 2. Biobehavioral influences* (National Research Council; pp. 173-244). Washington, DC: National Academy Press.

Brain, P. F., & Susman, E. J. (1997). Hormonal aspects of aggression and violence. In D. M. Stoff & J. Breiling (Eds.), *Handbook of antisocial behavior* (pp. 314-323). New York: John Wiley.

Bronfenbrenner, U. (1977). Toward an experimental ecology of human development. *American Psychologist, 32,* 513-531.

Bronfenbrenner, U. (1988). Interacting systems in human development: Research paradigms: Present and future. In N. Bolger & A. Caspi (Eds.), *Persons in context: Developmental processes. Human development in cultural and historic contexts* (pp. 25-49). New York: Cambridge University Press.

Brooks-Gunn, J., Duncan, G. J., Klebanov, P. K., & Sealand, N. (1993). Do neighborhoods influence child and adolescent development? *American Journal of Sociology, 99*(2), 353-395.

Carey, G. (1994). Genetics and violence. In A. J. Reiss, K. A. Klaus, & J. A. Roth (Eds.), *Understanding and preventing violence: Vol. 2. Biobehavioral influences.* Washington, DC: National Academy Press.

Carey, G., & Goldman, D. (1997). The genetics of antisocial behavior. In D. M. Stoff, J. Breiling, & J. D. Maser (Eds.), *Handbook of antisocial behavior.* New York: John Wiley.

Centers for Disease Control. (1986). *Homicide surveillance: High-risk racial and ethnic groups, 1970-1983*. Atlanta: Author.

Centers for Disease Control and Prevention. (1992). Physical fighting among high-school students, United States, 1990. *Morbidity and Mortality Weekly Report, 41*(6), 91-94.

Centers for Disease Control and Prevention. (1993). Years of potential life lost before age 65—United States, 1980-1991. *Morbidity and Mortality Weekly Report, 42*(13), 251-253.

Centers for Disease Control and Prevention. (1994a). Homicide among 15-19-year-old males. *Morbidity and Mortality Weekly Report, 43*(40), 725-727.

Centers for Disease Control and Prevention. (1994b). Weapon carrying among high-school students, United States, 1990. *Morbidity and Mortality Weekly Report, 40*(40), 681-684.

Centers for Disease Control and Prevention. (1996, June 7). Trends in rates of homicide–United States, 1985-1994. *Morbidity and Mortality Weekly Report, 45*, 460-464.

Cicchetti, D., & Lynch, M. (1993). Toward an ecological/transactional model of community violence and child maltreatment: Consequences for children's development. In Children and Violence [Special issue]. *Psychiatry: Interpersonal & Biological Processes, 56*(1), 96-118.

Coie, J. D., Dodge, K. A., Terry, R., & Wright, V. (1991). The role of aggression in peer relations: An analysis of aggression episodes in boys' play groups. *Child Development, 62*(4), 812-826.

Cook, P. J. (1991). *The technology of personal violence*. In M. Tonry (Ed.), *Crime and justice: A review of research* (Vol. 14). Chicago: University of Chicago Press.

Cooley, M. R., Turner, S. M., & Beidel, D. C. (1995). Assessing community violence: The children's report of exposure to violence. *Journal of the American Academy of Child and Adolescent Psychiatry, 34*(2), 201-202.

Cotten, N. U., Resnick, J., Browne, D. C., Martin, S. L., McCarraher, D. R., & Woods, J. (1994). Aggression and fighting among African-American adolescents: Individual and family factors. *American Journal of Public Health, 84*(4), 618-622.

Curry, G. D., & Spergel, I. A. (1992). Gang involvement and delinquency among Hispanic and African-American adolescent males. *Journal of Research in Crime and Delinquency, 29*(3), 273-291.

David, C., Steele, R., Forehand, R., & Armistead, L. (1996). The role of family conflict and marital conflict in adolescent functioning. *Journal of Family Violence, 11*(1), 81-91.

De Vos, E., Stone, D. A., Goetz, M. A., & Dahlberg, L. L. (1996). Evaluation of a hospital-based youth violence intervention. *American Journal of Preventive Medicine, 12*(Suppl.), 101-108.

DiLalla, L. F., & Gottesman, I. (1991). Biological and genetic contributors to violence: Widom's untold tale. *Psychological Bulletin, 109*(1), 125-129.

DiLalla, L. F., Mitchell, C. M., & Arthur, M. W. (1998). Aggression and delinquency: Family and environmental factors. *Journal of Youth & Adolescence, 17*(3), 233-246.

Durant, R. H., Pendergast, R. A., & Cadenhead. C. (1994). Exposure to violence and victimization and fighting behavior among urban black adolescents. *Journal of Adolescent Health, 15*, 311-318.

Elliot, D. S. (Ed.). (1997). *Blueprints for violence prevention*. Boulder: University of Colorado, Center for the Study and Prevention of Violence.

Embry, D. D., Flannery, D. J., Vazsonyi, A. T., Powell, K. E., & Atha, H. (1996). PeaceBuilders: A theoretically driven, school-based model for early violence prevention. *American Journal of Preventive Medicine, 12*(Suppl.), 91-100.

Evans, W. N., Oates, W. E., & Schwab, R. M. (1992). Measuring peer group effects: A study of teenage behavior. *Journal of Political Economy, 100*(51), 966-991.

Farrell, A. D., Meyer, A. L., & Dahlberg, L. L. (1996). Richmond Youth Against Violence: A school-based program for urban adolescents. *American Journal of Preventive Medicine, 12*(Suppl.), 13-21.

Farrington, D. (1997). A critical analysis of research on the development of antisocial behavior from birth to adulthood. In D. M. Stoff, J. Breiling, & J. D. Maser (Eds.), *Handbook of antisocial behavior*. New York: John Wiley.

Federal Bureau of Investigation. (1995). *Supplemental homicide report data tapes, 1980-1992*. Washington, DC: U.S. Department of Justice, Federal Bureau of Investigation.

Ferris, C. F., & De Vries, G. J. (1997). Ethological models for examining the neurobiology of aggressive and affiliative behaviors. In D. M. Stoff & J. Breiling (Eds.), *Handbook of antisocial behavior* (pp. 255-268). New York: John Wiley.

Fitzpatrick, K. M., & Boldizar, J. P. (1993). The prevalence and consequences of exposure to violence among African-American youth. *Journal of the American Academy of Child and Adolescent Psychiatry, 32*, 424-430.

Frederick, C. (1985). Children traumatized by catastrophic situations. In J. Laube & S. A. Murphy (Eds.), *Perspectives on disaster recovery* (pp. 10-30). New York: Appleton-Century-Crofts.

Friedlander, B. Z. (1993). Community violence, children's development and the mass media: In pursuit of new insights, new goals, and new strategies. In Children and violence [Special issue]. *Psychiatry: Interpersonal and Biological Processes, 56*(1), 66-81.

Gabriel, R. M., Hopson, T., Haskins, M., & Powell, K. E. (1996). Building relationships and resilience in the prevention of youth violence. *American Journal of Preventive Medicine, 12*(Suppl.), 48-55.

Garmezy, N. (1993). Children in poverty: Resilience despite risk. *Psychiatry, 56*, 127-136.

Gladstein, J., Rusonis, E. S., & Heald, F. P. (1992). A comparison of inner-city and upper-middle class youths' exposure to violence. *Journal of Adolescent Health, 13*, 275-280.

Glick, W. H., & Roberts, K. H. (1994). Hypothesized interdependence, assumed independence. *Academy of Management Review, 9*(4), 722-735.

Gordon, R. (1983). An operational classification of disease prevention. *Public Health Reports, 98*, 107-109.

Harries, K. (1995). The ecology of homicide and assault: Baltimore city and county, 1989-91. *Studies on Crime & Crime Prevention, 4*(1), 44-60.

Hawley, A. (1950). *Human ecology: A theory of community structure*. New York: Ronald Press.

Hawley, A. (1986). *Human ecology: A theoretical essay*. Chicago: University of Chicago Press.

Hodgins, S. (1995). Major mental disorder and crime: An overview. *Psychology, Crime, and the Law, 2*, 5-17.

Hudley, C., & Friday, J. (1996). Attributional bias and reactive aggression. *American Journal of Preventive Medicine, 12*(Suppl.), 75-81.

Huesmann, L. R., Maxwell, C. D., Eron, L., Dahlberg, L. L., Guerra, N. G., Tolan, P. H., VanAcker, R., & Henry, D. (1996). Evaluating a cognitive/ecological program for the prevention of aggression among urban children. *American Journal of Preventive Medicine, 12*(Suppl.), 120-128.

Huesmann, L. R., & Miller, L. S. (1994). Long-term effects of repeated exposure to media violence in childhood. In L. R. Huesmann (Ed.), *Aggressive behavior: Current perspectives* (pp. 153-186). New York: Plenum.

Huesmann, L. R., & Bacharach, R. S. (1988). Differential effects of television violence in kibbutz and city children. In R. Patterson & P. Drummond (Eds.), *Television and its audience: International research perspectives* (pp. 154-176). London: BFI Publishing.

Huesmann, L. R., & Eron, L. (1986). *Television and the aggressive child.* Hillsdale, NJ: Lawrence Erlbaum.

Iversen, G. R. (1991). *Contextual analysis* (Quantitative Applications in the Social Sciences, Vol. 81). Newbury Park, CA: Sage.

Kachur, S. P., Stennies, G. M., Powell, K. E., Modzeleski, W., Stephens, R., Murphy, R., Kresnow, M., Sleet, D., & Lowry, R. (1996). School-associated violent deaths in the United States, 1992-1994. *Journal of the American Medical Association, 275*(22), 1729-1733.

Kanarek, R. B. (1994). Nutrition and violent behavior. In A. J. Reiss, Jr., K. A. Miczek, & J. A. Roth (Eds.), *Understanding and preventing violence: Vol. 2. Biobehavioral influences* (National Research Council; pp. 515-539). Washington, DC: National Academy Press.

Kann, L., Warren, C. W., Harris, W., Collins, J. L., Williams, B. I., Ross, J. G., & Kolbe, L. J. (1996). Youth risk behavior surveillance, 1995. In CDC surveillance summaries, September 27, 1996. *Morbidity and Mortality Weekly Report, 45*(SS-4), 1-84.

Kelder, S. H., Orpinas, P., McAlister, A., Frankowski, R., Parcel, G. S., & Friday, J. (1996). The Students for Peace Project: A comprehensive violence-prevention program for middle school students. *American Journal of Preventive Medicine, 12*(Suppl.), 22-30.

Krug, E. G., Dahlberg, L. L., & Powell, K. E. (1997). Childhood homicide, suicide, and firearm deaths: An international comparison. *World Health Statistics Quarterly, 49*(3/4), 230-235.

Landau, S. F. (1984). Trends in violence and aggression: A cross-cultural analysis. *International Journal of Comparative Sociology, 25*, 133-158.

Levy, D. (1992). The liberating effects of interpersonal influence: An empirical investigation of disinhibitory contagion. *The Journal of Social Psychology, 132*(4), 469-473.

Lewis, D. O., Pincus, J. H., Bard, B., & Richardson, E. (1979). Neuropsychiatric, psycho-educational, and family characteristics of 14 juveniles condemned to death in the United States. *American Journal of Psychiatry 145*, 584-589.

Litt, S. (1972). Perinatal complications and criminality. *Proceedings of the Annual Convention of the American Psychological Association, 7*(Pt. 1), 239-240.

Loeber, R., & Hay, D. (1997). Key issues in the development of aggression and violence from childhood to early adulthood. *Annual Review of Psychology, 48,* 371-410.

Lowry, R., Sleet, D., Duncan, C., Powell, K., & Kolbe, L. (1995). Adolescents at risk for violence. *Educational Psychology Review, 7*(1), 7-39.

Martinez, P. E., & Richters, J. E. (1993). The NIMH Community Violence Project: II. Children's distress symptoms associated with violence exposure. *Psychiatry, 56,* 21-35.

Mednick, S. A., & Kandel, E. (1988). Genetic and perinatal factors in violence. In T. E. Moffitt & S. A. Mednick (Eds.), *Biological contributions to crime causation* (NATO Advanced Science Institutes Series D: Behavioral and Social Sciences, No. 40; pp. 121-131). Dordrecht, the Netherlands: Martinus Nijhoff.

Mercy, J. A., & Potter, L. B. (1996). Combining analysis and action to solve the problem of youth violence [Introduction]. *American Journal of Preventive Medicine, 12*(Suppl.), 1-2.

Mercy, J., & O'Carroll, P. (1988). New directions in violence prevention: The public health arena. *Violence and Victims, 3*(4), 285-301.

Mercy, J. A., Rosenberg, M. L., Powell, K. E., Broome, C. V., & Roper, W. L. (1993). Public health policy for preventing violence. *Health Affairs, 12*(4), 7-29.

Messner, S., & Tardiff, K. (1986). Economic inequality and levels of homicide: An analysis of urban neighborhoods. *Criminology 24,* 297-318.

Miczek, K. A., DeBold, J. F., Haney, M., Tidey, J., Vivian, J., & Weerts, E. M. (1994). Alcohol, drugs of abuse, aggression, and violence. In A. J. Reiss, Jr., & J. A. Roth (Eds.), *Understanding and preventing violence: Vol. 3. Social influences* (National Research Council; pp. 377-570). Washington, DC: National Academy Press.

Mirsky, A. F., & Siegel, A. (1994). The neurobiology of violence and aggression. In A. J. Reiss, Jr., K. A. Miczek, & J. A. Roth (Eds.), *Understanding and preventing violence: Vol. 2. Biobehavioral influences* (National Research Council; pp. 59-172). Washington, DC: National Academy Press.

Monahan, J. (1997). Major mental disorders and violence to others. In D. M. Stoff, J. Breiling, & J. D. Maser (Eds.), *Handbook of antisocial behavior.* New York: John Wiley.

Mrazek, P. J., & Haggerty, R. J. (1994). *Reducing risks for mental disorders: Frontiers for prevention intervention research.* Washington, DC: National Academy Press.

Mulvey, E. (1994). Assessing the evidence of a link between mental illness and violence. *Hospital and Community Psychiatry, 31,* 23-31.

Mungas, D. (1983). An empirical analysis of specific syndromes of violent behavior. *Journal of Nervous & Mental Disease, 171*(6), 354-361.

National Center for Health Statistics. (1997). Annual summary of births, marriages, divorces, and deaths: United States, 1995. *Monthly Vital Statistics Report, 42:13.* Hyattsville, MD: Public Health Service.

National Center for Injury Prevention and Control. (1993). *The prevention of youth violence: A framework for community action.* Atlanta, GA: Centers for Disease Control and Prevention.

National Center for Injury Prevention and Control. (1997). *1995—10 leading causes of death.* Atlanta, GA: Centers for Disease Control and Prevention.

Paquin, G. W., & Gambrill, E. D. (1994). The problem with neighbors. *Journal of Community Psychology, 22*(1), 21-32.

Powell, K. E., Dahlberg, L. L., Friday, J., Mercy, J. A., Thornton, T., & Crawford, S. (1996). Prevention of youth violence: Rationale and characteristics of 15 evaluation projects. *American Journal of Preventive Medicine, 12*(Suppl.), 3-12.

Pynoos, R. S., & Nader, K. (1989). Case study: Children's memory and proximity to violence. *Journal of American Academy of Child and Adolescent Psychiatry, 28,* 236-241.

Reiss, A. J., & Roth, J. A. (Eds.). (1993). *Understanding and preventing violence* (Vol.1) Washington, DC: National Academy Press.

Richards, J. M., Gottfredson, D. C., & Gottfredson, G. D. (1990). Units of analysis and item statistics for environmental assessment scales. *Current Psychology: Research & Reviews, 9*(4), 407-413.

Richters, J. E., & Martinez, P. E. (1993a). The NIMH Community Violence Project: I. Children as victims and witness to violence. *Psychiatry, 56,* 7-21.

Richters, J. E., & Martinez, P. E. (1993b). Violent communities, family choices, and children's chances: An algorithm for improving the odds. *Development and Psychopathology, 5,* 609-627.

Robins, L. N., & Regier, D. A. (1991). *Psychiatric disorders in America: The Epidemiologic Catchment Area Study.* New York: Free Press.

Roneck, D. (1981). Dangerous places: Crime and residential environment. *Social Forces, 60,* 74-96.

Sampson, R. J. (1985). Neighborhood and crime: The structural determinants of personal victimization. *Journal of Research in Crime and Delinquency 22*(1), 7-40.

Sampson, R. J., Raudenbush, S. W., & Earls, F. (1997). Neighborhoods and violent crime: A multilevel study of collective efficacy. *Science, 277,* 918-924.

Sampson, R. J., & Groves, W. B. (1989). Community structure and crime: Testing social-disorganization theory. *American Journal of Sociology, 94*(4), 774-802.

Schubiner, H., Scott, R., & Tzelepis, A. (1993). Exposure to violence among inner-city youth. Society for Adolescent Medicine National Meeting (1990, Atlanta, Georgia). *Journal of Adolescent Health, 14,* 214-219.

Shaw, C. R., & McKay, H. D. (1942). *Juvenile delinquency and urban areas.* Chicago: University of Chicago Press.

Smith, D. R., & Jarjoura, G. R. (1988). Social structure and criminal victimization. *Journal of Research in Crime and Delinquency, 25,* 27-52.

Tangney, J. P., & Feshbach, S. (1988). Children's television-viewing frequency: Individual differences and demographic correlates. *Personality and Social Psychology Bulletin, 14*(1), 145-158.

Taylor, R. B., & Covington, J. (1988). Neighborhood changes in ecology and violence. *Criminology, 26*(4), 553-589.

Tebbutt, J., Swanston, H., Oates, R. K., & O'Toole, B. I. (1997). Five years after sexual abuse: Persisting dysfunction and problems of prediction. *Journal of the American Academy of Child and Adolescent Psychiatry, 36*(3), 330-339.

Terr, L. (1990). *Too scared to cry: Psychic trauma in childhood.* Grand Rapids, MI: Harper & Row.

Tolan, P. H. (1996). How resilient is the concept of resilience? *The Community Psychologist, 29*(4), 12-15.

U.S. Department of Justice. (1992). *Criminal victimization in the United States, 1991* (Report No. NCJ-139563). Washington, DC: U.S. Department of Justice, Bureau of Justice Statistics.

U.S. Department of Justice. (1993a). *Age-specific arrest rates and race-specific arrest rates for selected offenses, 1965-1992.* Washington, DC: U.S. Department of Justice, Federal Bureau of Investigation.

U.S. Department of Justice. (1993b). *Criminal victimization in the United States, 1992* (Report No. NCJ-145125). Washington, DC: U.S. Department of Justice, Bureau of Justice Statistics.

U.S. Department of Justice. (1994). *Criminal victimization in the United States: 1973-92 trends* (Report No. NCJ-147006). Washington, DC: U.S. Department of Justice, Bureau of Justice Statistics.

Werner, E. E. (1989). High-risk children in young adulthood: A longitudinal study from birth to 32 years. *American Journal of Orthopsychiatry, 59,* 72-81

Werner, E. E., & Smith, R. S. (1992). *Overcoming the odds.* Ithaca, NY: Cornell University Press.

White, H. R. (1997). Alcohol, illicit drugs, and violence. In D. M. Stoff, J. Breiling, & J. D. Maser (Eds.), *Handbook of antisocial behavior.* New York: John Wiley.

Widom, C. S. (1989). Child abuse, neglect, and adult behavior: Research design and findings on criminality, violence, and child abuse. *American Journal of Orthopsychiatry, 59*(3), 355-367.

Widom, C. S. (1991). Avoidance of criminality in abused and neglected children. *Psychiatry, 54,* 162-174.

World Health Organization. (1995). *World health statistics annual, 1994.* Geneva: Author.

• CHAPTER 5 •

Television Violence and Children: Problems and Solutions

LEONARD A. JASON

LIBBY KENNEDY HANAWAY

ESTER BRACKSHAW

Television, one of the most beloved traditions of modern childhood, has in turn become one of the more vexing concerns of parenthood. On the one hand, parents know that television is a temptingly handy baby-sitter, one that seems to quiet the kids and deliver some quality entertainment to boot. On the other hand, observant parents must also admit that while it may keep children out of immediate trouble, habitual viewing also keeps them out of the real world—digging in dirt, riding bikes, playing the piano, and playing with friends. Moreover, they know that the wholesome likes of Mr. Rogers, Big Bird, and Bill Nye the Science Guy are often overshadowed by an enduring onslaught of sex jokes, commercialism, and tired, demeaning stereotypes. Most alarming, though, to many parents and other concerned individuals is the loud, rude presence of televised violence. From the warm comfort of their living rooms, kids are openly invited to view mob hits, serial killers, date rape, karate kicks, car bombs, drug busts, and all kinds of paranormal sleaze and slime. As many parents may uneasily suspect, such relentless exposure to life's violent side is not without effects.

Media Violence and Its Effect on Children

Children's fascination with televised violence often has the most innocent of roots. Toddlers giggle and grin as the hapless Wile E. Coyote gets steamrollered flat as a pancake by Road Runner at every turn. Never fear, for he is always back in full, furious form at the end of the commercial break! A few years later they tune in to watch morphed teenagers and masked turtles, the adored vigilantes who karate chop and flip-flop their way to the moral high ground. Alas, the adoration is temporary, for growing children will self-consciously realize that these shows are made for kids. Never mind that the young viewers are still kids—peer pressure and simple curiosity propels them on. At the next level of television violence the gates of adult fare swing wide open: knife-wielding sadists in tacky horror films, fleeing crack sellers on *Cops,* fiery car explosions on *Walker, Texas Ranger,* and stretchers bearing bloody victims on the 6 o'clock news.

These are the scenes children dutifully watch again and again. The litany of statistics is familiar, though still astonishing. A recent 5-year study by the American Psychological Association estimates that the average child has watched 100,000 acts of violence and 8,000 acts of murder by the time he or she leaves elementary school. By the end of high school, 200,000 acts of violence have flashed before most kids' eyes (Huston et al., 1992).

To be sure, scenes of violence vary greatly, ranging from a cartoon cat being blown to bits by Acme dynamite to the high psychological drama of a round of Russian roulette. Do both examples count as true TV violence? A team of researchers led by George Gerbner of the University of Pennsylvania subscribes to the following definition of violence: "The overt expression of physical force (with or without a weapon, against self or others) compelling action against one's will on pain of being hurt and/or killed or threatened to be so victimized as a part of the plot" (Gerbner, Gross, Morgan, & Signorielli, 1980). It is important to note that their standard does not omit violence occurring in an accidental, natural, humorous, or fantasy context, landing the cartoon cat and the Russian roulette in the very same category.

Using this broad definition, the research team conducted a nearly two-decade-long project analyzing the violence content of network television. Through the use of a "Violence Index," the researchers found that the frequency and patterns of violence remained remarkably stable over two decades. In the last year of the project, 1979, they found that 70% of all prime-time programs contained violence. Nearly 54% of all leading characters were involved in the violence—men typically as its perpetrators and women, particularly non-white and older women, as its most frequent victims. Shifting to children's weekend and daytime television, the team determined that over 90% of the programs contained violence, with nearly 75% of the leading characters inflicting or suffering it (Gerbner et al., 1980). More recently, in 1992 the American Psychological Association reported that violent incidents occur five to six times an hour on prime-time television and 20 to 25 times an hour on children's Saturday morning cartoons (Huston et al., 1992).

To be fair, the 1996-1997 network prime-time season scaled back on violence, but for reasons likely more economic than altruistic. Guns were temporarily set aside in favor of shows featuring hip, frisky young adults, a sign of the enduring and still profitable cloning power of *Friends* and *Seinfeld*. Aside from some obvious examples of both gratuitous and nongratuitous violent regular programming (*Walker, Texas Ranger; New York Undercover; The X-Files; NYPD Blue; Homicide; Nash Bridges; High Incident;* and *Profiler,* among others), the main network offenders now seem to be victim-oriented made-for-TV movies, edited films previously shown in theaters (*Under Siege* or *Home Alone,* for example), and commercials for current release films. In discussing the results of a 1996 violence study, one U.C.L.A. researcher noted that the television commercial for the theater-release film *Assassins* had 24 scenes of violence in 30 seconds (Mifflin, 1996).

With the exception of gradual shifts reflecting seasonal trends, the incidence of TV violence has remained fairly stable over the years. However, the nature of that violence has not. Over the years it has become more mean, more realistic, more random, and more sophisticated. Early westerns featuring dueling white and black hats seem refreshingly tame compared to today's fare. For example, the weaponry seen on TV is highly advanced and highly visible, with characters flashing pistols, Uzis, and M-60 machine guns with practiced regularity. Moreover, verbal and psychological violence are now regular programming themes, offering hostage situations, terrorist campaigns, and psycho-killers as familiar plot elements. And, finally, the hats have fallen off the good guys and bad guys, allowing their characters to take on increasing levels of moral ambiguity. While real people have never been as flat and predictable as television often portrayed them, TV characters are now swinging to the other extreme. Perhaps spurred on by a number of disillusioning news stories in recent years, television has responded with its own version of the human condition. There is now a plethora of "bad cops" roaming the TV streets, menacing both criminals and innocents alike. The thugs, on the other hand, have been infused with a strong measure of humanity and humor, further complicating questions of guilt and culpability. This shift in characterization is not a problem per se, for humans are complex creatures. Children, however, tend to see things in black and white, and those kids who routinely observe such heavily shaded characters may struggle with the issues of trust, integrity, and fear.

In addition to becoming more sophisticated and psychologically complex, media violence has also become more sexually oriented. Rape, sexual assault, and incest are now routine topics. Music videos are particularly adept at linking sex and violence. A University of Georgia study that examined the content of three music video programs and stations found violence occurring in 56.6% of the videos. Of these violent videos, a full 81% also depicted forms of sexual intimacy (Sherman & Dominick, 1986). Video games, computer software, and sites on the World Wide Web and the Internet further forge the relationship between sex and violence. In the video game "Night Trap," for example, men in dark masks terrorize five beautiful young women. In one scene, three men burst into the bedroom of a young woman dressed only in a skimpy negligee. Unless the player makes the right moves, the men drag her off and plunge an electric drill into her neck, then hang her on a meat hook.

Advances in electronic technology have also changed the face of violence. Cable and video options, for example, permit a highly flexible viewing schedule. In TV's pre-cable days, the dedicated viewer had to fight off yawns and sleepy eyes to watch scary stuff on *The Late, Late Show.* Concerned parents could in part monitor their children's violence intake by simply declaring an early bedtime. Today that approach is not nearly so effective as kids have 'round-the-clock, every-day-of-the-week access to gunshots and gore. This problem of access is exacerbated by the fact that cable programs and video movie selections enable children to see violence far more graphic than that allowed by network television. Violence that might once have been suggested by a menacing shadow is today shown in its full Technicolor glory. Blood squirts, eyeballs dangle, knives meet flesh, and skulls shatter in slow motion. The unspeakable stuff of nightmares is now played on the small screen over and over again.

Indeed, every raunchy slasher film ever created seems to find eternal life on a cable channel. These B-grade efforts represent only the extreme, however. The bulk of cable programming and video selections—from 24-hour cable news channels to the latest movie of the week—contain violence that is rarely so absurdly graphic, yet may be equally or perhaps more disturbing. And as increasing numbers of both major and minor cable channels squeeze their way into the cable line-up (or video selections find their way onto store shelves), the access grows even greater. This abundance creates a unique opportunity for the determined young viewer. Armed with a TV schedule and nimble channel surfing ability, he or she can watch virtually nonstop violence for hours on end. In an instant, a child can flip from the silly, blood spurting antics of the evil doll Chucky to the haunting scenes of *The Deerhunter* to news clips of the world's latest terrorist act. One form of violence becomes indistinguishable from another, and the essential lessons of motive and consequence are lost in the tense anticipation of another round of bloodletting.

If cable and video movies have expanded the options for violent television, video and computer games offer an entirely new arena. Though there are many popular educational and sports-related games on the market, a tremendous number of video games are based on openly violent premises. The goal in most of the violent games is simple enough: Obliterate one's enemy through whatever means necessary. A recent *New York Times* article describes the latest batch of so-called hack and whack games on display at the industry's annual trade show:

> Players could not only behead an opponent in "Mace," a new release for Nintendo and already a popular arcade game, but also kick around torsos—for fun, of course. Besides chopping people into pieces, popular pastimes included blasting zombies and cyborgs while running through creepy castles. . . . "Hexen II," a sequel from Id Software, had people waiting in line to slash monsters with virtual axes.

Such animated violence is mother's milk to the industry. (Elrich, 1997, p. C2)

Hundreds of other violent options already cram the shelves of video game retailers. Decorated with pictures of glinting knives, lightning bolts, and snarling mercenary types, the brightly packaged boxes are carefully designed to lure young purchasers. The box for Sega's "Dynamite Duke," for example, promises that the lucky player will "Tear through six levels of violence! . . . Get up close and nasty with elbow bashes, kicks, uppercuts, and gunstock smashes. Your bionic punch is vicious!"

As with television, there is growing concern that the playing of violent video games can lead to aggressive or antisocial behavior. Yet an important distinction exists between the two mediums: Whereas viewing television is a fairly passive experience, playing video games is highly interactive. Players actually participate in, control, and even "commit" the violence themselves. The competitive quality of the games, meanwhile, ensures that they will be played over and over and over again. Stripped of the immediate thrill and excitement, the image is disturbing.

The Public Responds

Children's exposure to televised and video violence has not gone by unchallenged. Perhaps more than any other feature of TV's content, violent images and storylines have fueled front-page headlines and politically savvy opposition. Over the past several decades, angry citizen and professional groups like Action for Children's Television (ACT), the National Council of Churches, the American Medical Association, the National PTA, and the American Psychological Association have become increasingly outspoken in their criticism. The topic has also become a staple on Capitol Hill. Congressional hearings on the subject are frequent, and a growing number of prominent lawmakers, like former Senator Paul Simon (D-Ill.) and Representative Edward J. Markey (D-Mass.), have placed TV violence near the top of their political agendas.

In 1993, political pressure against the violent content of television was so strong that the networks—ABC, NBC, CBS, and Fox, along with their affiliates—agreed to air warnings on shows that contain excessive violence. This was an unprecedented and much heralded move, though many in the antiviolence coalition complained that the warning labels were simply token gestures that had no teeth. To begin, they pointed out, the action erroneously assumes that most children watch television in a supervised environment in which a parent can flip the channel when such a warning appears. The measure also ignored a fundamental lesson in child psychology: Claim that it is bad for you, and kids will flock. Like the citizen groups, neither concerned legislators nor the current Attorney General seemed satisfied with the label system, and in the background the threat of further governmental regulation loomed large.

In fact, what was once just a low rumble has grown to a full-fledged debate about the next step in limiting the violent images and storylines. The topic of the moment revolves around the much ballyhooed V-chip (violence chip), a device that for all its controversy is not yet a working reality. The V-chip concept hinges on two major developments that have recently turned the entire industry on its ear: first, the television industry's implementation of a voluntary ratings system for violence and other potentially objectionable material and, second, in accordance with the 1996 Telecommunications Act, television manufacturers' obligation soon to include in their TVs an electronic chip that will read the encoded ratings. The hoped-for result? Parents will gain some control in the TV wars, allowing them to program their television sets to air only those shows rated within their comfort zone.

Though some see it as a logical approach, the prospect of allowing the federal government wide authority in regulating TV violence raises a number of thorny issues, not the least of which is First Amendment protection. Many in the industry assert that within the bounds of current Federal Communications Commission (FCC) regulations they are simply exercising free speech and creative liberty. In addition to claiming constitutional immunity, the networks, with plenty of advertising revenue behind them, argue that they are simply giving viewers what they want.

On the other hand, lawmakers must face an increasingly vocal constituency, one filled with parents weary from battling television's crude messages and images. In addition, many government leaders find it hard to ignore the possibility that violent programs may breed a violent society. The current TV violence debate comes at a time when crime—especially youth crime—seems epidemic.

According to a recent Justice Department survey, crime in America is now at its most violent point in 20 years. For youth, the picture is particularly grim. A few statistics tell the story:

- The rate of 15-year-old males arrested for murder increased 207% between 1985 and 1993.
- More than 2,900 children and youth between the ages of 10 and 19 were murdered with a firearm in 1993—an average of more than eight young people a day.
- Between 1984 and 1993, juvenile arrests for weapons violations increased 125%.
- Juveniles accounted for 19% of all violent crimes arrests in 1994. (Maguire & Pastore, 1995)

It would be naive and misleading to associate this increase in juvenile crime directly with televised violence. At the very least, though, these figures point to the volatile climate in which the TV violence debate is being conducted. As for more direct examples, there have been a few very high-profile copycat incidents that do seem to link televised violence with real-life, imitated violence. In 1977, a 15-year-old boy killed his elderly next door neighbor during a bungled burglary attempt, apparently as a conditioned response to what he repeatedly saw on shows like *Baretta, Kojak,* and *Starsky and Hutch.* The resulting trial was unprecedented by the fact that television was actually named as an "accessory to the crime." Similar cases have been documented. In 1974, a 9-year-old girl was attacked and raped on the beach by four teenagers in a nearly direct copy of a scene from the TV-aired movie *Born Innocent.* In 1993 a 5-year-old boy set fire to his 2-year-old sister. The mother claims her son got the idea from watching MTV's paean to teenage dysfunctionality, *Beavis and Butt-head.* Though many claim such linkages are sensational and circumstantial, these and other incidents continue to fuel a national debate on the subject of violence on television.

Of course, it is hardly fair to tag TV as the primary source of youth recklessness and lawlessness. Child abuse and neglect, poverty, the dissolution of the family, and educational issues certainly play a more direct role in adversely influencing a child's life. As for the above copycat incidents, television has never been implicated on legal grounds for inciting viewers to violent action. According to the arguments, the cited shows and movies did not purposefully invite imitation. Children, so the argument goes, should simply "know better" than to follow in Kojak's foolish footsteps, and if they are too young in age to make such discernment, their parents should not let them watch such shows in the first place.

Fair enough. Yet television cannot altogether escape responsibility. The primary age group that is killing and being killed today are major consumers of a medium that very attractively packages violence as an effective method of problem solving. When a character is insulted, his powerful right hook sends the offender sailing across the bar counter. With a POW! the problem is solved. Or when a character fears an ugly secret is headed for broad light, he chooses to "silence" a possible informant rather than come clean with the truth. With a BANG! the problem is solved. The issue of violent problem solving becomes particularly frustrating when TV heroes resort to violence to save the day. This common plot device has an unintentionally amusing twist on *The Mighty Morphin Power Rangers*. In a public service announcement that follows every show, the program's actors soberly advise kids not to use violence to solve their problems. Yet for the preceding 30 minutes the program has been showcasing witty, friendly, good-looking teenagers triumphing on the side of good with one well-placed karate-style kick. Which approach to life's troubles does the young viewer choose? Which approach seems to be more fun?

Television has a troubling knack for glamorizing violence. It's violence with a wisecrack. It's violence with rock music in the background. It's violence with spectacular special effects. It's also often violence without consequence. Despite a steady stream of gunshots, grenades, kidnappings, and beatings, few viewers see grieving families, hospital bills, prison time, lasting physical pain, or psychological damage. Such omissions heartily feed the myth of youthful invincibility.

Violence Research

Public interest in the issue of televised violence has been paralleled by, if not exceeded by, scientific interest in the topic. In the past 30 years, well over a thousand studies investigating the role of televised violence have been published by the scientific community. The bulk of the research focuses on one compelling question: Is there a link between viewing violent behavior on television and the viewer's own subsequent aggressive behavior? From the start, efforts at testing this hypothesis have triggered a rigorous debate. Complete with political intrigue and factious in-fighting, the history of consensus reaching in the field proves to be an engaging tale in itself.

Though studies on televised violence quietly dated back to as early as 1955, psychologist Albert Bandura brought the issue to the public's attention in the 1960s. In the 1963 *Look* magazine article, "What TV Violence Can Do to Your Child," Bandura put into popular form the theories and hypotheses that he and his students had been testing for several years. Though the initial intent of Bandura's work was to validate his evolving social learning theory, along the way he implicated television as a source of teaching aggression.

According to Bandura's social learning theory, children learn their personalities from experiences and interactions with culture, subculture, family, and peers. The process of *modeling,* in particular, plays a fundamental role in the child's social development. As a result, Bandura theorized, the best and most effective way to teach children new ways of acting is to show them the behavior you wish them to learn and display.

Though social learning experiments had been conducted with laboratory animals for years, Bandura set out to test the theory on humans. In a series of now-famous "Bobo" studies, Bandura and his students turned to the new and controversial medium of television, testing the correlation between a child's viewing novel aggressive behavior and the child's own subsequent aggressive actions. Though the experiments varied slightly in focus and execution, the premise was generally the same: In most tests, preschool-aged children watched a film projected on a simulated TV set in which an actor (or a "model") verbally and physically attacked a large inflated plastic clown. After viewing the film, the children were left to play with a similar Bobo doll and a variety of other toys for 10 minutes. Observers hidden behind a one-way mirror recorded any imitative aggressive actions. Over and over again, children viewing aggressive models were observed exhibiting similar aggressive behaviors.

Some of Bandura's specific experiments are noteworthy. In a 1965 study, he examined the effect that perceived consequences would have on children's aggressive actions. In the experiment, some aggressive models were punished for their actions, others were rewarded, and still others had no consequences. Children viewing the rewarded and no-consequence models exhibited significant imitative aggression, a troublesome finding in view of TV's consequence-free world. Moreover, even those who viewed the punished model were able to replicate the aggressive action upon request, indicating that the actions—though perhaps not immediately imitated—still had been acquired or learned (Bandura, 1965). In another experiment, Bandura studied how viewing an aggressive cartoon cat on television, as opposed to a human model, might affect children. The results showed that children learned as readily from Herman the Cat as they did from a human adult model, implicating television's seemingly innocuous cartoon creatures as models for aggression (Bandura, Ross, & Ross, 1963). While Bandura's early studies have been eyed critically for their low ecological validity (the viewing experience in the Bobo studies was hardly typical and the clown, after all, was not human), they provided an important window for further investigation and debate.

During this period of initial investigation, Bandura was joined by other researchers, including Leonard Berkowitz, Percy Tannenbaum, Seymour Feshbach, Robert Singer, and Leonard Eron. Despite the extent of their early research, clear answers on the relationship between children and televised violence were not forthcoming. Nevertheless, members of the public and a few key lawmakers continued to voice skittish opinions about the powerful medium. By the end of the decade, televised violence had become a bona fide public issue. In 1971, the government responded in typical fashion: It commissioned a study.

The Surgeon General's Report and Beyond

Though the government had held hearings on the topic of media violence in the 1950s and 1960s, this was the first instance in which it would sponsor and direct original research in the field. Prompted by a Senate request, the Department of Health, Education and Welfare tapped the Surgeon General's office for the job. It, in turn, appointed a 12-person committee of prominent researchers and television industry executives to conduct the research. Controversy rolled in swiftly, however, when it was revealed that certain researchers were "blackballed" (including Bandura, Berkowitz, Tannenbaum, and others concerned about TV violence), resulting in a committee stacked in favor of the television industry. From the start, the Surgeon General's Scientific Advisory Committee on Television and Human Behavior was mired in controversy.

Under the auspices of the National Institute of Mental Health (NIMH), 23 individual projects were undertaken to study television and children's social behavior. The studies included investigations of the levels of TV's violence content, levels of viewing, perceived reality, possible effects of viewing violent content, long-term effects of exposure to violence, and children's response to commercials. By early 1972 the research was in. The result was the highly publicized *Report of the Surgeon General's Advisory Committee on Television and Behavior,* or, as it was known by its published title, *Television and Growing Up: The Impact of Televised Violence.* Most simply referred to it as the "Surgeon General's Report."

Those seeking a mandate on the issue were surely disappointed, as the final report was inconclusive. Though there was general agreement on the *pervasiveness* of televised violence, the *impact* of such violence on children was still vigorously debated. Some participants found strong correlation between viewing violence and subsequent aggression, while others determined that the impact of televised violence was significant only on those children already "predisposed" to behave more aggressively. Industry-backed committee members, meanwhile, were beside themselves to quell a public backlash. Adding to the chaos, the Surgeon General's office was under pressure to produce a unanimous report that would settle the score once and for all. After much hedging and waffling, the result was merely unanimous ambiguity. In its wishy-washy summary, the report stated that while a causal relationship *might* exist, "a good deal of research remains to be done before one can have confidence in these conclusions" (*Television and Growing Up,* 1972). So much for a mandate.

Few appreciated the report's vague position. Hearings followed more hearings on the subject. The networks conducted their own research and, not surprisingly, televised violence was fully exonerated. At the same time, however, independent research continued to point in the opposite direction. Finally, in 1982 there was another opportunity for a definitive answer. Ten years after the publication of the Surgeon General's Report, the NIMH conducted a follow-up study titled *Television and Behavior: Ten Years of Scientific Progress and Implications for the Eighties* (Pearl, Bouthilet, & Lazar, 1982). Though the new report was primarily a review of previously published studies (many from the 1972 report were resurrected), televised violence was much more clearly implicated as a cause for aggressive behavior in children:

> Most of the researchers look at the totality of evidence and conclude . . . that the convergence of findings supports the conclusion of a causal relationship between televised violence and later aggressive behavior. The evidence is now drawn from a larger body of literature. Adherents to this convergence approach agree that the conclusions reached in the Surgeon General's program have been significantly strengthened by more recent research. (Pearl et al., 1982)

Network executives could hardly have been pleased.

Since that last major report, much research continues to be conducted on the topic. Though an ironclad conclusion still has not been reached, most research continues to show a positive correlation between televised violence and aggressive behavior. Moreover, despite the somewhat equivocal results in many general TV violence studies, there is nearly universal agreement when it comes to heavy viewers. Since children who watch television see inordinate amounts of violence, it seems likely that heavy viewing would be a contributing factor in resulting aggressive behavior and attitudes. Research confirms these suspicions. In a study involving pre-schoolers who watch excessive amounts of TV, particularly cartoons and action-adventure programs, there was a higher incidence of aggression during playtime (Singer & Singer, 1980a). Other studies show that heavy viewing by elementary students, especially those who watch violent shows, is correlated to later aggression, restlessness, and belief in a "scary world" (Singer, Singer, & Rapaczyniski, 1984). For older children, the conclusions are similar. Murray (1988), discussing a 1977 study by researchers Greenburg and Atkin, states the researchers gave 9- to 13-year-old boys and girls situations such as the following: "Suppose you are riding your bike and some other child comes up and pushes you off it. What would you do? Hit them, call them a bad name, tell your parents/teacher, or leave them?" The investigators found that physically or verbally aggressive responses were selected by 45% of the heavy television-violence viewers, compared to only 21% of the light violence viewers.

In recent years, researchers have been looking beyond the broad, general effects of televised violence on children. The primary question has shifted from "*Is* there a correlation between televised violence and aggression?" to "In *which* children and under *what* circumstances is that correlation manifested?" Despite mounds of research that indicate that children are affected by violence, social scientists know that not all children are affected by all forms of TV violence in the same way. Age and developmental level, for example, can be important indicators. Very young children rarely understand the motives and consequences of violence, and, being wonderful imitators, they delight in replicating the exciting action. Children around the ages of 9 to 12 appear to be most sensitive to TV violence, partly because that age range consumes such great quantities of television. As they mature, however, children in that age group begin to understand television better and view its violence as less realistic. They also tend to be more detached, respond less emotionally, and are less frightened by the violence, all of which gradually serves to reduce their levels of aggression (Van der Voort, 1986). Gender differences also factor in, but not as strongly. Though many recent studies have found that both genders can be impacted, boys generally remain more susceptible to televised aggression than girls. Researcher Leonard Eron (1980) claims that vulnerability to TV violence begins by age 3 for both genders, but by age 8 girls have learned other behaviors, have developed other interests, and seem less affected by the violence. In addition to age and gender, other variables like family background, personality characteristics, natural propensity for aggression, childhood disturbances, cognitive ability, and frequency of viewing impact levels of viewer aggression.

Though individual viewer variables are important, researchers also consider the action on the screen to be relevant. Certain forms and portrayals of violence elicit stronger and more predictable responses than others. Research points to four types of violence portrayals that are most likely to influence behavior:

1. *Social approval*. When violence appears justified and it does not elicit critical comment, the viewer may perceive the violence as being more socially acceptable.

2. *Efficacy.* When portrayals imply that a particular kind of violent behavior is likely to result in a reward—either social, such as approval by others, or material, such as monetary gain—the viewer may assign more utility or worth to the act.

3. *Relevance.* When portrayals are perceived as real and appropriate to the circumstances the viewer may attach more meaning to the act. (Importantly, this does not exclude cartoons, as many young viewers perceive animated action as realistic. Also, given the rash of real-life crime series on the air, this aspect gains further importance.)

4. *Arousal.* The more exciting the action on the screen (fast pace and quick scene changes, for example)—with or without violence—the more aroused viewers will be and thus more likely to behave aggressively (Comstock, 1980).

Equally important, each of these four factors also works in reverse; if the violence is punished or deemed socially unacceptable, the likelihood of viewer aggression decreases.

Though the relationship between televised violence and viewer aggression forms the heart of the violence debate, other important issues are now being explored. For example, researcher Joanne Cantor has been studying children's reactions to frightening TV shows and movies for the past 15 years. She cites the opening scene of the dinosaur adventure movie *The Lost World,* which features a young girl as a tender target for a group of hungry dinosaurs, as an example of terrifying action cloaked in the guise of family entertainment: "My research shows that one of the scariest things for a young child is when a child is a victim. And yet these programs are marketed to the entire family, and kids are begging to get in." Television, too, causes plenty of bedtime jitters. Cantor describes a 7-year-old boy who, after watching a particularly bizarre and frightening episode of *The X-Files,* "woke up in a fit and for a week insisted on sleeping with his parents" (Carvajal, 1997, p. E5).

On the flip side of fear is dispassion, an alternate and no less disconcerting response on the part of many young viewers. When guns are flashed and heads are blown off with such ho-hum regularity, it's hard to expect kids to see violence as anything but routine. And when habitual viewers become inured to small screen barbarity, they can in turn grow detached from the effects of real-life violence. Researchers Ronald Drabman and Margaret Thomas (1974) showed how easily children can become desensitized to violence. In their study, they exposed 44 third- and fourth-grade children to either a western with many violent scenes or to a no-film experience. Each child was then asked to "baby-sit" two younger children whose behavior the child could monitor by television. Contrary to appearances, the child was actually viewing a videotape in which the two children play quietly, then become progressively destructive, and finally erupt in a physical fight that demolishes the television camera. Those who saw the violent western tolerated greater violence before seeking adult help. Psychologist and TV violence expert Edward Donnerstein effectively sums up the problem:

> The notion that I watched a lot of violence on TV and never killed anybody doesn't mean that there aren't any other effects. We don't say everybody is going to go out and commit a rape, but they certainly might have a different attitude about victims of rape, or about what rape is. They might be desensitized about violence and have a callous attitude toward victims of violence which, given the events of our time, we should be concerned about. (Oldenburg, 1992, p. E5)

This observation points to what is perhaps the most important and least considered aspect of the violence debate. It is easy to grow smug, certain that one's own children would never lose their grip on reality and raise their fists or brandish a gun in imitation of their small-screen heroes. It is considerably more difficult to be certain that repeated exposure to violence won't change children's attitudes and beliefs, making them less compassionate and sensitive when life offers pain, suffering, and distress.

Mediating the Effects of Televised Violence

Once confronted with the issue of televised violence, many parents experience a growing sense of powerlessness, feeling abandoned in a sea of unsettling media messages. Especially in electronically advanced homes, complete with cable TV and the surging waves of the Internet, parents feel at a loss to control the tide of violent and aggressive images rushing toward their children.

Industry Efforts

While the most idealistic (or unambitious) of parents might still be hoping that the electronic entertainment industry will—on its own—work earnestly to create a safer media environment for kids, it's an unlikely scenario. The television industry (with the obvious exceptions of cable channels like Nickelodeon and the Disney Channel) is simply not interested in courting the seemingly unprofitable child audience. By deserting children and families during the traditional family hour, by bumping kid-friendly programming in favor of morning news shows and tacky afternoon talk shows, and by offering children's programs that are thinly veiled licensed-product merchandising efforts, network television has clearly indicated its priorities. Half-hearted efforts at governmental compliance complete the picture. In response to the demand for increased educational programming for children as stipulated in the Children's Television Act of 1990, local broadcasters blithely offered programs like *Donahue* and *The Jetsons* as examples of educational television. More recently, during the ratings and V-chip debate, the industry adopted a concept not unlike the fabled fox guarding the chicken coop, allowing network producers to rate their own shows on a fuzzy, nonspecific age-based standard.

On the other hand, parents should also become familiar with some of the solutions—and their respective limitations—offered by the industry. For example, as part of a voluntary effort, video, computer, and CD-ROM games now feature ratings that designate the games as suitable for young children, preteenagers, teenagers up to and over the age of 17, and adults only. Cable companies offer blocking options for channels subscribers deem undesirable. And beginning in 1998, television manufacturers will produce TV sets encoded with the infamous V-chip, a device that will read the much debated ratings established by the television industry.

These are promising steps, but they will carry consumers only so far. As solutions, they seek only to regulate or restrict the flow of material, rather than improve it in the first place. They are patches, so to speak, and for every patching solution offered there seems to be a serious leak. For example, despite video game ratings, many retail outlets sell or rent games to anyone of any age with cash in hand. As for the Internet, a source of serious concern for many parents, recent efforts at creating a kid-friendly cyberspace have proven inevitably weak given its breakneck rate of growth. There are now more than 30 million Web pages, but fewer than 200,000 are rated by the Recreational Software Advisory Council or Safe-Surf. Meanwhile, software products have been developed to block objectionable material and limit the times of day when kids can surf the Internet. Regrettably, most of these products can be defeated, and those that can't are fairly to extremely restrictive, preventing kids from getting most of their beneficial on-line experience.

As for the loudest debate of all, neither a rating system nor the V-chip is fully going to solve our problems with children's TV viewing. First, only new TV sets will have the V-chips within them, meaning that only those families who are willing or able to spend several hundred dollars will reap the benefits of this technology for the first several years. Further diluting the hoped-for strength of the V-chip are the time and energy demands it will require. The time-consuming task of evaluating the ratings and programming the set(s) to accommodate the needs of children of varying ages and levels of maturity means that only the most determined of parents will commit themselves to this end. Interview studies already indicate that very few parents are using the current rating system to alter or monitor their kids' viewing habits, either due to dissatisfaction with the vague content categories or because they would rather evaluate programs according to their values, not the networks'.

Parent Involvement

Either by design or by default, the media industry appears incapable of satisfying the concerns of parents wary of its influence. Where the industry leaves off, parents must be willing to jump in and pick up the slack. No one else is going to do the hard work of monitoring what kind and how much television children watch.

A Matter of Time. The average child in America spends an average of 4 hours viewing television a day—28 hours per week watching TV. By age 18 he or she will have watched 22,000 hours of TV—more time even than spent in the classroom (Rice, 1992). Add to these totals the time kids devote to ancillary electronic pursuits like video games and computer activities, and the result is a generation of kids who are missing out on many of life's richer experiences.

In the same way kids adore sugar-coated cereal and late bedtimes, we should not be surprised that children devote so much time to the electronic media. But like other appealing but non-edifying aspects of childhood, excessive indulgence in electronic entertainment is unhealthy and in some cases outright dangerous. The potential effects of televised violence represent only part of the problem. At risk for the TV-seasoned child are the failure to develop crucial social skills, the lack of meaningful family interaction, the sacrifice of reading time (which can affect cognitive development and academic achievement), the sacrifice of physical and imaginative play, and the faulty expectation that life should deliver easy, instant entertainment. Those who watch excessive amounts of television have little time for other critical life experiences.

Parents overwhelmed by the long reach of the media might be at a loss over where and how to start making a dent in its consumption. The most obvious step involves developing and maintaining consistently enforced rules regarding how much time kids can spend watching TV and pursuing video and computer activities. This is hard, unwelcome work, but sitting down with kids and presenting a fair but firm plan is an essential place to start. Though most experts suggest keeping the limit under 2 hours a day, families should individually consider their own goals and needs and come up with their expectations and strategy accordingly. Regardless how a family's rules actually take shape, logical consequences should consistently follow up any creative rule bending; on the other hand, kids who stick to the new plan deserve plenty of acknowledgment and praise (and maybe even a reward or two) for working to break a difficult habit.

As parents become increasingly aware of the negative effects of TV viewing, many have begun to take an active role in limiting their children's viewing. In one study, 83 families were surveyed to assess the techniques they used to limit viewing (Sarlo, Jason, & Lonak, 1988). Researchers reported that most of the parents tried to reduce the amounts of TV viewing by placing limits on the location of the set or the hours of viewing permitted, by making viewing conditional upon first completing some prosocial act, or simply by arguing with their children. Although some parents viewed these strategies as effective, parents whose children watched higher amounts of TV expressed a desire for alternative methods and/or a commercial device that would help them better control their children's TV viewing.

In response, researchers have developed several successful methods for reducing the amount of time children and adults spend engaged in this activity. Jason and Klich (1982) and Jason (1983) have reported that a self-monitoring technique was effective in reducing adults' and children's excessive television viewing. Wolfe, Mendes, and Factor (1984) implemented a program whereby children were given 20 unearned tokens each week, which could be exchanged for 10 hours of television viewing. Results indicate that children's viewing time decreased by more than 60% during this intervention. In another study, seven children in one family reduced their TV viewing by using a simple token exchange system whereby tokens were earned by engaging in a variety of school-, play-, or housework-related activities (Jason, 1984). Other studies have reported success with use of a token-actuated device (Jason, 1985; Jason & Rooney-Rebeck, 1984). For example, tokens were given to children in exchange for participation in certain positive activities such as reading, doing chores, or playing with friends. Each token, when placed in a small device attached to the TV, would allow the child to watch TV for 30 minutes (Jason, 1987). In another study, a device that requires the subject to ride a bicycle in exchange for TV viewing time has been effective in reducing television viewing. This device, attached to the wheel and corresponding wheel rim of a stationary bicycle, was programmed to require that the child ride the bicycle for 15 minutes to earn 30 minutes of television viewing time (Jason & Johnson, 1995).

Although studies using token-actuated devices have been effective, these products are not available to the general public. Several television locking devices have been manufactured and are marketed to the general public. Researchers are examining the efficacy of these products. Jason, Johnson, and Jurs (1993) reported a decrease in the amount of television viewed by two children in a study aimed at assessing the effectiveness of a device called The Switch. This device is a simple television lock that attaches to the cord of any TV set, allowing parents to "lock" the television with a key, thereby prohibiting television viewing. In another study, by Johnson and Jason (1996), a computerized television lock, called

SuperVision, was effective in reducing the hours spent watching television among two children in one family.

Though establishing clear rules and expectations is a natural start, the better and more enduring part of monitoring involves the clever art of diversionary tactics—that is, introducing children to pleasures beyond the small screen to make it less attractive in the first place (Jason & Hanaway, 1997). Homes that heartily encourage art, music, storytelling, reading, imaginative play, sports, and nature will find that television and other electronic entertainment naturally play less central roles in their kids' lives. This "liberal arts" approach to family life is easiest to institute when children are very young, but even families with older, dedicated viewers will see positive changes if new interests and opportunities are enthusiastically introduced.

A Matter of Content. If parents can commit to the hard work of monitoring *how much* time is spent watching TV and playing computer games, more than half the battle has been won. The other half of the equation—the issue of content—will have been mitigated in part simply by limiting the time of children's overall exposure. Yet even with time rules in place, content issues—especially those involving violence—must be carefully addressed.

Content is often a difficult arena to negotiate, in part because increasing numbers of kids actively lean toward sophisticated adult programming. As a sign of "cool" among their peers, young kids tune in shows like *Friends* and *The X-Files* and beg their parents to take them to violent films like *The Lost World* and *Face/Off.* Says one Warner Brothers executive,

> Children are the only demographic that aspires older. They were raised on the computer and they want the same explosions, special effects, originality, and edginess as adults. They know when a movie panders to them. Kids, even small kids, attack each choice with a level of sophistication and cynicism I've never seen before. (Weinraub, 1997, p. C10)

Parents often unwittingly spur the process on. For example, moms and dads often bemoan the violence that surges through their kids' video games, forgetting that they were the ones who made or allowed the purchase in the first place. This myopia occurs in any number of guises. As one father was recently complaining about the level of violence needed to keep his 4-year-old son's attention on the screen, he marveled at how the film *Jurassic Park* has been his son's favorite movie since he was 18 months old. Even as he spoke, he remained oblivious to the irresponsibility of introducing a 1½-year-old to a PG-13-rated film filled with terrifying moments. It's no surprise the child now needs extreme visual stimulation to remain entertained.

In addition to the need for wise general content guidelines, parents and caregivers also need to address specific content issues. One of the best ways parents can monitor television's content is simply by watching TV *with* their kids, serving as clarifiers, translators, and even censors when necessary. Not only does this keep TV on the level of an active family activity, it also serves as a great forum for values instruction. Demeaning stereotypes can be countered, positive messages can be applauded, consequence-free violence can be challenged, and delicate conversations on difficult topics like sex and racism can be broached. When confronting television violence, some of the following discussion starters might prove helpful:

- Do you think shooting that person was the only way for him to solve the problem?
- How else could he have gone about it?
- If someone in real life were shot in the arm (leg, belly), how long do you think it would take to heal? Do you think it would hurt very much? Did it look like it hurt him very much?
- Why do you think there is so much violence on TV?
- Do you think there is this much violence in the real world?

Parents also need to pay close attention to violence that appears from unexpected sources: news programs featuring the latest drive-by shooting or terrorist bombing, commercials for action-oriented TV or theater movies, and sporting events that erupt in fights among players. Moreover, parents and other caregivers should seek out opportunities to place violence in its proper context. For example, *The Lion King* video, filled with unsettling acts of violence, offers parents a great forum to discuss with their children the violence inherent in nature. A show featuring purely gratuitous violence, meanwhile, can be an object lesson on how *not* to respond to adversity.

TV violence is a serious concern, but parents need not go overboard and banish every aggressive scene from their living room. Violence is a part of life, plain and simple. It can be effectively addressed on television, and with care, maturity, and involvement on the part of parents and caregivers, children might learn its true lessons. In the absence of such efforts, though, television—with its typically flippant handling of the incidence of violence, the consequences of violence, and the value of human life—will have the last word.

References

Bandura, A. (1965). Influence of models' reinforcement contingencies on the acquisition of imitative responses. *Journal of Personality and Social Psychology, 1*, 589-595.

Bandura, A., Ross, D., & Ross, S. A. (1963). Imitation of film-mediated aggressive models. *Journal of Abnormal and Social Psychology, 66*, 3-11.

Carvajal, D. (1997, June 1). In kids' pop culture, fear rules. *New York Times*, p. E5.

Comstock, G. (1980). New emphases in research on the effects of television and film violence. In E. L. Palmer & A. Dorr (Eds.), *Children and the faces of television: Teaching, violence, selling* (pp. 129-148). New York: Academic Press.

Drabman, R. S., & Thomas, M. H. (1974). Does media violence increase toleration of real-life aggression? *Developmental Psychology 10*, 418-421.

Elrich, D. (1997, July 3). New video games: Despite promises, violence rules. *New York Times*, p. C2.

Eron, L. D. (1980). Prescription for reduction of aggression. *American Psychologist, 35*, 244-252.

Gerbner, G., Gross, L., Morgan, M., & Signorielli, N. (1980). The "mainstreaming" of America: Violence profile no. 11. *Journal of Communication, 30*, 11.

Huston, A. C., Donnerstein, E., Fairchild, H., Feshbach, N. D., Katz, P. A., Murray, J. P., Rubenstein, E. A., Wilcox, B. L., & Zuckerman, D. (1992). *Big world, small screen: The role of television in American society.* Lincoln: University of Nebraska Press.

Jason, L. A. (1983). Self-monitoring in reducing children's excessive television viewing. *Psychological Reports, 53*, 1280.

Jason, L. A. (1984). Reducing excessive television viewing among seven children in one family. *The Behavior Therapist, 7*, 3-4.

Jason, L. A. (1985). Using a token-actuated timer to reduce television viewing. *Journal of Applied Behavior Analysis, 18*, 269-272.

Jason, L. A. (1987). Reducing children's excessive television viewing and assessing secondary changes. *Journal of Clinical Child Psychology, 16*, 245-250.

Jason, L. A., & Hanaway, L. K. (1997). *Remote control: A sensible approach to kids, TV, and the new electronic media.* Sarasota, FL: Professional Resource Press.

Jason, L. A., & Johnson, S. Z. (1995). Reducing excessive television viewing while increasing physical activity. *Child & Family Behavior Therapy, 17,* 35-45.

Jason, L. A., Johnson, S. Z., & Jurs, A. (1993). Reducing children's television viewing with an inexpensive lock. *Child and Family Behavior Therapy, 15*(3), 45-54.

Jason, L. A., & Klich, M. (1982). Use of feedback in reducing television watching. *Psychological Reports, 51,* 812-814.

Jason, L. A., & Rooney-Rebeck, P. (1984). Reducing excessive television viewing. *Child and Family Behavior Therapy, 6,* 61-69.

Johnson, S. Z., & Jason, L. A. (1996). Evaluation of a device aimed at reducing children's television viewing [Letter to the Editor]. *Child and Family Behavior Therapy, 18,* 59-61.

Maguire, K., & Pastore, A. L. (Eds.). (1995). *Bureau of Justice Statistics: Sourcebook of criminal justice statistics—Federal Bureau of Investigation, uniform crime reports for the United States 1994.* Washington, DC: Government Printing Office.

Mifflin, L. (1996, October 16). Study says networks have cut violence. *New York Times,* pp. C11, C16.

Murray, J. P. (1988). Children's media: On TV violence. *Division of Child, Youth, and Family Services Newsletter,* American Psychological Association Division 37, *11*(3), pp. 1, 12-14.

Oldenburg, D. (1992, April 7). Primal screen: Kids—TV violence & real life behavior. *Washington Post,* p. E5.

Pearl, D., Bouthilet, L., & Lazar, J. B. (Eds.). (1982). *Television and behavior: Ten years of scientific progress and implications for the eighties: Vol. 1. Summary report* (p. 37). Washington, DC: Government Printing Office.

Rice, B. (1992). Mixed signals: TV's effect on children continues to stir debate. *American Health, 62,* 24-30.

Sarlo, G., Jason, L. A., & Lonak, C. (1988). Parent strategies for limiting children's television watching. *Psychological Reports, 63,* 435-438.

Sherman, B. L., & Dominick, J. R. (1986). Violence and sex in music videos: TV and rock 'n roll. *Journal of Communication, 36*(1), 79-93.

Singer, J. L., & Singer, D. G. (1980). Television viewing and aggressive behavior in preschool children: A field study. *Annals of the New York Academy of Science, 347,* 289.

Singer, J. L., Singer, D. G., & Rapaczyniski, W. S. (1984). Family patterns and television viewing as predictors of children's beliefs and aggression. *Journal of Communication, 34,* 274-278.

Television and growing up: The impact of televised violence—Report to the Surgeon General. (1972). Washington, DC: Government Printing Office.

Van der Voort, T. H. A. (1986). *Television violence: A child's eye view.* Amsterdam: North-Holland.

Weinraub, B. (1997, July 23). Fun for the whole family: Movies for children, and their parents, are far from "Pollyanna." *New York Times,* p. C9-C10.

Wolfe, D. A., Mendes, M. G., & Factor, D. (1984). A parent-administered program to reduce children's television viewing. *Journal of Applied Behavior Analysis, 17,* 267-272.

CHAPTER 6

Hating Those Different From Ourselves: The Origins of Racial, Ethnic, and Religious Hatred

WAYNE WINBORNE

RENAE COHEN

In a volume focusing on the nature of various types of violence in contemporary American society, a chapter addressing the origins of group hatred may seem to fit in easily. After all, is hatred not at the root of all forms of violence, at least to some degree? Yet even in this straightforward light, many questions are raised. The most basic of these is whether or not hate for the target is necessary for violence to occur. That is, is it clear that violence always stems from hate? Violence is, by definition, a concept that involves action or the expression of some feeling with one or more persons behaving aggressively toward another in a given situation, whether in the community, the home, the workplace, or elsewhere. Similarly, hate involves one or more persons having feelings against another or others. But is negative action against another person always a requisite for hate to be present?

There is a vast literature suggesting that negative thoughts and stereotypes are fairly common. Do negative stereotypes and negative beliefs constitute hate, or must the negative feelings be acted

AUTHORS' NOTE: The authors wish to thank Allison Smith for her research assistance, and Bart Meyers and Ken Stern for their review of an earlier draft. Portions of this research were supported by a grant from the Ford Foundation.

upon for hate to be present? Is hating a person for some individual reason (e.g., "I hate her because she is so mean to me") the same as hating someone based on his or her group membership (e.g., "I hate her because she is Black")? Exploring these questions will help to bring greater understanding to the concepts of individual hate and group hatred and also contribute to identifying their origins.

This chapter will examine these concepts within the context of American society and from a social scientific perspective. It will rely heavily on the literature of social psychology and other related disciplines, reviewing some key theoretical and research findings as they relate to hatred.[1] Using social psychological literature as a basis for approaching this subject permits an examination of processes that function at both the individual and group level, which in turn allows for some understanding of the most common ways in which hate can become manifest. The social psychological literature is also useful to understand the origins of hate because of its many research studies on the related concepts of attitudes, prejudice, and stereotyping and the theoretical importance it gives these concepts in developing a clear understanding of hate.

While we will attempt to identify some universal processes that influence the development of hate for others, it is clear that some hatreds—for example, racism and anti-Semitism—may have a life, depth, breadth, and future all their own. They may be seen as distinct from one another, although one may seek to understand and explain them in the context of more widely applicable social psychological processes. However, while the approach and focus of this chapter will be largely social psychological in orientation, that perspective is, we believe, but one way to understand the phenomenon of hatred in contemporary American society.

We have organized this chapter in the following manner: First, we offer various definitions of hate and discuss it as a continuum from milder to more extreme forms of negativity, suggesting a model that both allows for the understanding of hate as a multifaceted construct and integrates it with a number of related concepts. We then discuss the similarity between mild hate and prejudice, using this relationship as a springboard from which to examine more closely the related concepts of stereotyping and prejudice. Next, we identify and provide brief descriptions of a number of important theoretical approaches to understanding stereotyping and prejudice. Finally, we return to the distinctions between various definitions of hate and propose questions and directions for future consideration and exploration.

Definitions and Degrees

When we discuss hate, there may be the assumption that we are all discussing the same phenomenon, but what exactly is meant by the word *hate?*[2] It is useful to start with a standard definition. The *Random House Dictionary of the English Language* (1987) defines hate as "intense dislike; extreme aversion or hostility." It further specifies that "Hate, the simple and general word, suggests passionate dislike and a feeling of enmity." *Hatred* is defined as "the feeling of one who hates" (p. 876).

In his authoritative and groundbreaking book *The Nature of Prejudice* (1954), Gordon Allport, the noted social psychologist, explored the nature of hatred, classifying it as a "sentiment—an enduring organization of aggressive impulses toward a person or class of persons" (p. 363). Allport further points out that outgroups are often the object of hate, as opposed to individuals, with *outgroups* referring to members of some other group, not one's own. He writes, "people who hate groups in the abstract will, in actual conduct, often act fairly and even kindly toward individual members of the group" (pp. 363-364). Allport's belief may have stemmed in part from a field study conducted by LaPiere (1934), who toured the country with a Chinese couple, stopping at establishments along the way to see if they would be refused service. Although they were refused service only once, more than 90% of the hotels and restaurants that responded to the inquiry stated that they would not serve such a couple when asked by letter 6 months later. This result was also found by Kutner, Wilkins, and Yarrow (1952), who replicated LaPiere's study with two Black women.

Allport also highlights the distinction made by Eric Fromm (1947) between two kinds of hate, namely, "rational" hate and "character-conditioned" hate. Rational hate is said to serve an important biological function, arising "when fundamental natural rights of persons are violated. One hates whatever threatens his own freedom, life, and values. Also, if well socialized, he hates whatever threatens the freedom, lives, and values of other human beings" (p. 364). Character-conditioned hate is described as a "continuing readiness to hate" (p. 364), and, of the two forms of hate delineated by Fromm, Allport contends that it is character-conditioned hatred that is of concern. Allport writes,

> The sentiment has little relation to reality, although it may be the product of a long series of bitter disappointments in life. These frustrations may become fused into a kind of "free-floating hatred"—the subjective counterpart of free-floating aggression. The person carries a vague, temperamental sense of wrong which he wishes to polarize. He must hate *something*. The real roots of the hatred may baffle him, but he thinks up some convenient victim and some good reason. The Jews are conspiring against him, or the politicians are set on making things worse. Thwarted lives have the most character-conditioned hate. (p. 364)

In looking for a definition of hatred that is common to the literature of social psychology, it becomes clear that there is not one unifying, operational definition that covers all of the work in the field. An overview of the research and theory that relate to the area suggests that hate may be best described as a spectrum, with varying degrees of strength and meaning, all sharing the common component of negativity. For example, in examining hate, one researcher developed a checklist that is meant to measure love and hate based on the perceived actions of people toward one another (Parish, 1988). The so-called hateful adverbs or actions on the checklist included *cruelly, furiously, impolitely,* and *rudely* (findings of the study indicated that subjects' scores on the checklist were significantly correlated with their descriptions of their parents' loving actions). Another study examined the everyday conversations of a group of college undergraduates and married couples and revealed that "hate" was sixth on the list of most frequently named emotions discussed in conversations, following "love," "regret," "hope," "worry," and "anger" (Shimanoff, 1984). This result suggests that the salience of the word *hate* is far greater than one might think.

The above conceptions seem to focus on a watered-down version of the stronger, negative, and aggressive emotion discussed by Allport and explored by theologians and philosophers. In terms of the conception of hate as an emotion in contemporary America, hate crimes and hate speech appear to be at the other end of the spectrum from the recent empirical studies, with clearer expressions of hatred, of which violence is the most obvious. In a recent book on the subject, Levin and McDevitt (1993) define hate crimes as "offenses [that] are directed against members of a particular group simply because of their membership in that group"[3] (p. 4). They specify further that, "The basis for an attack may be a victim's race, ethnicity, religion, sexual orientation, or gender—indeed, any physical or cultural characteristic which, in the mind of the offenders, separates the victim from themselves. The victim's individual characteristics are, from the attacker's point of view, all but irrelevant" (pp. 4-5). Thus hate crimes, an extreme form of hatred in contemporary America, are based on the victim's group membership and, while directed against an individual, are based on some group characteristic of that individual such as race or gender. As such, hate crimes not only contrast with the milder forms of hate described above by several researchers (Parish, 1988; Shimanoff, 1984) but also highlight the role stereotyping can play in hatred due to the focus on characteristics the victim is perceived to have solely because of group membership. That is, the basis for the hate and for the resultant violent action is an extreme negative evaluation of a characteristic or set of characteristics that an individual may or may not possess in fact.

Levin and McDevitt (1993) delineate three different types of motivations for hate crimes: thrill, reactive, and mission. More specifically, thrill hate crimes are committed by offenders who are looking for excitement and attack the victims for the thrill; reactive hate crimes involve offenders who believe that they are protecting their turf (e.g., their neighborhood, their workplace, their college campus) from "outsiders"; and mission hate crimes—the rarest and also usually the most serious—involve offenders who commit their lives to bigotry, who may seek to eliminate members of a reviled group, and/or whose crimes may reflect their dedication to this cause. For example, in a more recent report, Levin and McDevitt (1995) cite the bombing of the federal office building in Oklahoma City as "probably the quintessential mission hate crime" (p. 9).

Certainly, manifestations of hate in the form of hate crimes—no matter what type of hate crime—differ considerably from the "hate" that may be mentioned in everyday conversations. Within the spectrum of hate, then, there lie hate crimes and hateful actions, hateful descriptions of everyday emotions, and hateful words. We also see in this spectrum a whole range of hateful and negative thoughts, beliefs, stereotypes, and attitudes, as well as the prejudice and discrimination with which they often occur. Hate is sometimes an emotion, at other times an attitude, and also at times a behavior, and the magnitude and severity of each is not the same. Thus, as we move forward to examine some of the key literature in social psychology, hate may be viewed as a spectrum, and what is described as hate by some researchers and theorists at one end of that spectrum may not be as frightening and potentially harmful as what is at the other end. This distinction is important in order to capture the range of phenomena that have occupied the interest of researchers regarding hate and the more common conceptualizations of hate.

Hating objects or things such as a television program or a place is obviously very different from hating your neighbor, which is also very different from hating a group of people such as Jews or Muslims. Yet, the research and theoretical literature rarely make clear distinctions between these various forms of hate. While hate has been found to be a fairly common and frequent concern for people (see Shimanoff, 1984), they nonetheless seem to distinguish implicitly between various forms of hate as illustrated by the range of value placed on different types of hate and the objects of hate.

Indeed, there is a difference in the extent to which individuals express and society accepts hatred of objects, things, places, or animals, as opposed to the hatred of other people or groups of people. The difference may exist because of the connection that people have to one another, the effort required to maintain hatred for another human being or group of human beings, and the behavioral implications of that maintenance. That is, maintaining hatred for another person or group requires a fair amount of mental energy and attention on a consistent basis and may increase the likelihood of some action, possibly violence, related to that hatred. Indeed, Allport (1954) stated, "The more intense the attitude, the more likely it is to result in vigorously hostile action" (p. 14). Hatred for objects may be less extreme and may require less cognitive, emotional, and behavioral involvement.

The notion of hate as a spectrum within which exist constructs such as attitudes, behavior, emotion, and speech—with all defined and bounded by a degree of negativity—is important because of the explicit link it provides to the more easily understood concepts of prejudice and stereotypes. One can view hate as a model that involves two intersecting dimensions: passive to active and thought to behavior, suggesting a fluid relation among the various forms of hate. While this hypothesized view of hatred does not explicitly include the affective or emotional component that also comes into play in the origins and expressions of hatred, it does allow for both an understanding of hate as a continuum and an understanding of the relationship of hatred to the related concepts of violence, prejudice, stereotypes, racism, and discrimination. Note that this hypothesized model of hate suggests only one possible framework for understanding its various forms discussed in the social scientific literature and among lay people. As mentioned earlier, both dimensions in the model (passive to active and thought to behavior) involve negative thoughts and behaviors (either passive or active), as opposed to behavior and thoughts that may be positive in nature.

This entire two-by-two dimensional spectrum of hate would include behaviors such as racially motivated violence and other hate crimes in the active/behavior quadrant, and personal stereotypes in the passive/thought quadrant. The examples of behaviors and thoughts provided here are exemplars of the activities associated with that particular quadrant of the model, but represent just a few of the possibilities. Other related constructs such as prejudice, discrimination, racism, anti-Semitism, bigotry, and hate writings could also be plotted within the spectrum defined by the two intersecting dimensions of hate.

As mentioned earlier, this model posits that the positions that people occupy on the dimensions are fluid such that people may move from one quadrant to another and back. For example, a person with very prejudiced personal attitudes may never actually discriminate against another person, perhaps because of a lack of opportunity. However, the degree of his or her prejudice may fuel a readiness to act. When presented with the opportunity, such as in an employment or promotion situation, this person may discriminate. This same person may never engage in violence, but might do so if placed in particular situation or if triggered by some external factor or factors. Obviously, there is a complex interaction among the attitudes, thoughts, and beliefs that may exist; constraints and catalysts within an individual; the readiness to act; and actually engaging in a behavior. In addition, external constraints and catalysts may cause movement from one quadrant of the hate spectrum to another—from the expression of hatred for another group to vandalism against someone's property to participating in an attack on an individual.

Related Concepts

While social psychological or social scientific theories do not often directly address the concept of hate, there are many theories that examine the related concepts of stereotypes and prejudice. To some, the relationship of stereotypes and prejudice to hate is understood implicitly, and it seems clear that the negativity associated with these concepts would underlie hate, certainly in its strongest form. Thus, in their book on hate crimes, Levin and McDevitt (1993), who write that "Learning to hate is almost as inescapable as breathing" (p. 21), draw a link between the negative stereotypes that abound in American society and hate crimes. However, the relationship between stereotypes and prejudice, as well as between prejudiced intergroup attitudes and discrimination, is vast, complex, and not always as straightforward as one might assume (see Duckitt, 1992, for a thorough review of these issues). While one finds variability in the definitions of these related constructs and in the interrelationships among them (depending on which theory is being explored), the following brief overview of these constructs allows us to move forward to examine the relevant literature in the field of social psychology. To the degree that hate can be viewed as an extremely negative attitude or feeling (recall Allport's definition of hate as a "sentiment"), an exploration of the related concepts of stereotyping and prejudice is appropriate.

In general, a stereotype may be thought of as a set of attributes or characteristics ascribed to a group and attributed to the individual members of that group (Heilman, 1983; Taylor, Fiske, Etcoff, & Ruderman, 1978). Ashmore and DelBoca (1981) defined a stereotype as "a set of beliefs about the personal attributes of a group of people" (p. 16). Thus, a person (or group of people) may be characterized in one way or another based on any one of a number of his or her features (or their group membership), such as religion, gender, race, ethnicity, or sexual orientation. Stereotypes, or the beliefs that people have about others based solely on their membership in a particular group, have been studied extensively over the years in a variety of different disciplines. While survey research indicates that some negative stereotypes of particular groups in America have diminished over the years, it is still the case that people are quite willing to ascribe characteristics—both negative and positive—to particular groups of Americans (Smith, 1998).

In recent years social psychology has focused extensively on cognitive-based theories and research with regard to stereotypes and prejudice (Brewer & Kramer, 1985). From this perspective, stereotypes are viewed as "cognitive categories that are used by the social perceiver in processing information about people" (Hamilton & Trolier, 1986, p. 128). Thus, stereotypes function as social categories that simplify the world by providing category-based information, and may be viewed as organizing the vast amount of information about a complex world that people have to process. Unfortunately, while ostensibly functional as organizing tools, it has been well documented that the use of and reliance on social stereotypes often leads to biases (see Hamilton & Trolier, 1986, for a review of some relevant research in the area).

Prejudice, too, has been studied extensively over the years, and many more definitions of prejudice than of hate exist within the field of social psychology. Duckitt (1992) provides an overview of various definitions of prejudice, concluding that there has been a shift to "nonevaluative definitions of prejudice as simply a negative intergroup attitude" (p. 23). Duckitt's review of the literature also explores discrepancies in the research findings and theories regarding the concept of attitudes. Thus, depending on the theoretical formulation of prejudice and attitudes that is being examined, stereotyped beliefs are thought to be linked to prejudiced attitudes in different ways. In one model, stereotyped beliefs lead to a prejudiced attitude (which in turn yields behavioral intentions that give rise to discriminatory behavior). Another model postulates that prejudiced attitudes consist of three components, namely, a cognitive component (i.e., stereotypes or beliefs), an affective component (feelings about the target; e.g., antipathy), and a behavioral component (action tendencies toward the target; e.g., social distance). The prejudiced attitude is then said to lead to a particular behavior. Yet a third model postulates that negative stereotypes (the cognitive component) and negative feelings (the affective component) lead to prejudice.[4] These various approaches postulate a variety of interrelationships among the concepts, and each may be linked in different ways to the hypothesized model of hate presented earlier in the chapter.

Theoretical Approaches

In a broad exploration of the causes of prejudice, Aronson (1992) reviewed four basic causes of prejudice that, he says, are not mutually exclusive. The causes of prejudice explored by Aronson are: *economic and political competition or conflict,* which leads the dominant group to exploit or derogate minority groups in order to gain some material advantage; *displaced aggression, or scapegoating,* with a scapegoat defined as "a relatively powerless innocent who is made to take the blame for something that is not his or her fault" (p. 317); *prejudiced personality, or a personality need,* which refers to the notion of individual differences in the tendency to hate; and *prejudice through conformity to existing social norms,* with people conforming to the social norms that exist in society with regard to prejudice. Among the four causes specified by Aronson are a number of social psychological variables that will be examined more closely below. At the same time, Aronson also cited variables that are not wholly psychological by definition. (Again, while the focus of the chapter is mainly on the social psychology literature, it is useful to bear in mind that this is but one discipline that has addressed the concepts of hate, stereotyping, and prejudice.)

Similarly, Dovidio and Gaertner (1986) reviewed the various conceptual approaches for studying prejudice, citing Gordon Allport's (1954, 1958) identification of six ways of explaining prejudice—the *historical* approach, which traces contemporary prejudice to slavery and proposes that its goal is to allow the exploitation of Blacks; the *sociocultural* approach, which emphasizes the society and culture within which prejudice survives; the *situational* approach, which studies the influence of immediate social forces, such as the particular nature of intergroup contact (e.g., cooperation or competition), on prejudice and discrimination; the *personality structure and dynamics* approach, exemplified by Adorno, Frenkel-Brunswick, Levinson, and Sanford's (1950) *The Authoritarian Personality,* which traces ethnocentrism and prejudice to earlier child-rearing practices and subsequent personality dispositions; the *phenomenological* approach, which examines how a variety of forces (i.e., society, culture, history, personality, and immediate context) influence people's experiences, perceptions, and ideas, and affect their attitudes and behavior; and the *stimulus-object* approach, which proposes that actual differences between groups are the basis for hostility and discrimination.

Dovidio and Gaertner also summarize Ashmore and DelBoca's (1976) classification of societal-level and individual-level approaches for studying prejudice. Among societal-level approaches, which focus on the nature of relationships between groups in the shaping of prejudice, researchers may examine motives for exploiting minorities or study the nature of intergroup contact as a contributor to attitudes. Among individual-level approaches, which focus on how an individual acquires and manifests prejudice, researchers may study intrapersonal factors such as personality, focusing on theories of projection, displacement, and/or the authoritarian personality; cognition, tracing prejudice to such processes as categorization rather than attributing these processes to prejudice; motivation, attributing prejudice to such factors as the need for cognitive consistency, that is, the need to confirm the expectation that outgroup members will have different attitudes than ingroup members; or interpersonal factors, such as socialization or conformity.

An integrative framework for classifying and examining the numerous psychological theories of prejudice was presented by Duckitt (1992), who identified four complementary processes that are involved in the causation of prejudice, with each particular causal theory of prejudice falling under one of the four processes. As summarized by Duckitt,

First, certain universal psychological processes build in an inherently human potentiality or propensity for prejudice. Second, social and intergroup dynamics describe the conditions and circumstances of contact and interaction between groups that elaborate this potentiality into normative and socially shared patterns of prejudice. Third, mechanisms of transmission explain how these intergroup dynamics and shared patterns of prejudice are socially transmitted to individual members of these groups. Fourth and finally, individual-difference mechanisms determine individual susceptibility to prejudice, and so operate to modulate the impact of these social transmission mechanisms on individuals. (p. 62)

These four processes are useful for understanding and categorizing the theories on causes of prejudice and for understanding the complementary and non-exclusive roles that these causes may play. Thus the first causal process, which examines universal psychological mechanisms that underlie prejudice, includes theories of projection, displacement, and social categorization. The second causal process, which looks at social and intergroup dynamics, includes theories of social dynamics and realistic group conflict. Mechanisms of transmission, the third process specified by Duckitt, includes theories of socialization, conformity, and attribution. The last process, individual-difference dimensions that influence susceptibility to prejudice, includes consideration of frustration, authoritarianism, and cognitive factors. We will explore below a number of the more prominent theories and approaches in social psychology that attempt to explain the phenomenon of prejudice.

The Authoritarian Personality (Adorno et al., 1950) is among the most well-known explorations of prejudice in the field of social psychology. Following the Holocaust, Adorno and his colleagues attempted to uncover the psychological foundations for anti-Semitism and fascism. A broader pattern forming the authoritarian personality emerged from this investigation. A dimension of personality that varies from individual to individual, authoritarianism is said to underlie the tendency to prejudice and ethnocentrism. Thus, authoritarianism is described as a personality syndrome that encompasses a number of variables, such as ethnocentricity, anti-Semitism, dislike of outgroups, and political conservatism. Research into the authoritarian personality assumed that prejudiced people displace their aggression onto scapegoats who might belong to a range of groups. This work drew heavily upon psychodynamic concepts, particularly projection. Adorno et al. designed the F scale, a questionnaire that measures nine traits of the authoritarian personality including conventionalism, authoritarian submission, and authoritarian aggression.

The authoritarian personality reportedly develops as a result of particular parenting styles on the part of an individual's parents. These parenting styles are theorized to have a profound impact on the child and the adult personality he or she eventually manifests. Duckitt (1992) writes,

> strict and punitive parental socialization sets up an enduring conflict within the individual. Resentment and hostility toward parental authority, and by extension all authority, is repressed and displaced because of a fear of and a need to submit to that authority. These psychodynamics are given expression at the surface of personality in a syndrome of nine covarying traits. It is this constellation of traits that constitutes the authoritarian personality per se. Finally, these traits are expressed in certain social beliefs, attitudes, and behaviors, most notably in those implicitly antidemocratic beliefs sampled by the F scale. (p. 196)

In terms of the origins of intergroup hostility and prejudice, the authoritarian personality theory points to particular parenting styles that set into motion a series of events that lead to the authoritarian syndrome. This theory conceptualizes prejudice, negativity, and hatred for others as rooted in deep and broad personality factors. Indeed, research on the authoritarian personality indicated that, "People who hated one group tended to hate many, not by coincidence, but because bigotry addressed and, to some extent, resolved their deepest needs" (Kressel, 1996, p. 221). While the research and theory have been subject to numerous methodological concerns and critiques over the years (see Duckitt, 1992, and Kressel, 1996, for overviews), it remains a powerful and original exploration of prejudice, hate, fascism, and ethnocentrism.

A much more recent investigation of a personality variable that is said to contribute to intergroup tensions and hostilities and that may be seen as related to authoritarianism in that regard has been conducted by Pratto and her associates (Pratto, Sidanius, Stallworth, & Malle, 1994). Postulating that "societies minimize group conflict by creating consensus on ideologies that promote the superiority of one group over others" (p. 741), they state that "hierarchy-legitimizing myths"—ideologies that say that one group is better than another and deserves more than another—contribute to stabilizing oppression against particular groups. The theory proposes that individuals vary in their level of "social dominance orientation" (SDO), that is, their desire for ingroup domination and superiority. The researchers see social dominance orientation as "the central individual-difference variable that predicts a person's acceptance or rejection of numerous ideologies and policies relevant to group relations" (p. 742). Thus, the theory predicts that people with stronger SDO orientations will tend to support hierarchy-enhancing ideologies and policies and will join institutions and choose roles that contribute to social inequality, whereas people with weaker SDO orientations will tend to favor hierarchy-attenuating views and will choose institutions and roles that reduce inequality.

As with the research and theory on the authoritarian personality, this newer investigation of a personality variable that influences prejudice and hatred has been subject to critique (Kressel, 1996). Specifically, Kressel points out that the biggest problem with this line of inquiry is the way the authors define their terms: "They define social dominance in a way that seems to measure in part how much one disagrees with liberal ideology" (p. 229). Moreover, because of their apparent liberal bias, the social dominance theorists fail to extend the research to isolate the true psychological attributes underlying mass hatred on all sides of the political spectrum. Kressel does concede that the concept of social dominance seems to be important and should continue to be studied, but without political bias.

While the authoritarian personality and the newer examination of social dominance orientation represent personality-based explorations of and explanations for prejudice, other explorations of prejudice have focused on variables that are not specifically linked to personality. For example, recent advances by researchers in an area of social psychology called social cognition have examined stereotypes as one type of *role schema*. *Schemas* are cognitive structures that represent knowledge about a concept or type of stimulus, including its attributes and the relations among those attributes (see Fiske & Taylor, 1991, for a complete review). Fiske and Taylor write, "One can think about stereotypes as a particular kind of role schema that organizes people's expectations about other people who fall into certain social categories" (p. 119). Schemas are thought to influence several aspects of social information processing, including encoding, memory, retrieval, inference, evaluation, and utilization of information (see e.g., Ajzen, Timko, & White, 1982; Fiske & Neuberg, 1990; Fiske & Taylor, 1991;

Higgins & King, 1981; and Taylor, 1981, for a complete review). It is important to note that this approach represents a non-evaluative conception of stereotypes and, to some degree, emphasizes the functionality of stereotypes, although much of the research into schemas has examined how bias might occur and the implications of such errors (see e.g., Brown, Schmidt, & Collins, 1988; Maass, Salvi, Arcuri, & Semin, 1989; Wilder, 1986).

Brewer and Kramer (1985) summarize the results of a number of studies that have examined the cognitive effects of stereotyping. Among the findings of such research are: People are more likely to recall a category member's stereotype-relevant behavior than non-stereotype-relevant behavior (Brewer, Dull, & Lui, 1981; Cohen, 1981; Lui & Brewer, 1983); when people expect a category member to behave in a certain way, they may interact with that person in a manner that elicits stereotype-confirming behaviors (Skrypnek & Snyder, 1982); pictures of ambiguously aggressive behaviors are interpreted as more hostile when performed by a Black person than by a White person (Sagar & Schofield, 1980); stereotypes are resistant to disconfirming behaviors on the part of category members since people may disassociate a stereotype-disconfirming individual from his or her category or may ignore the disconfirming behavior (Weber & Crocker, 1983); and, in the "illusory correlation" effect, people tend to overestimate how often they have seen pairings between two stimuli that they expect to go together, which helps entrench stereotypes (Hamilton & Rose, 1980; McArthur & Friedman, 1980). Thus, the biasing effect of social stereotypes is demonstrated by research in the area of social cognition.

The development of stereotypes, prejudice, and intergroup hostility was examined in a series of classic studies in social psychology conducted by Sherif and his associates at a boys' camps in Oklahoma (see Sherif, Harvey, White, Hood, & Sherif, 1961). The researchers, disguised as camp personnel, divided the 11- and 12-year-old boys, who were all middle-class, white, and Protestant, into two groups roughly matched for camping experience, athletic and intellectual ability, and popularity prior to leaving for the campsite. The boys had no preexisting friendships, and social affiliation was limited to ingroup members for the first week. During the second week, the researchers had the groups engage in competitive activities, with the winners receiving rewards. Intergroup hostility emerged. During the third week, the researchers brought the two groups into contact with each other for noncompetitive activities, but this manipulation produced no positive effect or change in the existing group identifications. The researchers then introduced superordinate goals such as intergroup cooperation to purchase a movie or fix broken plumbing. Intergroup hostility eventually decreased, but only after a series of successes on common goals. The researchers found that the boys' friendship choices subsequently became much less group oriented.

This classic research demonstrated that some of the major components of intergroup conflict, such as devaluing outgroup members, loyalty to ingroup members, stereotyping, and hostility toward outgroups, could be created experimentally. In essence, group hostility was created experimentally *without actually establishing any previous substantive differences* between the groups (see Forbes, 1997; Sherif et al., 1961; Sherif & Sherif, 1953).

These classic studies provided much of the early support for Allport's contact hypothesis, which postulated that contact between equally situated groups of Blacks and Whites in pursuit of common goals would reduce prejudice (Allport, 1954). Allport went on to theorize that, "The effect is greatly enhanced if this contact is sanctioned by institutional supports" (p. 281). The Sherif studies also led to elaborations on the contact hypothesis that would become known as realistic group conflict theory, which broadly defined refers to the notion that actual conflict over competing group interests causes intergroup conflict (see e.g., Campbell, 1965; Forbes, 1997).

Realistic group conflict theory is important because it formed the basis for much of the thinking in the 1960s and 1970s regarding the improvement of intergroup relations and identified key components of interaction between and among differing groups necessary for reduced hostilities. Although considered to be more of a broad framework of general principles than a specific theory, realistic group conflict theory has been examined in a number of studies using various samples and situations (e.g., Blake & Mouton, 1979; Turner, 1981). The most basic conclusions from Sherif's work are that competitive group goals cause conflict and intergroup hostility, while superordinate goals cause cooperation and positive relations. Turner (1981) did note that there are certain conditions of intergroup contact that do not lead to improved relations and may instead result in cooperating groups exhibiting more negative relations than competing groups.

Campbell (1965) similarly suggested an important addition to the basic definition of realistic group conflict, noting that awareness of and reaction to the underlying conflict of group interests brings about the phenomenon of ethnocentrism. However, Forbes (1997) cautions against overgeneralizations of this notion and raises the question of the applicability of realistic group conflict to the United States:

> Perhaps the only interesting question is whether this realistic perspective has any role to play in explaining prejudice and discrimination *within* a society like the United States, where the relevant ethnic groups are not organized for competition as rival states are (with armies, navies, and so on) and do not have clear territorial or ideological ambitions. (p. 31)

Realistic group conflict theory is an interesting framework for understanding the ways in which conflict and hostilities between persons and groups over material resources can occur, can organize social cognitions like prejudice and hate, and can precipitate their behavioral expressions.

Prior to the development of the contact hypothesis, an important line of inquiry flourished in this country that suggested that frustration incited aggression. This perspective shaped the thinking of a range of researchers interested in understanding the causes of group-based violence. Like authoritarian personality research, these studies built upon psychodynamic constructs, particularly the notion of projection. The idea was that aggression that could not be directed at the source of the frustration would be displaced to a scapegoat or substitute. Originally developed in the 1930s (e.g., Dollard, Doob, Miller, Mowrer, & Sears, 1939; MacCrone, 1937), the frustration-aggression hypothesis has been explored in a number of empirical studies and is a respected approach to this issue (see Duckitt, 1992, for a review). It provides another framework for understanding some of the ways in which the extreme emotion of hate might be formed and its behavioral implications.

The frustration-aggression hypothesis is also considered more of a general approach than a full theory because it does not answer the basic question of why some groups become scapegoats and not others and does not include the social factors needed to explain the selection of these scapegoats (Berkowitz, 1962; Zawadski, 1948). Duckitt (1992) does note that the theory provides a robust, general approach to prejudice that provides plausible explanations for its pervasiveness as a fairly consistent component of the human psyche. It also provides a testable theory that resonates in public discourse and has had some influence on researchers in areas other than group conflict, including economics and labor studies (see Hovland & Sears, 1940). Despite mixed support in the extensive research literature examining the relation among frustration, prejudice, and aggression (Brown & Turner, 1981; Koneci, 1979; Lindzey, 1950; Young-Breuhl, 1997), the theory remains an important stepping-stone effort for understanding how and under what circumstances hate-related violence will arise.

The hypothesized link between prejudice and hate described above suggested a progressive movement from the relatively benign personal attitude to the more aggressive and overtly manifested hate that is reflected by racial, ethnic, gender, and religious violence. The approaches identified in this section represent a few of the more prominent and well-researched theories of the origins, form, and manner of prejudice. Taken together, these theoretical approaches present a number of alternative ways of understanding hate and hate-related violence by hypothesizing, delineating, describing, and researching the relations among prejudice, behavior, and a variety of other constructs.

Conclusions

While we have explored a number of the theories that relate to stereotyping and prejudice, they need not be viewed as mutually exclusive. Indeed, the development and manifestation of stereotypes, prejudice, and hate is likely a complex process that varies across individuals and is best described by a synthesis of different theories. For example, while stereotypes may indeed be one type of neutral cognitive structure that is functional in many situations, the role they play as the content of a range of prejudices implicates them in their progressive impact on hate and hate crimes. Such a formulation requires a synthesis of several lines of inquiry, yet is still fairly unrelated to theories of hate and the origins of hate. In an examination of prejudice, Young-Breuhl (1997) takes the entire field of social psychology to task for its clichéd approach, overreliance on unproven assumptions, generalizations, and unidimensional definitions. She argues for an approach that is broad in its sweep and that incorporates learnings from a range of fields including psychoanalysis, feminism, literary criticism, as well as more traditional areas such as social psychology. Adopting this type of approach to studying hate and attempting to understand its origins is useful precisely because of the current lack of agreement on the definition of hate and its related constructs.

This lack of agreement is not necessarily an indictment of the state of the field, however. Rather, it may reflect the fact that while exclusively negative, hate involves a range of phenomena both psychological and behavioral in nature and as such demands examination from multiple viewpoints. It is also true that there is so little research examining hate and its related aspects in the social scientific literature that one must look closely at related areas such as prejudice and stereotyping to begin to build a useful body of work on hate. Yet, that body of work will still need to be diverse in its content and flexible in its embrace of emerging areas of inquiry. Theories need to strive to synthesize insights from areas such as religion, philosophy, and literature. Similarly, research delineating active hate from prejudice and demonstrating an explicit relation between prejudice and hate, or identifying prejudice as a mild form of hate, is also needed.

The two-dimensional model of hate (passive to active and thought to behavior) that was presented earlier should also be explored for its utility in furthering understanding of hate and hate-related violence. A fuller description of and elaboration on the framework we describe, as well as research into the constructs that exist within the framework (such as stereotypes, prejudice, discrimination, and violence), may prove helpful in understanding the relationship between the various forms of hate.

Notes

1. While we are primarily concerned with the literature of social psychology in the exploration of hate, there have been many psychoanalytic examinations of the

concept of hatred (see Galdston, 1987; Kernberg, 1989; Lipschitz, 1986; Parens, 1991).

2. In this chapter, attention will be focused specifically on hate and hatred, rather than on self-hatred, except as self-hatred is mentioned as a factor in the development of hatred for others (see Marrow, 1951, for one examination of the concept of self-hate).

3. Levin and McDevitt point out that in a 1990 FBI definition, hate may be only a partial motivation for a hate crime. Thus, the FBI defines a hate crime as a "criminal offense committed against a person or property which is motivated, in whole or in part, by the offender's bias against a race, religion, ethnic/national origin group, or sexual orientation group." In this definition, the link between the behavior toward an individual and the feeling toward the group is an explicit requisite for their identifying the crime as one of hate.

4. See Duckitt, 1992, for a complete overview and evaluation of this literature.

References

Adorno, T. W., Frenkel-Brunswick, E., Levinson, D. J., & Sanford, R. N. (1950). *The authoritarian personality*. New York: Harper.

Ajzen, I., Timko, C., & White, J. B. (1982). Self-monitoring and the attitude-behavior relation. *Journal of Personality and Social Psychology, 42*, 426-435.

Allport, G. W. (1954). *The nature of prejudice*. Reading, MA: Addison-Wesley.

Allport, G. W. (1958). *The nature of prejudice*. Garden City, NY: Doubleday/Anchor.

Aronson, E. (1992). *The social animal* (6th ed.). New York: Freeman.

Ashmore, R. D., & DelBoca, F. K. (1976). Psychological approaches to understanding intergroup conflicts. In P. A. Katz (Ed.), *Towards the elimination of racism* (pp. 73-123). Elmsdale, NY: Pergamon.

Ashmore, R. D., & DelBoca, F. K. (1981). Conceptual approaches to stereotypes and stereotyping. In D. Hamilton (Ed.), *Cognitive processes in stereotyping and intergroup behavior* (pp. 1-36). Hillsdale, NJ: Lawrence Erlbaum.

Berkowitz, L. (1962). *Aggression: A social psychological analysis*. New York: McGraw-Hill.

Blake, R. R., & Mouton, J. S. (1979). Intergroup problem solving in organizations: From theory to practice. In W. G. Austin & S. Worchel (Eds.), *The social psychology of intergroup relations* (pp. 19-32). Monterey, CA: Brooks/Cole.

Brewer, M. B., Dull, V., & Lui, L. (1981). Perceptions of the elderly: Stereotypes as prototypes. *Journal of Personality and Social Psychology, 41*, 656-670.

Brewer, M. B., & Kramer, R. M. (1985). The psychology of intergroup attitudes and behavior. *Annual Review of Psychology, 36*, 219-243.

Brown, R. J., & Turner, J. C. (1981). Interpersonal and intergroup behaviour. In J. Turner & H. Giles (Eds.), *Intergroup behaviour* (pp. 33-65). Oxford: Basil Blackwell.

Brown, J. D., Schmidt, G. W., & Collins, R. L. (1988). Personal involvement and the evaluation of group products. *European Journal of Social Psychology, 18*, 177-179.

Campbell, D. (1965). Ethnocentric and other altruistic motives. In D. Levine (Ed.), *Nebraska Symposium on Motivation, 1965: Vol. 13. Current theory and research on motivation* (pp. 283-311). Lincoln: University of Nebraska Press.

Cohen, C. E. (1981). Person categories and social perception: Testing some boundaries of the processing effects of prior knowledge. *Journal of Personality and Social Psychology, 40,* 441-452.

Dollard, J., Doob, L., Miller, N. E., Mowrer, O., & Sears, R. (1939). *Frustration and aggression.* New Haven, CT: Yale University Press.

Dovidio, J. F., & Gaertner, S. L. (1986). Prejudice, discrimination, and racism: Historical trends and contemporary approaches. In J. F. Dovidio & S. L. Gaertner (Eds.), *Prejudice, discrimination, and racism.* Orlando, FL: Academic Press.

Duckitt, J. (1992). *The social psychology of prejudice.* Westport, CT: Praeger.

Fiske, S. T., & Neuberg, S. L. (1990). A continuum of impression formation, from category-based to individuating processes: Influences of information and motivation on attention and interpretation. In M. P. Zanna (Ed.), *Advances in experimental social psychology* (Vol. 23, pp. 1-74). New York: Academic Press.

Fiske, S. T., & Taylor, S. E. (Eds.). (1991). *Social cognition* (2nd ed.). New York: McGraw-Hill.

Forbes, H. D. (1997). *Ethnic conflict: Commerce, culture, and the contact hypothesis.* New Haven, CT: Yale University Press.

Fromm, E. (1947). *Man for himself.* New York: Rinehart.

Galdston, R. (1987). The longest pleasure: A psychoanalytic study of hatred. *International Journal of Psycho-Analysis, 68*(3), 371-378.

Hamilton, D. L., & Rose, T. L. (1980). Illusory correlation and the maintenance of stereotypic beliefs. *Journal of Personality and Social Psychology, 39,* 832-845.

Hamilton, D. L., & Trolier, T. K. (1986). Stereotypes and stereotyping. In J. F. Dovidio & S. L. Gaertner (Eds.), *Prejudice, discrimination, & racism.* Orlando, FL: Academic Press.

Heilman, M. (1983). Sex bias in work settings: The lack of fit model. In B. Straw & L. Cummings (Eds.), *Research in organizational behavior* (Vol. 5). Greenwich, CT: JAI.

Higgins, E. T., & King, G. A. (1981). Accessibility of social constructs: Information-processing consequences of individual and contextual variability. In N. Cantor & J. F. Kihlstrom (Eds.), *Personality, cognition, and social interaction* (pp. 69-122). Hillsdale, NJ: Lawrence Erlbaum.

Hovland, C., & Sears, R. (1940). Minor studies of aggression V1. Correlation of lynchings with economic indices. *Journal of Psychology, 9,* 301-310.

Kernberg, O. F. (1989). The psychopathology of hatred. *Journal of the American Psychoanalytic Association, 39*(Suppl.), 209-238.

Kressel, N. J. (1996). *Mass hate: The global rise of genocide and terror.* New York: Plenum.

Koneci, V. J. (1979). The role of aversive events in the development of intergroup conflict. In W. Austin & S. Worchel (Eds.), *The social psychology of intergroup relations* (pp. 85-102). Monterey, CA: Brooks/Cole.

Kutner, B., Wilkins, C., & Yarrow, P. (1952). Verbal attitudes and overt behavior involving racial prejudice. *Journal of Abnormal and Social Psychology, 47,* 649-652.

LaPiere, R. T. (1934). Attitudes versus actions. *Social Forces, 13,* 230-237.

Levin, J., & McDevitt, J. (1993). *Hate crimes: The rising tide of bigotry and bloodshed.* New York: Plenum.

Levin, J., & McDevitt, J. (1995, August). Landmark study reveals hate crimes vary significantly by offender motivation. *Klanwatch Intelligence Report,* Southern Poverty Law Center.

Lindzey, G. (1950). An experimental examination of the scapegoat theory of prejudice. *Journal of Abnormal and Social Psychology, 45,* 297-309.

Lipschitz, F. (1986). Love and hate: Conservation and change. *Contemporary Psychotherapy Review, 3*(1), 69-85.

Lui, L., & Brewer, M. B. (1983). Recognition accuracy as evidence of category-consistency effects in person memory. *Social Cognition, 2,* 89-107.

Maass, A., Salvi, D., Arcuri, L., & Semin, G. (1989). Language use in intergroup contexts: The linguistic intergroup bias. *Journal of Personality and Social Psychology, 57,* 981-993.

MacCrone, I. D. (1937). *Race attitudes in South Africa: Historical, experimental and psychological studies.* London: Oxford University Press.

Marrow, A. J. (1951). *Living without hate—Scientific approaches to human relations.* New York: Harper & Brothers.

McArthur, L. Z., & Friedman, S. A. (1980). Illusory correlation in impression formations: Variations in the shared effect as a function of the distinctive person's age, race, and sex. *Journal of Personality and Social Psychology, 39,* 615-624.

Parens, H. (1991). A view of development of hostility in early life. *Journal of the American Psychoanalytic Association, 39*(Suppl.), 75-108.

Parish, T. S. (1988). The love/hate checklist: A preliminary report. *Psychological Reports, 63*(1), 67-70.

Pratto, F., Sidanius, J., Stallworth, L. M., & Malle, B. F. (1994). Social dominance orientation: A personality variable predicting social and political attitudes. *Journal of Personality and Social Psychology, 67,* 741-763.

Random House dictionary of the English language. (1987). [Second edition, unabridged]. New York: Random House.

Sagar, H. A., & Schofield, J. W. (1980). Racial and behavioral cues in Black and White children's perceptions of ambiguously aggressive acts. *Journal of Personality and Social Psychology, 57,* 539-551.

Sherif, M., & Sherif, C. W. (1953). *Groups in harmony and tension.* New York: Harper.

Sherif, M., Harvey, O. J., White, B. J., Hood, W. R., & Sherif, C. W. (1961). *Intergroup conflict and cooperation: The Robber's Cave experiment.* Norman: University of Oklahoma Press.

Shimanoff, S. B. (1984). Commonly named emotions in everyday conversations. *Perceptual and Motor Skills, 58*(2), 514.

Skrypnek, B. J., & Snyder, M. (1982). On the self-perpetuating nature of stereotypes about men and women. *Journal of Experimental Social Psychology, 18,* 277-297.

Smith, T. W. (1998). Intergroup relations in contemporary America: An overview of survey research. In W. Winborne & R. Cohen (Eds.), *Intergroup relations in the United States: Research perspectives* (pp. 69-155). New York: National Conference for Community and Justice.

Taylor, S. E. (1981). A categorization approach to stereotyping. In D. L. Hamilton (Ed.), *Cognitive processes in stereotyping and intergroup behavior* (pp. 88-114). Hillsdale, NJ: Lawrence Erlbaum.

Taylor, S. E., Fiske, S. T., Etcoff, N. L., & Ruderman, A. J. (1978). Categorical and contextual bases of person memory and stereotyping. *Journal of Personality and Social Psychology, 36,* 778-793.

Turner, J. C. (1981). The experimental social psychology of intergroup behaviour. In J. C. Turner & H. Giles (Eds.), *Intergroup behaviour* (pp. 66-101). Oxford, UK: Basil Blackwell.

Weber, R., & Crocker, J. (1983). Cognitive processes in the revision of stereotypic beliefs. *Journal of Personality and Social Psychology, 45,* 961-977.

Wilder, D. A. (1986). Social categorization: Implications for creation and reduction of intergroup bias. In L. Berkowitz (Ed.), *Advances in experimental social psychology* (Vol. 19, pp. 291-355). New York: Academic Press.

Young-Breuhl, E. (1997). *The anatomy of prejudices.* Cambridge, MA: Harvard University Press.

Zawadski, B. (1948). Limitations of the scapegoat theory of prejudice. *Journal of Abnormal and Social Psychology, 43,* 127-141.

CHAPTER 7

Mental Illness and the Myth of Violent Behavior

MICHAEL M. FAENZA

ROBERT W. GLOVER

GAIL P. HUTCHINGS

JAMES A. RADACK

Are people with mental illnesses dangerous? Do mental disorders cause violence? Can we predict violence by people with mental illnesses?

These questions frame the important and controversial debate about the implied, and often erroneous, link between mental illness and violence. This relationship is perhaps the most damaging and stigmatizing notion associated with mental illnesses and the individuals who suffer from them. The confusion about the relationship has generated significant misunderstanding and fear among the general public and policymakers.

The purpose of this chapter is to: (a) review the current research on the relationship between mental illnesses and violence; (b) explore the impact of myths and stereotypes; (c) identify tools for risk assessment and predictors of violence utilized by the field; (d) describe effective treatment strategies and community responses; and (e) discuss the increased victimization of persons with mental illnesses.

The debate exploring a causal relationship between mental illness and violence is not new. Indeed throughout history, there have been countless references to "madmen" terrorizing towns and villages. Over time, these frequently inaccurate portrayals have created—and perpetuated—the perception that people with mental illnesses are violent, unpredictable, and dangerous.

This perception is now firmly rooted in the American psyche. A 1993 *Parade Magazine* survey found that 57% of Americans thought that people with mental illnesses were more likely to commit acts of violence than others (American Psychiatric Association, 1994). The media and entertainment industries have helped to perpetuate these attitudes. In his book *Media Madness* (1995), Dr. Otto Wahl examined mass media images of mental illness and the extent to which they helped form public perceptions. He found that portrayals of people with mental illnesses were repeatedly overrepresented in movies, television, and books as villains and violent characters. Wahl (1995) concluded that "there is a strong, unmistakable, and repeated warning . . . that people with mental illnesses are particularly dangerous, are compelled to violence, are walking time bombs" (p. 60). He noted that 72% of all characters with mental illnesses in prime-time drama were portrayed as violent and over one fifth (21%) of the same characters were killers (Wahl, 1995).

Likewise, Wahl (1995) reviewed the news industry's tendency to report on people with mental illnesses and violence. According to Wahl (p. 67), in a 1991 study of the content of United Press International stories, researchers found that the majority of newspaper stories dealing with psychiatric patients involved the commission of violent crimes. Wahl also found these overwhelming violent images in popular literature, comics, and children's programming.

Another disturbing conclusion of Wahl's (1995) review was the acceptable violence against people with mental illnesses in television shows and other media. According to research on television content, 81% of characters with mental disorders end up as victims of violence, and 23% are killed.

The public also makes the connection between mental illness and violence through the exposure that the press gives to criminal cases involving the insanity defense. *Insanity* is a legal term that concerns criminal intent and competency to stand trial. These pleas usually attract excessive and protracted media attention. However, it is raised in only about 1% of all major felonies and roughly three quarters of those pleas fail (Wahl, 1995).

The link between mental illness and violence is also raised when a suspected criminal is ordered to undergo a psychiatric evaluation. The public also sees a potential threat when anyone is released from a psychiatric hospital. These perspectives may lead to inappropriate commitment, extended incarceration, and the punishing stance of special legislation that is implemented to deal with children and adults with serious mental illnesses.

Hence, it is not difficult to understand why the actual facts concerning mental illness and violence are confused and distorted through the onslaught of negative imagery. Methodologically sound research conducted over the past decade, however, has repeatedly demonstrated the inaccuracies of these images. Indeed, the current state of expert consensus is perhaps best stated by Monahan (1997): "clearly, mental health status makes at best a trivial contribution to the overall level of violence in society" (p. 315).

The research has explored the link between mental illness and violence by looking at the prevalence and predictors of violent behavior, and the findings are seldom in agreement with the media portrayals discussed above. Key findings of the research discussed in this chapter include: (a) the vast majority of people with mental illnesses are not violent, nor criminals; (b) mental illness is not a good indicator of violence—substance abuse, age, and gender are more reliable predictors; and (c) persons with mental illnesses are more likely to be *victims* of crime. Although, sadly, a small number of people with severe mental illnesses do become violent, these episodes, whether caused by paranoid ideation or uncontrollable anger, are normally the result of unrecognized and untreated symptoms.

The great divide between myth and fact has dangerous consequences for those who have mental illnesses, as well as for their families. These attitudes have added to the general fear and misunderstanding that surround mental illness and reinforced the continued discrimination against people with mental disorders in public policy, health care, housing, and employment. Indeed, recent attention to violence in the workplace combined with the myths conveyed by the media that much of violence in society is committed by people with mental illness bodes poorly for the employment futures of people with mental illness.

The collective fear and misunderstanding among the general public translates into stigma and, ultimately, barriers to accessing treatment. Indeed, this stigma keeps some policymakers and insurance companies from providing adequate and fair treatment options and thus prevents many people from getting the treatment they need.

Examining the Research Base

Like the *Parade* survey, scientific studies confirm that many people in the United States believe that there is a strong, direct connection between violence and mental illness (Monahan & Arnold, 1996; Steadman & Cocozza, 1978). In other words, there is a public perception that people with mental illnesses are likely to commit violent acts. According to Monahan and Arnold (1996), public perceptions that mental illness is strongly linked to violent behavior are important for two reasons.

First, such beliefs drive the formal laws and policies by which society attempts to control the behavior of people with mental illness and to regulate the provision of mental health care. For example, the authors point out that the assumption of a connection between mental health and violence has played a major role in the formulation of the following policies: (a) the prominence of "dangerous to others" as a criterion for civil commitment; (b) the commitment of people acquitted of crime by reason of insanity; (c) the creation of special statutes for the extended detention of prisoners with mental illnesses; and (d) the imposition of tort liability on psychologists and psychiatrists who fail to anticipate the violence of their patients.

The second reason why beliefs in the violence potential of people with mental illnesses are important, say Monahan and Arnold (1996), is that they not only drive formal law and policy but they also determine our informal responses and modes of interacting with individuals who are perceived to have a mental illness. For example, the authors cite a study by Link, Cullen, Frank, and Wozniak (1987) in which the extent to which a person's status as a former mental patient fostered social distance on the part of others, was measured by questions tapping the willingness of the respondent to have as a co-worker or neighbor someone described in a vignette as having once been a patient in a mental hospital. Findings indicated that the more respondents associated mental illness with violence, the more they opposed having the former patient as a neighbor or co-worker.

Thus, the importance of setting the record straight on the nature of the link between violence and mental illness is a crucial and necessary step in reducing the stigma of mental illness. Likewise, the debate surrounding much of these discussions involves some of the most fundamental tenets of society: self-protection versus the preservation of civil liberties and freedom from discrimination for all people, including those with mental illnesses.

Despite the considerable debate and speculation about the dangers people with mental illnesses pose to the general population, the bottom line is that the relationship between mental illness and violence can also be tested as an empirical issue rather than one situated solely in the realm of public discourse. Yet, until recently, the data necessary for adequately answering this empirical question were at best weak. In the past decade, however, a remarkable amount of epidemiological and clinical research on violence among people with mental illness and on mental illness among people who are violent has become available for the first time (Monahan & Arnold, 1996; also see reviews by Monahan, 1992, and Mulvey, 1994). Although research exploring a connection between mental illness and violence dates back beyond the past decade, it was not without its limitations. While studies from the 1950s and 1960s generally found that discharged patients were no more violent than the general public, studies from the 1970s and 1980s concluded that discharged patients were more violent than others in the community. As emphasized by Monahan (1997) and others, the findings of earlier research that focused strictly on inpatient samples are problematic. Recent research findings do not support the public view that people with mental illness categorically pose a danger to others in the community (Swanson et al., 1997). According to Swanson et al. (1997), images of irrational volatility—etched in the public imagination and reinforced by media caricatures of "psychopathic killers"—are inaccurate stereotypes, deeply offensive to people with mental illnesses and their advocates. For example, Swanson (1993) reviewed the findings from the National Institute of Mental Health (NIMH) Epidemiological Catchment Area (ECA) study and found that 90% of people with a current mental illness are not violent. Furthermore, statistics show that only up to 3% of violence in the United States is committed by persons with mental disorders (Monahan, 1992).

In addition, studies that neglect to control for various demo-graphic factors can confound the findings concerning the influence of mental illness on violent behavior (Junginger, 1996). Although Steadman and Felson (1984) found that 22% of former psychiatric patients reported at least one incident of striking someone in the previous year, compared with 15% of a random community sample, these differences were found to be no longer significant when demographic factors were statistically controlled. Likewise, Mona-han and Steadman (1983) reviewed over 200 studies on crime and mental illness and concluded that the association between the two tends to "disappear" when factors such as age, sex, race, and social class are controlled.

However, according to Monahan and Arnold (1996),

> the answer provided by this research depends on the question put to it. If the question is, "Is there *any* relationship between mental illness and the commission of violent behavior?" the answer provided by the current research would be, "Yes." This is because some individuals with mental illness *do* commit violent acts. But if the question is "Is there a strong relationship between mental illness and the commission of violence?" the answer emerging out of recent studies is clearly, "No." (p. 69)

Indeed, the empirical evidence consistently demonstrates that *most* people with mental illnesses do not commit violent acts (Link, Andrews, & Cullen, 1992; Monahan, 1992; Swanson, Holzer, Ganju, & Jono, 1990). Thus, the nuances of the empirical data can be easily confused or manipulated.

One fact that has become clear in the most recent research is that while the majority of people with mental illness do not exhibit violent behavior, there is a subpopulation with severe symptoms that are prone to violence. In other words, the likelihood that *some* people with severe mental illnesses may commit assaultive acts is a legitimate risk that needs to be managed in the community (Swanson et al., 1997). For example, there is substantial evidence that a significant amount of violence observed in people with severe mental illness is associated with specific psychotic symptoms (Junginger, 1996). Thus, what this suggests is that it is not simply the presence of mental illness that induces violence, but rather the presence of particular symptoms.

For example, some data suggest that psychotic symptomatology, particularly symptoms of perceived threat and the overriding of internal cognitive controls (i.e., Threat/Control Override or TCO) may be largely responsible for the higher rates of violence found among some people with mental illnesses (Link & Strueve, 1995; Swanson, Borum, Swartz, & Hiday, 1996; Swanson, Borum, Swartz, & Monahan, 1997).

Likewise, researchers have reported that increased episodes of violence are associated with substance abuse—especially among persons who have co-occurring mental health and substance use disorders (Steadman et al., 1998). Indeed, evidence suggests that when substance abuse—especially alcohol abuse—is combined with major mental disorder, particularly with psychotic symptoms, the likelihood of violence increase significantly (Swanson, 1993, 1994; Swanson et al., 1996). According to Swanson et al. (1996), consistent with these findings, Mulvey, Gardner, Lidz, Graus, and Shaw (1996) recently found, in a prospective study of 520 psychiatric patients, that symptoms including hostility, paranoid ideation, psychoticism, and substance abuse were the most significant predictors of violence.

Similarly, in a study that recruited individuals from psychiatric treatment settings, Estroff, Zimmer, Lachincotte, and Benoit (1994) found that people who felt threatened or who perceived hostility in their relationships were at greater risk of engaging in violence (see Swanson et al., 1996). In addition, in looking at people with mental illnesses in the community, one study found that the only difference between those who were violent and those who were not involved early onset substance abuse on the part of those who were violent (Fulwiler, Grossman, Forbes, & Ruthazer, 1997; Steadman et al., 1998). Thus, recent investigations have more clearly specified some of the clinical symptom patterns that are associated with higher risk for violent behavior.

When violence by a person with a mental illness does occur, a family member is more likely to be a target. It is very rare for strangers to be the victims of these acts. People with severe mental illnesses often rely on their families for some level of care. The individual who is directly involved with the caregiving is found to be most at risk. According to one study, 65% of patients admitted to psychiatric hospitals who had attacked people during the time near their admission, had assaulted a family member (Tardiff,

1984). However, there is limited information on the situational factors that lead to violence against family members. One study found that psychiatric patients who attacked family members were more likely to live with their victims, but also noted age, marital status, limit setting, paranoid delusions, and substance abuse as significant risk factors (Straznickas, McNeil, & Binder, 1993).

According to Swanson et al. (1996), while recent research provides a partial promise for achieving a better clinical understanding of the relationship between mental illness and violence, many studies are still limited by an almost exclusive focus on the *individual* with a mental disorder and the *binary risk* of any violent acts rather than on the complex relationship between mental disorder and violence risk.

Risk Assessment and Predictions of Violence

The results of exciting new research conducted by the MacArthur Foundation Violence Risk Assessment study and the National Institute of Mental Health have just been published. The study examined how much, if any, of the relationship between violence and mental illness exists by comparing rates of violence among people with mental illness to violence rates in the general population. Steadman et al. (1998) found that patients discharged from psychiatric facilities who did not have co-occurring substance abuse disorders were no more violent than their neighbors. However, substance abuse raised the rate of violence among discharged patients by nearly five times, whereas it caused the rate only to triple for the general population.

According to Monahan (1997), the next wave of research on violence and mental illness will accept that a relationship does exist between the two and will focus on discovering the extent and parameters of such. He contends that both the MacArthur study and other research are likely to yield important information on using actuarial techniques to improve on the accuracy of predicting violence.

In the area of risk assessment, the issue is: Can violence be predicted? As previously noted, mental illness is not a good predictor of violence. Past antisocial and violent behaviors, substance abuse, age, and sex are among the most important factors to consider when attempting to predict violence (Benda, 1993; Cirincione, Steadman, Robbins, & Monahan, 1994; Harris & Rice, 1997). Yet assessing risk of violence accurately is a complex process (Monahan & Steadman, 1994).

Research concerning the validity of clinical violence risk assessments has demonstrated that such assessments are only modestly better than chance at predicting violent behavior among people with mental illnesses (Monahan, Steadman, & Robbins, 1997). Nor does that research identify ways in which the accuracy of clinical risk assessments could be readily improved. According to Monahan et al. (1997), the Research Network on Mental Health and the Law of the John D. and Catherine T. MacArthur Foundation identified four problems that limit the ability of existing studies to provide information about risk assessment that is useful to either clinicians or policymakers:

- The range of predictor variables studies has been very narrow, often no more than chart diagnosis or simple demographic information
- The measures of the criterion variable—violence in the community— have been very weak, typically arrest or rehospitalization for a new violent crime
- The patient samples analyzed have been highly restricted, usually to males with prior history of violence
- Past research efforts have been fragmented and have lacked coordination

One of the objectives of the MacArthur Study (Steadman et al., 1998) was to address these problems. It was designed with three purposes in mind: (a) to improve the validity of clinical risk assessment; (b) to enhance the effectiveness of clinical risk management; and (c) to provide information on mental disorder and violence useful in reforming mental health law and policy (Monahan et al., 1997).

Clinicians face difficulties in assessing the likelihood of a behavior as complex and multidetermined as violence in a population as diverse and poorly understood as those with mental illnesses (Steadman et al., 1994). In that manner, according to Steadman et al. (1994), the validity of clinical risk assessments and the effectiveness of clinical risk management could be appreciably improved.

Preliminary Conclusions

Based on a review of current research, both on prevalence and risk assessment, Mulvey (1994, pp. 663-665) developed a series of summary statements that can be made about an association between violence and mental illness:

- Mental illness appears to be a risk factor for violence in the community. A body of research, taken as a whole, supports the idea that an association exists between mental illness and violence in the general population.
- The size of the association between mental illness and violence, while statistically significant, does not appear to be very large. Also, the absolute risk for violence posed by mental illness is small.
- The association between mental illness and violence is probably significant even when demographic characteristics are taken into account. However, no sizable body of evidence clearly indicates the relative strength of mental illnesses as a risk factor for violence compared with other characteristics such as socioeconomic status or history of violence.
- Active symptoms are probably more important as a risk factor than is simply the presence of an identifiable disorder.
- No clear information about the causal paths that produce the association between mental illness and violence is available.

Implications of Mental Illness as a Risk Factor for Violence in the Community

As stated earlier, public assumptions of a connection between mental illness and violence and the suggestions of the research findings have played a major role in the formulation of the following policy: (a) the prominence of "dangerous to others" as a criterion for civil commitment; (b) the commitment of people acquitted of crime by reason of insanity; (c) the creation of special statutes for the extended detention of prisoners with mental illnesses; and (d) the imposition of tort liability on psychologists and psychiatrists who fail to anticipate the violence of their patients (Monahan & Arnold, 1996). These assumptions also lead to increased rates of incarceration among people with mental illnesses.

In fact, there are more people with mental illnesses in U.S. jails today than ever before (Steadman, Morris, & Dennis, 1995). Researchers have documented that the prevalence of severe mental disorders is significantly higher in jails than in the general population (Abram & Teplin, 1991). In addition, people with mental illnesses serve longer sentences for lesser crimes. For example, a 1992 study revealed that psychotic men in a county jail who had been arrested for misdemeanor offenses served sentences that were up to six times longer than those of their nonpsychotic counterparts. The finding was not related to whether or not they actually committed the offense (guilt or innocence) nor to dangerousness or seriousness of the crimes (Axelson & Wahl, 1992).

The explanation for these trends lies partially in the "criminalization" of mentally disordered behavior. Instead of being treated, people with mental illnesses are sent to jail for behaviors that fall outside that which society accepts. Criminalization of people with mental illnesses is thought to be the unintended consequence of deinstitutionalization, more stringent commitment criteria, and inadequate community mental health resources (Abram & Teplin, 1991). However, one cannot overlook the connection between criminalization of mental illness and the assumption concerning links between mental illness and the potential of violence.

The dramatic increase in the numbers of jail beds in the United States has placed a fiscal strain on state budgets and state systems (Bureau of Justice Statistics, 1993). What is unclear, however, is the number of persons who are inappropriately placed in jail and other criminal justice settings who should be served in mental health settings. It appears society is facing a fundamental conflict in distinguishing between treatment and rehabilitation versus punishment via incarceration—and the current result is that the lines are getting blurred. References to persons who commit crimes and have mental health problems being "sentenced" to state psychiatric facilities continue—yet what does this say about how society views treatment?

Many advocates have been quick to point out that despite the recent eras of deinstitutionalization and state psychiatric hospital closings, more people with mental illnesses are institutionalized now than ever before—the only thing that has changed is the locus of their confinement from state psychiatric hospitals to jails and prisons. In Texas, for example, more people with mental illness are in prisons than in state psychiatric hospitals on any given day. A study of urban county jails in Texas suggests that 20% to 35% of inmates are mentally ill (Texas Citizens' Planning and Advisory Committee, 1994).

The juvenile justice system is also warehousing large numbers of youth with serious emotional disturbances. From intake interviews, the U.S. Department of Justice found that 73% of youth in the juvenile justice systems have mental health problems (Parent et al., 1994). A study by Emory University (Marsteller et al., 1997) estimated that 61% of children in the Georgia system have a mental or emotional disorder.

Many urban county jails, state penitentiaries, and juvenile correctional facilities have become increasingly crowded during the past 10 years. There are more people, youth and adults, incarcerated in this country than at any other time in history. There are many factors that come into play regarding the increase of populations in secure facilities. They include jurisdictions enacting stiffer penalties for a range of controlled substance violations, and legislation such as the "three strikes" bills that have federal and many state implications. In recent years, huge amounts of federal and state general fund allocations have also been used to build large numbers of secure facilities for children and adult offenders. From 1980 to 1992, state government expenditures for the construction of correctional institutions grew by 275% (Bureau of Justice Statistics, 1997). Many local and state jurisdictions have not been able to build capacity fast enough to handle the tidal wave of new admissions to facilities.

Many mental health advocates in urban centers across the United States claim that despite the proliferation of programs to serve people who are homeless in many cities, increasing numbers of people, including women and children, are accessing homeless shelters and other emergency services. Although the data are incomplete, it appears that the number of people with mental illnesses and substance use disorders who live on our urban streets and shelters is growing. One of the consequences of so many people with severe mental illness entering our streets is that many end up in jail for violations ranging from disturbing the peace to loitering to petty theft. However, most of these individuals actually receive inadequate care and are often vulnerable to victimization in jails and prisons.

Identifying Effective Interventions

The increased interaction between mental health and criminal justice systems has led to increased resource demands on both. People who are incarcerated and are entitled to mental health services represent an additional demand for already scarce resources in both systems.

The positive aspects of this trend, however, are emergent models of systems integration and other interventions including jail diversion programs that focus on avoiding inappropriate incarceration or entry into the criminal justice system. When effective, not only do these measures yield important savings to systems and budgets, but they mitigate the additional trauma and stigma that may otherwise accrue to consumers of mental health services and their families. If the positive aspects of this trend continue, then so too must the development of cross-training of police officers, jail and other criminal justice personnel, judges, and others to raise their awareness of effective responses to mental health consumers who come into contact with the criminal justice system.

The lack of recent contact with a community mental health provider has also been found to be related to violent acts committed by persons with mental illness (Swanson et al., 1997). One team of researchers contends that a key tool in risk management involves using intensive case management techniques in the community that reduce violence committed by people with mental illness. They point out the importance of meaningful systems coordination among mental health and criminal justice systems at the local level along with case managers who have low case loads and are accessible on a 24-hour basis. Access to services in the community is also an important factor in minimizing the risk of dangerousness (Dvoskin & Steadman, 1994). Effective local programs continue to demonstrate that mental health consumers with low risks of violence can be served better in community-based settings than in costly jails (Center for Mental Health Services, 1995). Yet our review of the existing literature indicates that the efficacy of such programs for consumers judged to be at high risk for violence remains undiscovered and would benefit from future research inquiry.

Co-Occurring Mental Health and Substance Use Disorders

Because the research is clear on the increased likelihood of violence when substance abuse becomes involved and on the high incidence of co-occurring substance use disorders among people with mental illnesses (Steadman et al., 1998), the need for effective treatment strategies for this population is evident. Researchers such as Abram and Teplin (1991) have clearly identified a disproportionately high incidence of co-occurring mental health and substance use disorders in jail populations. The results of their study of 728 randomly selected urban jail inmates revealed that an "extraordinarily high" 72% of subjects with a current severe mental illness also had a co-occurring substance abuse problem. Of concern, over the course of a lifetime, the rate of co-occurring disorders for those subjects jumped to 94%. The implications for public policy, specifically the delivery of mental health and substance abuse services, brought on by these findings cannot be overemphasized. As stated by Abram and Teplin (1991), "patients with multiple problems are persona non grata to many treatment facilities, and they may be arrested as a way to manage their disorders" (p. 1036).

Responding With Community-Based Programs

Many states and communities have invested heavily in the development of new ways to approach old problems that have plagued mental health and criminal justice systems. These programs vary in their emphases on different aspects of the criminal justice system ranging from prearrest, jail diversion, in-jail or in-prison, and postincarceration programs. The goals of these programs are to reduce inappropriate arrests, divert persons with mental illnesses from jails to more appropriate services and settings, and reduce recidivism after release from jails or prisons.

Steadman et al. (1995) define jail diversion programs as those that: (a) screen detainees for mental disorder; (b) rely on mental health professionals to provide assessments of those identified; (c) emphasize cross-systems collaborations and negotiations with a range of criminal justice stakeholders including prosecutors, defense attorneys, and the courts together with local mental health service providers to work toward a mental health disposition that results in an alternative to prosecution or reduced charges; and (d) provide direct referrals for detainees to local providers.

In Maryland, for example, 18 of the state's 23 counties participate in a program begun by the state Mental Hygiene Administration designed to break the cycle of criminal justice recidivism, hospitalization, and homelessness for people with mental illness and co-occurring mental health and substance abuse disorders. The Maryland Community Criminal Justice Treatment Program, initiated in 1993, identifies eligible program participants in county jails through screening and assessment tools. The program's goal is to remove persons who have been inappropriately jailed and to provide them with a range of services and supports in the community, including housing and case management services. The program places a heavy emphasis on interagency collaboration and pooled funding at the state and local level, and cross-training as well. During the first 5 years of the program's operation it has served more than 2,000 clients, and less than 10% have returned to jail, hospitals, or homelessness (National Technical Assistance Center for State Mental Health Planning, 1998).

Another example of a collaborative response includes the Denver County Jail, which relies on full-time psychiatric nurses to provide screening and assessments for new detainees and, where appropriate, to divert arrestees to community-based services. The Rensselaer County Jail in New York partners with the county mental health department and funds a full-time staff person who provides mental health services at the jail (National Technical Assistance Center for State Mental Health Planning, 1998).

Training for law enforcement officials also offers hope for directing people with mental illnesses toward appropriate treatment settings. The lack of knowledge on the part of police officers about mental illness and violence can contribute to the further criminalization, forced committal, and victimization of people with mental illnesses. In addition, on a basic level, the sight of a uniformed officer can either have a calming effect, or just the opposite, causing even greater fear. The National Mental Health Association (NMHA) has published a manual for law enforcement on aiding people in conflict, which provides suggestions for police officers on how to deal with a person with a mental illness who may be violent (National Mental Health Association, 1992). An NMHA affiliate, the Mental Health Association in Greater St. Louis, conducts regular training with local police forces and is working with the Missouri Mental Health department to expand this program statewide (Personal communication, March 11, 1998).

These initiatives seek to break the cycle of crime, incarceration, and homelessness. When effective, not only do these measures yield important saving to systems and budgets, but they mitigate the additional trauma and stigma that may otherwise accrue to consumers of mental health services and their families. If the positive aspects of this trend continue, then so too will the systematic development of cross-training of police officers, jail and other criminal justice personnel, judges, and others to raise their awareness of effective responses to mental health consumers who come into contact with the criminal justice system.

Victimization of People With Mental Illness

Because of the continuing stigma associated with mental illness and the widely held belief among the public that people with mental illness are violent, little attention has been paid to the criminal victimization of people with mental illness and its consequences. A sad irony is that people with mental illness are much more likely to become the *victim* of violence than they are the perpetrator. The violent victimization of young people and adults with mental illnesses is a very old but only modestly acknowledged phenomenon, especially during the past 30 years. In fact, the modern-day mental health movement can trace its roots back to the victimization of one man who suffered from bipolar disorder: Clifford Beers. Beers, who later founded NMHA, experienced physical abuse and degradation during his stays in public and private psychiatric hospitals early in this century. His autobiography, *A Mind That Found Itself* (1907), exposed this cruel treatment and brought attention to the need for reform in psychiatric care.

The deinstitutionalization of people with mental illnesses from giant, overcrowded facilities that began in the 1950s was partially the result of advances in new medications and of social security funds being made available for people with disabilities. However, there probably was no more powerful force behind the movement of people out of huge institutions than the media coverage of the terrible conditions that patients were forced to experience. One of those conditions was physical violence perpetrated on patients by their caregivers.

Homelessness and victimization as it relates to people with mental illness have been found to be related in two fundamental ways: Homelessness can result from victimization (particularly domestic violence) and, alternatively, victimization is a frequent experience of homeless people (Fischer, 1992). Indeed, there has been a call for a reexamination of the causes of mental illness and homelessness, particularly among women, that gives serious consideration to the contributions of physical and sexual abuse toward this state (Koranda, 1991).

One of the most egregious forms of violence against people with mental disorders appears to be taking place in state correctional facilities for juvenile offenders. As stated earlier, a 1994 report by the U.S. Department of Justice (DOJ) concluded that in their intake interviews, 73% of youth in the juvenile justice systems reported mental health problems (Parent et al., 1994). Twenty percent have a serious disorder (Cocozza, 1997). The DOJ also said the mental health screening and treatment at juvenile justice facilities do not adequately address children's mental health treatment needs (Parent et al., 1994).

It is worth noting that 94% of children in the juvenile justice system have committed nonviolent offenses (Federal Bureau of Investigation, 1996). They are involved with the system for offenses like breaking windows, stealing, and running away from home. Many incarcerated children have been physically and sexually abused. About 60% of children in the system abuse drugs and/or alcohol; many of their parents are addicted. Fifty percent have clinical depression; half have conduct disorders; and up to 45% have attention deficit/hyperactivity disorder. An overwhelming number of the children are poor; minorities are overrepresented (Edens & Otto, 1997).

In the secure juvenile corrections facilities in Louisiana, Georgia, and Kentucky, the DOJ reported serious deficiencies ranging from a severe shortage of mental health services for youth with serious psychiatric problems to punishment of youth for seeking medical care. In Louisiana, the DOJ (U.S. Department of Justice, 1997) found:

- Rampant physical abuse of youth by staff and other youth. Children are hit and kicked by officers; officers pay children to beat other children; children are sprayed with Mace while in handcuffs; children are punished for seeking medical attention.
- Insufficient psychiatric coverage for assessments and medication monitoring. Children or parents give no consent to be medicated; children get no psychotherapy.
- Some children are put in isolation for up to a month, others are isolated or beaten for refusing to take medications.

In Georgia, the DOJ (U.S. Department of Justice, 1998) found:

- Mental illness is addressed almost solely through discipline, isolation, and restraint. Youth are often disciplined for manifestations of their mental illness. Discipline includes being restrained, shackled, hit, put in restraint chairs, sprayed with pepper spray, involuntarily injected with psychotropic drugs, shackled to beds or to toilets.
- Inappropriate handling of suicidal children. Suicidal youth are locked in disciplinary facilities, stripped of clothing and bedding, and monitored, not transferred for hospital treatment.
- Gross overcrowding, mixing of young children with older adolescents, with no programs to address physical and sexual abuse or substance abuse.
- Excessive use of force and routine use of restraints as punishment.

An even more recent trend has centered on the very limited dialogue that has begun to focus on the impact of trauma in the lives of people with mental illness. The developing literature base continues to demonstrate the pervasive impact of physical and sexual abuse and the mental health consequences of this on women, children, and men alike (Goodman, Dutton, & Harris, 1997). Other research has demonstrated that 50% of women and significant numbers of men who receive services in psychiatric hospitals have physical and/or sexual abuse histories (Bryer, Nelson, Miller, & Krol, 1987; Carmen, Rieker, & Mills, 1984; Craine, Henson, Colliver, & MacLean, 1988). Even now, however, these discussions are rarely held in the context of "criminal justice system" issues, yet the fact is that these are crimes committed against persons.

The boundaries of this dialogue are only beginning to be explored—What treatment and services are most effective? Where and when do mental health systems retraumatize consumers? How do we ensure a "no wrong door" approach where regardless of how a trauma survivor "enters" any of a number of systems—criminal justice (including victim assistance), mental health, social welfare—she will have access to the highest quality treatment, services, and supports? In the context of the costs of violence to society, it has been estimated that 10% to 20% of mental health care costs in the United States are spent on treating victims of violence (Miller, Cohen, & Wiersema, 1996).

The promise for improvements in this area of responding to the needs of trauma survivors is immense. Several states are pioneering efforts to address the needs of trauma survivors and are making great strides. The Massachusetts Department of Mental Health has issued clinical guidelines for psychiatric hospitals under its jurisdiction that require assessing clients for histories of abuse or neglect (Massachusetts Department of Mental Health, 1996). Model standards on alternatives to the use of seclusion and restraint in state hospitals is another important example of this progress. The point here is simple—there is a need to broaden the discussion of mental health and violence not only to include people who commit crimes, but the victims of crimes as well.

Conclusion

The substantial mythology surrounding people with mental disorders and their alleged propensity to violence has existed in all forms of public expression. This mythology has been perpetuated in more recent times by television, movies, news coverage, and other facets of popular culture.

On the other hand, for many years the mental health community has been eager to deny or contradict any relationship between mental illness and violence. This stance was used to confront the enormous stigma that is associated with mental illness. However, this viewpoint has not stemmed the overriding public perception of a connection nor has it convinced policymakers nor deterred incorrect media images of people with mental illnesses. Ideas about the association between mental illness and violence, though, are beginning to change.

The knowledge that is continuing to develop based on research on violence and mental illness creates opportunities to inform the debate. While the emergent findings show a minimal, if any, relationship between mental illness and violence, the overall evidence is that the majority of people with mental illnesses are neither dangerous nor violent. Again, however, there does appear to be a small subpopulation of individuals with mental illnesses who commit violence. The MacArthur study shed important insight on the association and provided helpful data on the potential for risk assessment.

Any attempts to counter the damaging perception of people with mental illnesses as overwhelmingly violent will depend on the continued objective and systematic study of this issue. The National Academy of Sciences estimates that the federal government spends a total of $20 million a year on violence research (Monahan, 1993). This expenditure pales in comparison with the large sums this country spends on the by-products of violence: incarceration, health care, and other societal costs. The nation must invest more resources into scientific research on the link between mental illness and violence. Some of the areas for future research that are needed include the following.

1. Co-Occurring Substance Abuse Disorders: It is clear that substance abuse is a pivotal factor in violence, but this is true in the general population as well; is it higher still for people with mental illnesses who use substances?

2. Victimization: What is the incidence of victimization of adults with serious mental illnesses and children with serious emotional disturbances?

3. Efficacy of Systems Integration: Do coordinated approaches among systems result in better services/outcomes and fiscal savings?

4. Social Supports: What is the importance of social supports in preventing violence?

5. Research Designs: Longitudinal studies that follow people over time are needed. There is also a paucity of published literature incorporating the perspective of persons with mental illnesses and their families. The design models of future research will also have to

address socioeconomic status, diagnosis, use of psychiatric medications, and selection and exclusion criteria.

6. Family Violence: Are incidents of family violence involving a family member with mental illness as underreported as domestic violence is in the general population? More risk assessment research could help families intervene and deal with potential violence.

7. Involuntary Commitment: Should the threshold for "harm to self or others" standard be examined?

8. Problems in the Definition and Measurement of Dangerousness: The majority of studies have used arrest rates. This poses problems for accurate findings because studies have shown that persons with mental illnesses may be arrested at a disproportionately higher rate than people who do not self-identify, thus overestimating the criminality of people with mental illnesses.

9. Self-Harm and Suicide Rates: These acts of violence should also be considered when examining the association between mental illness and violence.

10. Impact of Involuntary Interventions on Violence: Do interventions such as seclusion, restraint, and forced medication reduce or exacerbate problems?

One of the few pathways to lessening the erroneous assumptions that surround the issue of violence and its relationship to mental illness is to insist firmly that public policy decisions are made based on empirical data. Without this informed decision-making process, the harm that has been unfairly inflicted on people with mental illnesses and their families will continue to thrive due to the continued perpetuation of myths and the stigma this creates. Similarly, efforts to reduce the stigma associated with mental illness will be furthered by research that continues to explore the causes and consequences of violence that is engaged in by the small subgroup of people with mental illness (Torrey, 1994).

The new research offers tremendous hope for a major shift in attitudes about and policies concerning people with mental illnesses. When these findings are brought to bear on public policy and public opinion, individuals and communities may better understand and no longer fear people with mental illnesses. Then, effective solutions to violence and to the country's wholesale neglect of children and adults with mental health needs will be possible.

References

Abram, K., & Teplin, L. (1991). Co-occurring disorders among mentally ill jail detainees: Implications for public policy. *American Psychologist, 46*(10), 1036-1045.

American Psychiatric Association. (1994). *Violence and mental illness fact sheet.* Washington, DC: Author.

Axelson, G., & Wahl, O. (1992). Psychotic versus nonpsychotic misdemeanants in a large county jail: An analysis of pretrial treatment by the legal system. *International Journal of Law and Psychiatry, 15,* 379-386.

Beers, C. (1907). *A mind that found itself.* New York: Longmans, Green.

Benda, B. (1993). Predictors of arrests and service use among the homeless: Logit analyses. *Psychosocial Rehabilitation Journal, 17*(2), 145-161.

Bryer, J., Nelson, B., Miller, J., & Krol, P. (1987). Childhood sexual and physical abuse as factors in adult psychiatric illness. *American Journal of Psychiatry, 144*(11), 1426-1430.

Bureau of Justice Statistics. (1993). *Jail inmates, 1992.* Washington, DC: U.S. Department of Justice.

Bureau of Justice Statistics. (1997). *Justice expenditure and employment extracts, 1992.* Washington, DC: U.S. Department of Justice.

Carmen, E., Rieker, P., & Mills, T. (1984). Victims of violence and psychiatric disorders. *American Journal of Psychiatry, 141*(3), 378-383.

Center for Mental Health Services, Substance Abuse and Mental Health Services Administration. (1995). *Double jeopardy: Persons with mental illness in the criminal justice system.* Rockville, MD: SAMHSA.

Cirincione, C., Steadman, H., Robbins, P., & Monahan, J. (1994). Mental illness as a factor in criminality: A study of prisoners and mental patients. *Criminal Behavior and Mental Health, 4,* 33-47.

Cocozza, J. (1997). Identifying the needs of juveniles with co-occurring disorders. *Corrections Today, 12,* 146-149.

Craine, L., Henson, C., Colliver, J., & MacLean, D. (1988). Prevalence of a history of sexual abuse among females psychiatric patients in a state hospital system. *Hospital and Community Psychiatry, 39*(3), 300-304.

Dvoskin, J. A., & Steadman, H. J. (1994). Using intensive case management to reduce violence by mentally ill persons in the community. *Hospital and Community Psychiatry, 45*(7), 679-684.

Edens, J., & Otto, R. (1997). Prevalence of mental disorders among youth in the juvenile justice system. *Focal Point: A National Bulletin on Family Support & Children's Mental Health,* Portland State University, *11*(1), 6-7.

Estroff, S., Zimmer, C., Lachincotte, W. S., & Benoit, J. (1994). The influence of social networks and social support on violence by persons with serious mental illness. *Hospital and Community Psychiatry, 45*(7), 669-678.

Federal Bureau of Investigation. (1996). *Crime in the United States 1995.* Washington, DC: Government Printing Office.

Fischer, P. J. (1992). Victimization and homelessness: Cause and effect. *New England Journal of Public Policy, 8*(1), 229-246.

Fulwiler, C., Grossman, H., Forbes, C., & Ruthazer, R. (1997). Early-onset substance abuse and community violence by outpatients with chronic mental illness. *Psychiatric Services, 48*(9), 1181-1186.

Goodman, L., Dutton, M., & Harris, M. (1997). The relationship between violence dimensions and symptom severity among homeless, mentally ill women. *Journal of Traumatic Stress, 10*(1), 51-71.

Harris, T. H., & Rice, M. E. (1997). Risk appraisal and management of violent behavior. *Psychiatric Services, 48,* 1168-1176.

Junginger, J. (1996). Psychosis and violence: The case for a content analysis of psychotic experience. *Schizophrenia Bulletin, (22)*1, 91-103.

Koranda, A. (1991, September). *Violence as a precursor to mental illness and homelessness.* Paper presented at the National Advisory Mental Health Council National Mental Health Leadership Forum Public Hearing: Mental Illness and Homelessness, Chicago.

Link, B., Andrews, H., & Cullen, F. (1992). The violent and illegal behavior of mental patients reconsidered. *American Sociological Review, 57*(June), 275-292.

Link, B., Cullen, F., Frank, J., & Wozniak, J. (1987). The social rejection of former mental patients: Understanding why labels matter. *American Journal of Sociology, 92,* 1461-1500.

Link, B., & Stueve, A. (1995). Evidence bearing on mental illness as a possible cause of violent behavior. *Epidemiologic Reviews, 17*(1), 1-10.

Marsteller, F., Brogan, D., Smith, I., Ash, P., Daniels, D., Rolka, D., & Falek, A. (1997). *The prevalence of substance use disorders among juveniles admitted to regional youth detention centers operated by the Georgia Department of Children and Youth Services.* Atlanta, GA: Emory University.

Massachusetts Department of Mental Health. (1996). *Task force on the restraint and seclusion of persons who have been physically or sexually abused report and recommendations.* Boston: Author.

Miller, T., Cohen, M., & Wiersema, B. (1996). *Victim costs and consequences: A new look.* Washington, DC: U.S. Department of Justice, National Institute of Justice.

Monahan, J. (1992). Mental disorder and violent behavior: Perceptions and evidence. *American Psychologist, 47*(4), 511-521.

Monahan, J. (1993). Causes of violence. In *Drugs and violence* (pp. 77-85). Washington, DC: United States Sentencing Commission, Government Printing Office.

Monahan, J. (1997). Clinical and actuarial predictions of violence. In D. Faigman, D. Kaye, M. Saks, & J. Sanders (Eds.), *Modern scientific evidence: The law and science of expert testimony* (Vol. 1, pp. 300-318). St. Paul, MN: West.

Monahan, J., & Arnold, J. (1996). Violence by people with mental illness: A consensus statement by advocates. *Psychiatric Rehabilitation Journal, 19*(4), 67-70.

Monahan, J., & Steadman, H. (1983). Crime and mental disorder: An epidemiological approach. *Crime and Justice, 4,* 145-189.

Monahan, J., & Steadman, H. (Eds.). (1994). *Violence and mental disorder: Developments in risk assessment.* Chicago: University of Chicago Press.

Monahan, J., Steadman, H., & Robbins, P. (1997, January). *The MacArthur Violence Risk Assessment Study.* Presented at Pivotal Issues in Mental Health Law: Competence, Risk and Coercion Conference, Phoenix, AZ.

Mulvey, E. P. (1994). Assessing the evidence of a link between mental illness and violence. *Hospital and Community Psychiatry, 45,* 663-668.

Mulvey, E. P., Gardner, W., Lidz, C. W., Graus, J., & Shaw, E. C. (1996). *Symptomatology and violence among mental patients.* Pittsburgh, PA: University of Pittsburgh.

National Mental Health Association. (1992). *Aiding people in conflict.* Dubuque, IA: Kendall/Hunt.

National Technical Assistance Center for State Mental Health Planning. (1998, Spring). Focus on the states: Maryland seeks to break cycle of crime, hospitalization and homelessness. *Networks Newsletter,* p. 6.

Parent, D., Leiter, V., Kennedy, S., Livens, L., Wentworth, D., & Wilcox, S. (1994). *Conditions of confinement: Juvenile detention and corrections facilities, research summary.* Washington, DC: U.S. Department of Justice, Office of Juvenile Research and Delinquency Prevention.

Steadman, H., & Cocozza, J. (1978). Selective reporting and the public's misconceptions of the criminally insane. *Public Opinion Quarterly, 41*(4), 523-533.

Steadman, H. J., & Felson, R. B. (1984). Self-reports of violence. *Criminology, 22*(3), 321-342.

Steadman, H., Monahan, J., Appelbaum, P., Grisso, T., Mulvey, E., Roth, L., Robbins, P., & Klassen, D. (1994). Designing a new generation of risk assessment research. In J. Monahan & H. Steadman (Eds.), *Violence and mental disorder: Developments in risk assessment* (pp. 297-318). Chicago: University of Chicago Press.

Steadman, H., Morris, S., & Dennis, D. (1995). The diversion of mentally ill persons from jails to community-based services: A profile of programs. *American Journal of Public Health, 85*(12), 1630-1635.

Steadman, H., Mulvey, E., Monahan, J., Robbins, P., Appelbaum, P., Grisso, T., Roth, L., & Silver, E. (1998). Violence by people discharged from acute psychiatric inpatient facilities and by others in the same neighborhoods. *Archives of General Psychiatry, 55,* 1-9.

Straznickas, K., McNeil, D., & Binder, R. (1993). Violence toward family caregivers by mentally ill relatives. *Hospital and Community Psychiatry,* (4), 385-387.

Swanson, J. (1993). Alcohol abuse, mental disorder, and violent behaviors: An epidemiological inquiry. *Alcohol Health & Research World, 17,* 123-132.

Swanson, J. (1994). Mental disorders, substance abuse, and community violence: An epidemiological approach. In J. Monahan & H. Steadman (Eds.), *Violence and mental disorder: Developments risk assessment* (pp. 101-136). Chicago: University of Chicago Press.

Swanson, J., Borum, R., Swartz, M., & Hiday, V. (1996, February). *Characteristics of violent events among people with severe mental disorder.* Paper presented at the Biennial Meeting of the American Psychology-Law Society, Hilton Head, SC.

Swanson, J., Borum, R., Swartz, M., & Monahan, J. (1996). Psychotic symptoms and disorders and the risk of violent behavior in the community. *Criminal Behavior and Mental Health, 6,* 309-329.

Swanson, J., Estroff, S., Swartz, M., Borum, R., Lachincotte, W., Zimmer, C., & Wagner, H. (1997). Violence and severe mental disorder in clinical and community populations: The effects of psychotic symptoms, comorbidity, and lack of treatment. *Psychiatry: Interpersonal and Biological Processes, 60*(1), 1-22.

Swanson, J. W., Holzer, C. E., Ganju, V. K., & Jono, R. T. (1990). Violence and psychiatric disorder in the community: Evidence from the Epidemiological Catchment Area surveys. *Hospital and Community Psychiatry, 41,* 761-770.

Tardiff, K. (1984). Characteristics of assaultive patients in private hospitals. *American Journal of Psychiatry, 141,* 1232-1235.

Texas Citizens' Planning and Advisory Committee. (1994). *Persons with mental illness and mental retardation and the criminal justice system: Issues, models, recommendations.* Austin: Texas Department of Mental Health and Mental Retardation.

Torrey, E. F. (1994). Violent behavior by individuals with serious mental illness. *Hospital and Community Psychiatry, 45*(7), 653-662.

U.S. Department of Justice, Civil Rights Division. (1997, June). Letter from Isabelle Katz Pinzler to the Honorable Mike Foster, Governor of Louisiana. *Findings of investigation of secure correctional facilities for juveniles in Louisiana. Summary of findings regarding conditions at the juvenile facilities in Louisiana.* Washington, DC: Author.

U.S. Department of Justice, Civil Rights Division. (1998, February). Letter from Bill Lann Lee to the Honorable Zell Miller, Governor of Georgia. *Findings of investigation of state juvenile justice facilities.* Washington, DC: Author.

Wahl, O. F. (1995). *Media madness: Public images of mental illness.* New Brunswick, NJ: Rutgers University Press.

• CHAPTER 8 •

Effective Youth Violence Prevention

DANIEL J. FLANNERY

LAURA WILLIAMS

Despite recent declines in the overall rate of violent behavior, violence among young people continues to rise. This is especially worrisome because the number of 15- to 19-year-olds is expected to increase by about 20% in the next 5 years. For the first time since the 1970s, violent acts against strangers occur more frequently than violence between individuals who know each other (Hughes & Hasbrouk, 1996). It makes sense, then, that rates of exposure to violence and victimization from violence are also steadily increasing (Finkelhor & Dziuba-Leatherman, 1994), especially among young people.

What Constitutes Youth Violent Behavior?

Youth violent behavior takes on many different forms and is described using a variety of labels. This is an important place to begin our discussion of effective youth violence prevention because one first needs to know what one is targeting, trying to reduce or prevent. A definition of *violence* can include conflict between two individuals; the perpetration of physical harm resulting in injury; or criminal behavior, which includes theft, property offenses and vandalism (Goldstein, Apter, & Hartoonian, 1984). Studies of violent behavior also use various terms, depending on the focus and perspective of the study: *aggression, conflict, delinquency, conduct disorders, criminal behavior, antisocial behavior,* and *violence.*

In defining youth violent behavior, we need to consider violence along a continuum of behavior within a developmental framework. For example, violent behavior for young elementary school children consists primarily of aggressive behaviors such as kicking, hitting, spitting, or name calling. As children grow older, behavior becomes more serious, characterized by bullying, extortion, and physical fighting. Aggressive or violent adolescents may engage in assault against their peers or adults, sexual harassment, gang activity, and weapon carrying. Considering violent behavior along a developmental continuum permits an examination of how different forms of violence exposure and victimization affect children at different ages, at different developmental levels, and how children are challenged to meet various developmental tasks. These issues are essential to consider if we are to implement effective violence prevention strategies.

What Is Prevention?

In a public health model, prevention takes place at three levels: primary, secondary, and tertiary. Primary prevention aims to keep violence from occurring in the first place. In a primary prevention program, the entire population is exposed to the intervention. Most primary prevention or universal programs occur at school, since this is a convenient way to reach a large population, although many of the highest-risk children rarely attend school on a regular basis (Flannery, 1997). Secondary prevention targets individuals identified as being "at risk" for engaging in violence and providing them services that reduce the chances that they will become further involved in violence. Tertiary-level prevention efforts engage those who have already perpetrated violence, and seek to reduce the chances that they will engage in violence again (Graham, 1994). Decisions about the level of prevention will also determine the type of program that is implemented, the complexity of risk that individuals bring to the situation, the factors associated with success or failure, and the short- and long-term prognosis for participants.

The public health model has been criticized on various grounds for not adequately distinguishing among strategies with different epidemiological justifications and because both secondary and tertiary approaches are more like treatment than prevention (Bower, 1987; Gordon, 1983). Gordon (1983), and more recently the Institute of Medicine (IOM; 1994) propose a strategy that divides prevention strategies into those that are *universal* and those that are *targeted*. Universal or populationwide prevention is designed to reach all individuals of a particular age in a specified area or setting. There are two types of targeted preventive interventions. Selected interventions are targeted strategies for those identified as being at risk for developing a disorder based on factors external to the targeted individuals, including biological, psychological, or social factors. Indicated preventive interventions are designed to reach individuals considered to be at risk for a particular disorder by virtue of specified current characteristics of the individuals themselves, or internal factors, including for example low-birth weight, social skill deficits, or poor impulse control (Peters & McMahon, 1996).

The Mental Health Consequences
of Violence Exposure and Victimization

The need to engage in effective youth violence prevention is highlighted by the significant impact that exposure to violence and victimization from violence has on child mental health. Recent work has illustrated quite convincingly that victimization and exposure are related to children experiencing post traumatic stress disorder (PTSD) symptoms such as anxiety, anger, depression, and dissociation (Martinez & Richters, 1993; Singer, Anglin, Song, & Lunghofer, 1995). Studies also consistently show that younger children are victimized at higher rates than older children at school, at home, and in their neighborhood. This has important implications for understanding when and how we must intervene to prevent violence.

Boney-McCoy and Finkelhor (1995) conducted a national telephone survey of adolescents age 10 to 16 and found that one out of three had been victims of an assault at least once in their lives. Adolescent victims reported significantly more psychological distress and behavioral symptomatology than their nonvictimized peers. These problems included more PTSD symptoms, increased sadness, and more behavioral difficulties at school. Singer, Miller, Guo, Slovak, and Frierson (1998) have recently demonstrated the same strong relationship between violence exposure and PTSD symptoms for elementary school aged children, a relationship that held for children and adolescents across urban, suburban, and rural settings (Singer et al., 1995; Singer et al., 1998).

How do adolescents cope with violence exposure and victimization? The most frequently endorsed coping strategy is listening to music, followed by being with a friend (Singer & Flannery, 1997). Rarely do adolescents talk to a teacher or counselor, one of the least frequently endorsed methods of coping. For both boys and girls, increased exposure to violence is associated with higher levels of maladaptive coping strategies such as getting angry, sleeping, saying something mean to other people, and using alcohol or drugs (Flannery, Singer, Williams, & Castro, 1998). Knowledge about the impact of exposure and victimization on child mental health and coping can influence our choices about prevention strategies, particularly targeting multiple risk factors and efforts to increase resilience and improve coping.

A Developmental Perspective

To understand risk for violence along a developmental continuum, and to provide a framework for effective prevention efforts, it is essential to understand risk factors for aggression and violence. The complement of risk, of course, is an understanding of the "protective" factors that can be promoted and supported as a way to reduce risk. The American Psychological Association (APA; 1993) concluded recently that violence is predominantly a learned behavior. This does not mean that physiological or temperamental factors are unrelated to the manifestation of aggressive or violent behavior, because we now know that these are important influences (Tolan & Guerra, 1994; Perry, 1997). If violence is primarily learned, however, then we should be able to teach children how to behave and react in nonviolent ways.

Children at risk for aggression and violence are cognitively, imitatively, and socially different from their more socially competent peers (Embry, Flannery, Vazsonyi, Powell, & Atha, 1996). Recognizing that violent behavior is a complex phenomenon that is manifested in many different ways, we briefly review major risk factors that may inform our prevention efforts. These categories are not meant to be comprehensive or exhaustive. The six categories of risk presented here include: (a) temperament and perinatal risk; (b) cognitive abilities and factors influencing school achievement and attachment to school; (c) the stability and early onset of aggressive behavior; (d) family factors; (e) exposure to violence and victimization from violence; and (f) the influence of the media on aggressive and violent behavior. Several excellent reviews examine risk factors for aggression and violence (Earls, 1994; Elliott, 1994; Farrington, 1991; Fraser, 1996; Reiss & Roth, 1993; Yoshikawa, 1994).

Temperament and Perinatal Risk. The literature in this area is limited, mostly due to the necessity to track children over a long period of time to determine whether perinatal risk factors are associated with violence later in life. Several studies have demonstrated an association among low-birth weight, number of delivery complications and birth trauma, and later conduct problems (Cohen, Velez, Brook, & Smith, 1989) and violent behavior (Kandel & Mednick, 1991). More recent studies have shown perinatal risk to be associated with violent behavior only in conjunction with other rearing and environmental factors such as maternal rejection (Raine, Brennan, & Mednick, 1994; Werner, 1994). Birth complications can result in neurological dysfunction that can predispose a person to violent behavior (Moffitt, 1990; Perry, 1997).

There also exists a relationship between aggressive and violent behavior and childhood impulsivity and child temperament (Brier, 1995). A "difficult" temperament is associated with school failure and delinquency. Having a temperament characterized by high activity levels, being inflexible, having difficulty with transitions, being easily frustrated, and being distractible usually means a child will be more noncompliant, out of control, and impulsive. Some of these children will meet the diagnostic criteria for disorders such as Attention Deficit Hyperactivity Disorder, or Oppositional Defiant Disorder. There exists a significant relationship between ADHD and ODD and risk for delinquency and violence (Moffitt, 1990). Young children who suffer from a combination of a Mood Disorder (e.g., Major Depression, Bipolar Disorder), Conduct Disorder, and associated Attention Deficit Hyperactivity Disorder, are also at particularly high risk for criminal offending, school failure, and incarceration as adolescents and young adults (Farrington, 1991).

Cognitive Abilities and School Achievement. Longitudinal research has consistently demonstrated the relationship between low verbal intelligence (e.g., poor problem-solving skills) and risk for aggression and violence (Eron & Huesmann, 1990), an association that holds even after controlling for the influence of poverty, from age 8 through age 30. Children who do poorly at school and lack attachment to school are also more likely to be rejected by their peers, increasing their risk and opportunity for engaging in delinquent, violent behavior. The combination of "failure" of peer group relations and academic skills has been described as an essential feature of an "early starter" model of delinquency and violence (Patterson, Reid, & Dishion, 1992).

Another problem for aggressive, violent youth is their tendency to make cognitive misattributions and to have impaired social judgment (Dodge, Price, Bachorowski, & Newman, 1990). These youth are more likely to interpret or label ambiguous or neutral events as hostile, and expect that aggressive solutions will gain them tangible rewards (Durant, Cadenhead, & Pendergast, 1994).

The Early Onset and Stability of Aggression. One of the most consistent findings in the risk factor literature is that we can predict with a high degree of accuracy which children will be aggressive and violent in adolescence by their behavior in kindergarten and first grade (Loeber et al., 1993; Tremblay, Kurtz, Masse, Vitaro, & Phil, 1995). Aggression is a relatively stable, self-perpetuating behavior that begins early in life (Huesmann & Moise, 1999). Children who engage in highly aggressive, violent behavior at an early age (before age 10) are most at risk for chronic offending (Hawkins et al., 1992; Hawkins, Von Cleve, & Catalano, 1991).

Family Factors. Parents of aggressive children punish more frequently, but inconsistently and ineffectively. They also tend to negatively reinforce coercive and manipulative child behavior and fail adequately to reinforce positive, prosocial behavior. Children learn that aggressive behavior often leads to parents and others giving them what they want. Parents who are harsh, rejecting, and neglecting also have children at higher risk for engaging in aggressive, violent behavior (Gorman-Smith & Avery, 1999). Children who are victims of maltreatment and abuse at home during childhood are also at significantly higher risk of being violent in adolescence than their nonmaltreated peers (Thornberry, 1994). Conversely, parents who monitor their child effectively and who are more actively involved in their child's school activities are more likely to have prosocially competent children (Walker, Colvin, & Ramsey, 1995).

Exposure to Violence and Victimization. Both exposure to violence and victimization from violence are associated with increased risk of perpetrating violence (Thornberry, 1994; Widom, 1989). Rivara, Shapherd, Farrington, Richmond, and Cannon (1995) showed that adolescents victimized by assault were more likely to have a history of criminal activity or to engage in criminal behavior subsequent to their assault. Widom (1989) found that youth who were abused or neglected were 38% more likely to be arrested for a violent crime by the time they were adults compared to children who had not been mistreated. Singer et al. (1995) showed that even after controlling for demographic variables, parental monitoring, and watching aggressive television, recent violence exposure was the most significant predictor of self-reported violent behavior among third to eighth grade students.

Media Influences. Several large scale studies have concluded that exposure to violence in the media is strongly associated with a child's risk for engaging in aggressive and sometimes violent behavior (APA, 1993; Derksen & Strasburger, 1996; Eron, Gentry, & Schlegel, 1993; Gerbner & Signorielli, 1990). There are three main effects of violence in the media. First, children who are exposed to high levels of media violence are more accepting of aggressive attitudes and, after watching violence, behave more aggressively with peers (Centerwall, 1992). Second, more chronic and long-term exposure to violence can lead to desensitization toward violence and its consequences. Third, children who watch a lot of violence on television seem to develop a "mean-world syndrome" in that they increasingly fear being victimized by violence and come to view the world as a mean and dangerous place where they can trust no one.

Other Macrosocial Influences. Recently several large studies have linked adolescent violence to neighborhood factors such as levels of disorganization, high mobility rates, a high ratio of children to parents, and levels of drug use and gang activity (Coulton, Korbin, & Su, 1996). Conversely, collective efficacy, defined as social cohesion among neighbors combined with their willingness to intervene on behalf of the common good, has been associated with reduced violence (Sampson, Raudenbush, & Earls, 1997).

Developmental Continuum

Figure 8.1 provides a developmental sequence for violent behavior. This developmental sequence reflects the continuum of risk factors, from perinatal risk and parental history of antisocial behavior and family management practices, to peer rejection and academic problems in elementary school. The developmental sequence highlights several aspects of risk for violent behavior and implications for prevention. First, risk factors are interdependent. Few risk factors operate singularly or in a vacuum to predict violent, delinquent behavior in adolescence. Second, risk factors for violence do not suddenly emerge in early or middle adolescence, but are present even before a child is born. We are learning more and more about the importance of the first 3 years of life for neuronal and neurobiological development (Perry, 1997) and the impact of early and chronic exposure to violence and victimization from violence on child adjustment (Osofsky, 1997). Third, as children mature, the intrapersonal and interpersonal factors associated with their aggressive, violent behavior increase significantly in complexity. As children grow older, the window of opportunity for intervening and effecting positive change grows significantly smaller. The social, economic, and personal costs of intervening increase exponentially as the complexity of the presenting problems and the multiple manifestations of aggression and violence emerge. Finally, the model for a developmental sequence of aggressive and violent behavior illustrates that there are many "choice points" for potential preventive intervention efforts. Given what we know about the etiology of aggression and violence, it makes little sense to wait until adolescence to identify at-risk youth and attempt to intervene. While school is a logical starting point for many universal and

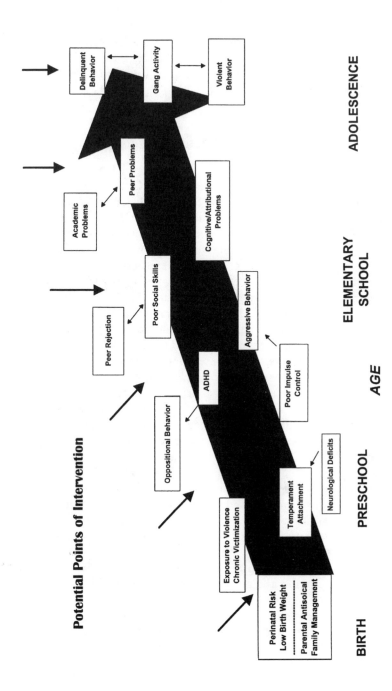

Figure 8.1. Proposed Developmental Sequence of Violent Behavior

targeted preventive intervention efforts, there is also much evidence that risk for aggression and violence can be identified prenatally for some youth and in infancy and toddlerhood for others (Osofsky, 1997).

What Constitutes Effective Prevention?

Any approach to violence prevention needs to be a multicomponent and multicontext intervention (Tolan, Guerra, & Kendall, 1995). An effective approach will include parents, children, school, media, law enforcement, local businesses, and community-based organizations. Time-limited approaches are not effective over the long term. Approaches that focus on only one risk factor (e.g., self-esteem) are also less effective over time. Research has shown that the most potentially effective programs go beyond a focus on individual children and attempt actually to change the climate or culture of the entire school. This is not to say that individual child focused programs are ineffective and should be discontinued. They are a valuable violence prevention tool (Tolan et al., 1995). They do not, however, address the contextual/environmental or social ecology factors that contribute to the incidence of violence. Programs also typically need to last at least 2 years before they demonstrate change in behavior that is sustainable over time (Yoshikawa, 1994). As we have discussed, aggressive behavior is very stable and chronic, making it very difficult to change with short-term, singular, limited interventions.

Of course, the effectiveness of any intervention will depend on its usefulness in the real world versus the way it might be designed in a textbook, whether the components of the intervention are transportable to other populations in other contexts, whether the intervention fits with other services being provided to children in a school, for example, and whether the program is accepted and supported by parents and others in the neighborhood. The following are some principles and guidelines to consider when implementing a violence prevention strategy:

1. *Violence Is Learned Behavior.* If violence is learned behavior, then we can also teach children prosocial competence. Positive coping skills, competencies, and strategies can be taught to very

young children so they can deal more effectively with their frustrations and anger. This makes schools both a logical and necessary setting to implement, systematically and over the long term, universal prevention strategies to reduce aggression and violence. Purposely focus on and reinforce a child's positive behaviors and use a simple, common language to help generalize learning across settings (Embry & Flannery, 1999).

2. *Start Early*. If a child is identified as being aggressive and at risk for academic failure at an early age, chances are that child will continue to struggle over time, and the factors contributing to adjustment problems will grow in number, in intensity, and in complexity. As children mature and grow older, we have a shrinking window of opportunity to intervene in an effective manner. The earlier we are able to intervene, the greater our chances of success. The resources (measured in time, money, and effort) that we spend by waiting until a child is in adolescence compared to intervening early in a child's life are enormous. The pool of available resources to do this is rapidly shrinking.

3. *Make Interventions Developmentally Appropriate*. A violence prevention program will be less effective and may lead to iatrogenic effects (i.e., make things worse) if the program fails to take into account the developmental appropriateness of the program components and the target behaviors. Let's take an extreme example: a violence prevention program for kindergartners that focuses on reducing gang involvement or firearm violence may be misguided. Reduced gang involvement may be a laudable long-term goal, but very difficult to demonstrate in the short term regarding program outcome efficacy. A focus on knowledge and attitudes may be one aspect of a program's target goals, but funders are increasingly looking for behavior change as indication of a program's impact. The intervention, therefore, needs to be clear about what behaviors, developmentally, are appropriate to target (either to increase or decrease), and the intervention strategy should be developmentally appropriate given a child's existing competencies, cognitive abilities, social skills, and behavior.

4. *Effective Prevention Is Systematic and Long Term*. Prevention strategies must be systematic and long term, not time-or risk-actor

limited. This is directly related to the stability and chronicity of aggressive behavior and the challenges related to changing one's environment. It may be unreasonable to accomplish either goal with short-term, limited, and rigid approaches. Recent reviews of delinquency prevention programs suggest that interventions need to last a minimum of 2 years before positive, sustainable behavior change is realized (Yoshikawa, 1994).

5. *Focus on Increasing Social Competence, Problem Solving, and Prosocial Behavior.* To be effective, efforts must be aimed at increasing prosocial competence and protective factors (Kellam & Rebok, 1992; Werner, 1994), not just on reducing aggression, crime, and violence. It is easy and natural to pay attention to a child's negative behaviors. Assault, vandalism, bullying, and theft are all behaviors that contribute to fear and insecurity. The need to reduce and eliminate these behaviors from our schools and neighborhoods is paramount to ensuring a safe environment for our children. There are at least three difficulties with relying on this approach. First, these negative behaviors are very difficult to eliminate altogether, so some of these will occur at least some of the time in most settings. Second, a relatively small portion of youth account for a large number of the discipline problems and violent, criminal acts. Merely focusing on reducing negative behaviors puts a great deal of emphasis on a small group of children, perhaps differentially reinforcing their negative behavior, and ignores the large majority of students who are doing well. Third, in the absence of focusing on improving social competence, children will not have the skills necessary to sustain positive behavior change.

6. *Alter the Environment.* Programs that work over the long term attempt to change the climate or culture of the environment. This is not to say that paying attention to individual children at risk for engaging in problem behaviors is ineffective. Rather, utilizing a strategy that identifies and treats individual children should be one component of the systematic strategy that also attempts to change the environment and alter the social ecology that contributes to violence.

7. *Be Comprehensive, Intensive, and Flexible.* Programs that are successful are comprehensive, intensive, and flexible. Programs that

work are intensely sensitive to the needs of the children and families that they serve and the unique circumstances that must be addressed in that school, for those children, for those staff members, and in that neighborhood. We can learn much from the effectiveness of other programs. Many of the basic principles we have discussed here are necessary and will be effective across contexts, time, and settings. However, in implementing any prevention program one must not be overly rigid, as every situation is different, the timing and circumstances vary, and the sociocultural climate varies across sites, even within the same neighborhood, school system, or city.

A second implication of the need for comprehensive preventive interventions is the evidence for the effectiveness of "dosage level" prevention programs that combine both universal and targeted preventive interventions. This strategy is most consistent with a developmental perspective on youth violence prevention. There is no single approach that will prevent aggression and violence for all children in all settings and at all grade levels. In order to be effective systematically and over the long term, it will be necessary to implement both universal strategies and targeted interventions for at-risk youth.

8. Increase Children's Attachment to School. Promote their involvement in school activities and focus on academic achievement. Children who are disengaged from school have little or no investment in acting appropriately while they are there. A tremendous amount of energy goes into paying attention to children who are truant from school, who daily receive disciplinary referrals to the principal's office, and children who are at risk of failing academically. If children are more attached to and involved in school, we may decrease daily truancy rates. Children cannot learn when they are not in school. Chronic truancy in kindergarten through second grade significantly and negatively impacts a child's chances of being successful in school and increases the risk of dropping out. This in turn increases risk for associating with a deviant peer group and engaging in delinquent behavior and violence. Parents who model and encourage school attachment and academic achievement have children who are less likely to become involved with violence (Steinberg, 1996).

Violence prevention programs may also increase attendance at school and decrease truancy, especially for children who stay home from school because they fear for their safety. If more at-risk children are actually in school, this increases the school's ability to effect change for a child and increases the chance that the violence prevention program will actually benefit the children most in need of the attention.

9. *Take Into Account the Impact of Victimization.* The impact of victimization from violence affects child learning, motivation, teachability, adjustment, and ability to attain appropriate developmental tasks. Being exposed to violence or being victimized by violence may take on many forms and may affect children in many different ways. Witnessing a friend being shot or being shot at oneself may be a different form of exposure or victimization than constant harassment by a bully at school. Nevertheless, both forms of violence may result in increased distractibility, irritability, anxiousness, and anger. These can be the "masked effects of violence" (Flannery, 1996). What looks like Attention Deficit Hyperactivity Disorder may really be the manifestation of Post Traumatic Stress brought on by chronic exposure to violence. Staying home from school with a stomachache may be the way a child is coping with fear for his or her safety at school. Constantly getting into fights with peers may be a reaction to a perceived threat from others rather than because a child is engaging in predatory aggressive behavior.

10. *Evaluate Your Program's Effectiveness.* Base what you do on what is known to work effectively. Evaluation research, even if it is conducted at a very basic level, is an essential component of an effective violence prevention strategy (Webster, 1993). Programs that demonstrate effectiveness in one school, community, age group, or ethnic/culture milieu may not be effective in another. The pressure to evaluate program effectiveness to respond to funders, parents (we are doing something that works), and policymakers (school boards, state legislatures) is steadily increasing.

11. *Involve Others.* Involve parents and other community members and organizations in your school's violence prevention efforts. Whatever the constellation of a family, we know that caregivers and others at home play a critical role with respect to modeling and teaching children appropriate social skills, coping strategies, and

competencies (Gorman-Smith & Avery, 1999). Home is also where the most common form of victimization, sibling assault, occurs. Parents remain influential role models for children through adolescence, and they can model both appropriate and inappropriate behavior and problem-solving strategies to children (Resnick, Bearman, Blum, et al., 1997). Having parents and schools on the same page with respect to discipline strategies and safety concerns, as well as involving parents directly in the provision of service at the school, is essential to a program's support structure and long-term viability.

12. School-Based Prevention Programs. School-based prevention programs should be integrated into teacher training or orientation discussion or preparation for issues related to school safety, discipline, student victimization and its impact, and general teaching strategies that we know contribute to a more prosocial school climate. Teachers are often unprepared to address the complex school discipline issues they encounter in the classroom. New teachers may need help in identifying behavior patterns that may be related to violence exposure or victimization.

13. Involve Peers. Involve peers in a way that promotes and rewards prosocial peer interactions. Peers play an important role in sustaining a positive environment for a youngster. Peer groups are also important sources of influence on a young person's behavior. At-risk children can learn from their more socially competent peers.

14. Model Hopefulness. Be hopeful, and model this hopefulness to children. There exists longitudinal evidence spanning many years that most children are extremely resilient and overcome a great deal of hardship and turmoil in their lives, growing up to be high-functioning, well-adjusted, and productive adults (Werner, 1994). Hopelessness is one of the most disparaging and difficult-to-overcome aspects of youth's reactions to the violence encountered daily in their lives. If they are hopeless and don't expect to live long, then their day-to-day behavior, goal orientation, and motivation to succeed will reflect this attitude and way of being.

Examples of Effective Prevention Programs

Historically there have been many attempts at quick fixes, an emphasis on maintaining social control rather than on prevention, and a dependence on approaches that have lacked any empirical data on effectiveness. Fortunately, many organizations and schools have begun to shift their strategy. Part of the change is out of necessity—these historical approaches haven't worked very well, and the problem of youth violence is continuing unabated. The need to garner additional resources has also increased. These resources will not come from the business community, foundations, or the federal government without quality evaluation data for program effectiveness, even if the data are of a pilot nature and short term.

Many school-based violence prevention programs focus on individual children identified by teachers or peers as aggressive or at risk for school failure (Coie, Lochman, Terry, & Hymna, 1992; Hawkins et al., 1992; Tremblay et al., 1995). School violence, or the potential for school violence, is then reduced by decreasing individual risk of perpetrating violence at school. For example, if a program reduces a child's aggressive behavior and increases that child's problem-solving ability and social skills, the school will decrease the likelihood of that child instigating a fight with a peer or reacting with hostility to one of the many conflicts that occur at a school (Grossman et al., 1997). Some programs combine a focus on individual risk with family risk by integrating their school-based programs with efforts to work with parents and families, peers, or involving community members (Huesmann et al., 1996; Kellam & Rebok, 1992). Still other programs integrate individual risk with attempts to change the culture or environment of the school. These programs tend to place a lot of emphasis on the compatibility of their strategies across people, settings, and places (Embry et al., 1996; Grossman et al., 1997). The focus on changing the environment is meant to provide the positive, long-term reinforcement to sustain individual behavior change (Walker et al., 1995). Most programs have a dual focus: increasing student social skills and prosocial competence, and reducing aggressive behavior (Kazdin, 1994).

In this section, we present as illustrative examples some violence prevention programs that show promise as effective strategies.

Three criteria generally guided the choice of examples. First, we want to provide some examples of programs at the elementary, middle, and high school levels because these programs are generally very different in their focus, content, and purpose. Second, we want to focus on programs that are relatively well established. This is not to say that they are necessarily old, but that most have been adopted in many different locations. Even though we must recognize that few programs will work equally well in all settings and all geographic locations, there is also no need to reinvent wheels. Third, we want to present programs that have undergone some level of evaluation of program effectiveness. Intensive evaluation of violence prevention programs (school based or otherwise) is a relatively new phenomenon, as most of the effort has been put into creating and implementing the programs rather than on evaluating them. By no means are these programs the only ones, and they are not necessarily the best models for all contexts and all situations. They should be viewed as specific, singular components of a comprehensive, long-term strategy to reduce school violence. There exist several resources that review other school-based violence prevention programs (Act Against Violence, 1995; Crawford & Bodine, 1996; Eron et al., 1993; Hoffman, 1996; Powell & Hawkins, 1996; U.S. Department of Justice, 1995). We have summarized some of the most promising and well-established youth violence prevention programs in Table 8.1. Examples of universal, targeted, and comprehensive programs are presented, depending on whether they generally focus on elementary, middle, or high school-aged youth. The table is by no means comprehensive; there certainly exist many valuable violence prevention programs across the country not represented here.

Elementary School Programs. Below we briefly review three elementary school-based programs: PeaceBuilders, which originated in Tucson, Arizona; Second Step, which originated in Seattle, Washington; and the Young Ladies/Young Gentlemen Clubs, from Cleveland, Ohio.

The PeaceBuilders program is a school-wide violence-prevention program for students in kindergarten through fifth grade (Embry et al., 1996; Embry & Flannery, 1999). It is currently being implemented in more than 375 schools in Arizona, California, Utah, Oregon, and Ohio. The program incorporates a strategy to change

(text continued on p. 233)

Table 8.1 Examples of Universal and Indicated Prevention Programs

Elementary School Based Programs

Program	Age Groups	Program Components	Outcomes
P.A.T.H.S. (Promoting Alternative Thinking Strategies) (Greenberg, Kusche, Cook, & Quamma, 1995)	Grades 1 through 5	60-lesson curriculum aimed at teaching emotional competence, self-control, and problem solving.	Positive effects for regular and special education students on the social competence skills targeted. Lower rates of self-reported conduct problems at 1-year follow-up.
PeaceBuilders (Embry & Flannery, 1999; Embry, Flannery, Vazsonyi, Powell, & Atha, 1996; Flannery et al., 1997)	Kindergarten-5th grade 375; schools in Arizona, California, Utah, Oregon, & Ohio	Implemented by staff and students. Aim is to promote prosocial behavior, reduce child aggressive behaviors, and improve social competence. Five universal principles are taught and utilized.	Initial evaluation results indicate increases in social competence according to teacher ratings for intervention schools. Both teacher and child self-reports show significant decline in male aggressive behavior over first 2 years of intervention.
D.A.R.E. (Drug Abuse Resistance Education) (Ringwalt et al., 1994)	Usually 5th and 6th grades. Has been used with all grades. Program used by 70% of nation's school districts, reaching approximately 25 million students.	17-lesson core curriculum focusing on teaching skills to recognize and resist peer pressure to use drugs. Also teaches lessons on self-esteem, decision making, alternatives to drugs, and anger management skills.	Ringwalt et al. (1994) summarize the evaluations of D.A.R.E.'s short-term effects. Short-term effects on drug use are nonsignificant. Effects on risk factors for drug use are small. Does not appear to work as a method for reducing substance use. Not as comprehensive as other programs in teaching social competence and social problem solving.

Second Step (Grossman et al., 1997)	Grades 1 through 3 (includes modules for students through 8th grade)	30-lesson curriculum utilizing activities to teach empathy, impulse control, problem solving, and anger management	Students in intervention group rated by observers as less physically aggressive than control group. Some change still noticeable at 6-month follow-up. No significant behavior change rated by teachers or parents.
Metropolitan Area Child Study (MACS) (Huesmann et al., 1996)	16 schools in the Chicago area ($N = 4,507$).	Three levels of intervention delivered in 2-year segments: (a) Level 1: classroom enhancement aimed at increasing cultural sensitivity, classroom management, and instruction focusing on mitigating aggressive development; (b) Level 2: Small group session focusing on peer relationship skills for high-risk children; (c) Level 3: a 1-year family relationship intervention focused on enhancing emotional responsiveness and parenting skills.	Schools were assigned to a control group or one of the three intervention levels. There are no outcome data to date, as the intervention and evaluation are ongoing. Baseline data indicate that children in the study have higher levels of aggression and elevated clinical levels of psychopathology compared to national averages. There are no differences across the four intervention groups with regard to ethnic composition, SES, aggressive behavior, and beliefs about aggression.

Middle School Based Programs

ALERT (Ellickson, Bell, & McGuigan, 1993)	7th graders from 30 junior high schools in California and Oregon	8-lesson curriculum taught 1 week apart followed by 8 booster sessions. Targets social resistance skills.	Assessed improvements after 6th, 8th, 9th, & 10th grades. Showed effects for both low- and high-risk adolescents, including a drop in marijuana use. Follow-up studies showed that once program stopped, so did the effect on drug and alcohol use.

Middle School Based Programs (cont.)

L.S.T. (Life Skills Training) (Botvin et al., 1989)	7th graders followed by booster session in Grades 8 and 9	16 sessions targeting resistance skills training and general life skills development. Groups led by older students or teachers	More recent studies examined L.S.T. use in 10 suburban New York junior high schools. Students in the peer-led groups reported less marijuana use and excessive drinking. Effects of program decreased without booster sessions. In peer-led group with booster sessions, effects for alcohol and marijuana use were maintained at the end of the 8th grade.
G.R.E.A.T. (Gang Resistance Education and Training) (Esbensen & Osgood, 1996)	Middle school students	9-week program developed by the Phoenix Police Department. Curriculum focuses on the impact of crime on victims, cultural differences, conflict resolution skills, and how to meet one's needs without a gang. Does not teach social competence skills.	Outcome studies compared 2,600 participating students with 3,200 controls. Results showed decreases on delinquency and drug use but effect sizes were small so findings must be viewed cautiously.
PACT (Positive Adolescent Choices Training) (Hammond & Yung, 1992)	Designed specifically for African American youth.	Students received two 50-minute training sessions per week for a semester. Techniques included using videotapes and role playing.	Examination of school records indicated that physical and verbal aggression decreased during the semester of participation and the semester after. Experimental youth also had lower rates of juvenile court-recorded criminal offenses at follow-up than comparison youth. Chronically truant youth were excluded from participation so study groups were not comparable. Findings must thus be viewed cautiously.

L.R.E. (Law-Related Education) (Johnson & Hunter, 1985)	Has been implemented in elementary, middle, and high schools	Curriculum has been in use for nearly three decades and is designed to teach children about the country's laws, legal processes, political participation, and moral-ethical values.	Several outcome evaluations of this program were conducted during the 1980s. Results indicated good effects for student acquisition of law-related factual knowledge. Effects on delinquency were minimal. At one strong site (i.e., strong program implementation), effects for certain risk factors (e.g., attachment to school & attitudes toward violence) were improved. There was no impact on other risk behaviors (e.g., associating with delinquent peers).
Richmond Youth Against Violence: Responding in Peaceful and Positive Ways (Farrell & Meyer, 1997; Farrell, Meyer, & Dahlberg, 1996)	Developed for use with 6th grade students.	School-based curriculum consisting of 16, 40-minute workshops to be taught once per week. Taught a 7-step problem-solving model.	School data and self-reports are being assessed for outcomes. There were some baseline differences between the groups: A high percentage of boys had exposure to community violence, and many had engaged in high-risk behaviors. For boys, participation resulted in significant post-intervention differences in frequency of violence and other problem behavior. Girls did not benefit from the program.

High School Based Interventions

Resolving Conflicts Creatively Program (RCCP) (Aber et al., 1996)	Developed for children and adolescents in Grades K-12	A conflict and mediation program that begin in NYC in 1985 and has expanded to four other school systems across the country. The program has several key components: classroom lessons stressing modeling nonviolent alternatives for coping with conflict, negotiation and other resolution skills, and weekly practice of these skills; mediation program aimed at providing strong peer models and principles negotiation; teacher training and development, providing 24 hours of after-school training to teachers; and school administrator training.	A 2-year evaluation of approximately 9,600 children ages 5-12 is currently under way. Data from baseline instruments indicate that means on constructs such as aggressive fantasies and hostile attributions increase with grade level. While the program has been in existence for over 10 years, the results of the more recently developed empirical evaluation are needed in order to examine the program's efficacy in changing attributions and behavior problems.
Dealing With Conflict (Bretherton, Collins, & Ferretti, 1993)	Targeted high school students in three Australian secondary schools.	Teachers presented 1-hour weekly sessions in class for 10 weeks. Classes focused on building group cohesion, trust, respect, self-esteem, self-disclosure, and on barriers to communication, causes of conflict, and ways to resolve conflict.	A pretest/posttest model was used to examine change. At posttest, participating students reports decreases in violent behavior and more appropriate responses to hypothetical situations. There were no differences between experimental students and controls in attitudes toward violence and aggression or on other cognitive measures.

INDICATED

Elementary School Based Programs

Program	Age Groups	Program Components	Outcomes
Cities in Schools (Rossman & Morley, 1995) *Selected*	Elementary and middle school children	Drop-out prevention program for high-risk students. Has been implemented at 665 sites in 197 communities nationwide. Caseworkers assigned to groups of problem students in inner-city schools. Provide case management, individual group counseling, tutoring, attendance monitoring, and self-esteem building. No established curriculum.	Evaluators could not quantify level of program implementation. Analysis of dropout and absences indicates that the program was not effective in preventing these occurrences. Using retrospective child reports, results indicated that students were most likely to improve slightly or report no change as opposed to getting worse.
FAST Track (Families and School Together) (Dodge, 1993) *Targeted*	Elementary school students identified at risk for the development of conduct disorder, based on teacher and parent ratings of behavior problems in kindergarten.	A comprehensive, theory-based, implemented intervention in four cities. Provides training for parents in family management, home visits by staff, social skills training for children, academic tutoring, and a classroom instructional program for social competence and classroom management.	Only preliminary data are available regarding measured outcomes. Results indicate positive effects on targeted behaviors, including improved parent involvement in child's education. Findings also suggest significant improvement in child problem behaviors.

Elementary School Based Programs (cont.)

Young Ladies/Young Gentlemen Clubs (Cleveland, OH) (Flannery & Williams, 1997) *Targeted*	Elementary school children in high-risk elementary schools identified and referred by classroom teachers for problematic behavior and/or poor attendance and low academic performance.	Children participate in group sessions several times per week during the course of the school year. Group leaders employ a series of activities aimed at improving self-concept, developing peer relationship skills, and encouraging attachment to school.	A year-long evaluation of the program was recently completed. Data were gathered from children, teachers, group leaders, and parents. Teachers and group leaders rated improvements in child social competence and peer relationship skills. Children reported improvements in social competence. Regression analyses indicated that length of time in the program (e.g., exposure to the intervention) significantly predicted decreases in child self-report and group leader ratings of aggression and teacher ratings of declines in delinquency.

Middle School Based Programs

Aggression Replacement Training (ART) (Goldstein & Glick, 1987)	ART: 3-component intervention that includes (a) skillstreaming, (b) anger control training, (c) moral education.	The authors have conducted a series of investigations to examine the program's efficacy. Results indicate that participating students gained new skills, managed anger better, and had improved moral reasoning. Other outcomes were reduction in rearrests and enhanced community functioning. Studies of the ART program by other groups have yielded similar results.

Program	Target	Description	Evaluation
The Prepare Curriculum (Goldstein, 1999) *Targeted*	Targets adolescents with aggressive and delinquent behaviors	Prepare 10-step curriculum including the 3 steps from ART and adding problem solving training, situational perception training, stress management, cooperation training, recruiting supportive models, and understanding/using group processes.	A matched control was used to examine change among participants. Students in the program showed decreases in referrals for problem behaviors after participating. There were no main effects for measures of anger, aggression, or attitudes toward delinquency and violence.
Think First anger-control and problem-solving training program (Larson, 1992) *Selected*	Students designated as high risk	Students receive 50-minute session two times per week for 5 weeks. Uses modeling, role-playing, and self-instructional methods of anger and aggression control. There are incentives for attendance and completion of homework.	

High School Based Programs

Program	Target	Description	Evaluation
The Omega Boys Club; Joseph Marshall, Jr., Executive Director *Selected*	Targets African American youth at high risk for violence and delinquency. Designed for boys and girls who are in trouble at school or with law enforcement.	Uses a combination of mentoring and peer counseling to help high-risk youth become more responsible members of their community. New members pledge not to use drugs and to avoid violence. The club emphasizes improved school performance by providing study halls, tutoring, and academic counseling. The club also incorporates meetings with extended family of the participating youth.	No formal evaluation of the club has been conducted to date, so empirical evidence of the efficacy of the program is not available. Currently, the program has expanded to include a weekly radio talk show that focuses on helping youth to discuss their problems, including crime, gang violence, teenage pregnancy, and drug use. Because of the program's widespread appeal, it has been expanded to include listeners from Los Angeles twice a month. *The New Yorker* referred to the program as, "a kind of electronic parent for violence-prone young people."

High School Based Programs (cont.)

Violence Prevention Curriculum for high school students. (Prothrow-Stith, 1987). *Targeted*	Targeted high school students in four inner cities across the country.	Teachers received 1 day of training in the curriculum. Classes focused on risk factors for violence, anger management, negative consequences of violence, and alternatives to violence.	Teachers administered pretests 2 weeks before the curriculum and posttests 1 week after the program ended. There were no differences between experimental and comparison students from pretest to posttest for knowledge about violence, attitudes about how to handle conflict, acceptance of violence, locus of control, self-esteem, fighting, drug use, or weapon carrying. There was also a greater attrition rate in the experimental group.

the school climate, and is implemented by both staff and students. PeaceBuilders aims to promote prosocial behavior among children and staff, to enhance child social competence, and to reduce child aggressive behavior. Children learn five simple principles: (a) praise people; (b) avoid put-downs; (c) seek wise people as advisers and friends; (d) notice and correct the hurts we cause; and (e) right wrongs. Adults reinforce and model the behaviors at school, at home, and in public places. PeaceBuilders attempts to create a common language and culture that is easily transferable across people, settings, and time. The program provides extensive materials to teachers and parents, and incorporates community involvement and media as resources to effect long-term systematic change.

PeaceBuilders is different from most school-based programs in that it is not curriculum based, but is meant to become a "way of life" in a school. Some of the materials utilized by PeaceBuilders include "praise notes" for student positive behaviors and "referrals" to the principal's office for good behavior. Students identify with a Hero (themselves in comic books and activities) who resolves conflict and problem situations as a PeaceBuilder. Schools have a "wise person" lunch table where business and community leaders join PeaceBuilder-nominated students for lunch. Recently, materials have been developed to utilize PeaceBuilder principles with at-risk and special needs children, as well as to address individual differences (e.g., cultural and religious issues).

The program is currently in the middle of a 6-year longitudinal evaluation funded by the Centers for Disease Control and Prevention (1995). The evaluation consists of both process and outcome data, including reports from students, teachers, and parents, and archival data from the schools and the local police department. Information on program implementation and utility is also being gathered, along with observations of playground behavior. The initial evaluation results from the program are very encouraging. Using growth curve analyses, we have found that teachers rate significant increases in social competence for both kindergarten through second grade children and third through fifth grade children in the initial intervention schools. Both teacher and child self-reports also show a significant decline in male aggressive behavior over the 2 years of intervention (Flannery, Huff, & Manos, 1996; Flannery et al., in press). Intervention schools have also experienced reductions in student visits to the nurse's office for treatment of injuries compared to control schools (Krug, Brener, Dahlberg, Ryan, & Powell, 1997).

The Second Step program also targets young children in Grades 1 to 3 (Grossman et al., 1997), although it has modules for students through Grade 8. Second Step is designed to prevent aggressive behavior by increasing prosocial behavior, reflected by competence in peer interactions and in interpersonal conflict resolution skills. Based on the "habits of thought" model that violence can be unlearned, Second Step includes activities to help students acquire empathy, impulse control, problem-solving, and anger management skills. A recent comprehensive and well-designed evaluation of the Second Step program showed that 2 weeks after the 30-lesson curriculum, students in the intervention group were rated by behavioral observers to be less physically aggressive and to engage in more neutral/positive behaviors on the playground and in the lunchroom (but not in the classroom) than students in the control group. Some of the changes persisted at 6 months postintervention, although neither teachers nor parents rated significant behavior change (Grossman et al., 1997).

The third program is not as large or comprehensive as the other two, but illustrates an approach of early identification of at-risk youth. The Young Ladies/Young Gentlemen Clubs (YLYG) in the Cleveland Public Schools target youth in Grades 1 to 6 who are identified by teachers and principles as at risk for school failure and drop-out and who engage in problem behavior in the classroom. Students attend a group session several times per week throughout the year. The group is run by an adult who also serves as a mentor to the students and as a liaison between the student's family and the school (i.e., by conducting home visits). The group focuses on developing problem-solving and social skills, as well as on character education and discipline. Students learn how to respect and care for themselves, each other, and adults. The utilization of music therapy has proven to be a valuable component to the program's success. YLYG, developed by the Partnership for Safer Cleveland, has been in existence since the mid-1980s and has served as a model for similar programs in other school districts throughout the country.

YLYG has undergone several (albeit limited) evaluations. In the most recent one-year longitudinal evaluation, children and teachers reported significant improvements in child social competence, and group leaders reported significant gains in child prosocial behavior accompanied by decreases in aggressive behavior. Analyses of grade card data found statistically significant improvements in positive classroom behaviors, self-control, and general attachment to school. Parents also reported program benefits: 96% said YLYG helped their child perform better at school, 92% said that the club had helped their child's behavior at home, and 97% felt the YLYG is an important part of their child's education (Flannery & Williams, 1997).

Middle School Programs. One of the most common approaches to violence prevention in middle schools and high schools is conflict mediation or conflict resolution programs. One of the most widely known is the Resolving Conflicts Creatively Program (RCCP) in New York City. RCCP is somewhat unique among conflict resolution programs in that it has models for implementation for children in kindergarten through Grade 12. In existence since 1985, RCCP is a comprehensive school-based program in conflict resolution and intercultural understanding (Aber, Brown, Chaudry, Jones, & Samples, 1996). Teachers and students are trained to address conflict with nonviolent alternatives and negotiation skills. The curricula also contain strategies to promote multicultural acceptance and global peace. Teachers are trained first, then student mediators. Mediators work in pairs during lunch periods and recess to identify and resolve disputes. Since its inception, the program has trained over 2,000 student mediators and served more than 60,000 students in over 150 schools.

Conflict resolution programs, while extremely popular and widespread, have not fared very well in the face of intensive evaluation (Webster, 1993). While several intensive longitudinal evaluations of RCCP are ongoing and the final word is still out, early research on conflict mediation programs showed few long-term effects in reducing violent behavior or risk of victimization. One potential problem faced by conflict mediation programs is that they tend to focus on mediating only the most serious conflicts, which differentially reinforces them when they occur. This is not to say that the conflict resolution and problem-solving strategies students and staff learn are not helpful and beneficial. Caution, however, is the word for schools that rely solely on conflict resolution programs as their panacea for youth violence and crime. This caution is shared by

RCCP, for example, which promotes the program as only one component of an effective violence prevention strategy.

Other examples of promising middle-school-based programs include the Students for Peace Project (Kelder et al., 1996), the Richmond Youth Against Violence Project (Farrell, Meyer, & Dahlberg, 1996), PACT (Hammond & Yung, 1993), and Peer Culture Development programs (Gottfredson, Gottfredson, & Cook, 1983; see Table 8.1). Students for Peace seeks to modify the school environment, promote peer leadership, and educate parents and students about violence prevention. The Richmond Project focuses on African American middle school students in an urban setting. The 16-session program "Responding in Peaceful and Positive Ways" promotes positive and healthy alternatives to interpersonal and situational violence. Both of these programs are currently undergoing intensive longitudinal evaluations.

High School Programs. While many high school students are also exposed to conflict mediation programs, several other kinds of interventions are more prevalent with older students. These include job training programs, mentoring programs, and "Rites of Passage" programs. Violence prevention at the high school level, such as the Omega Boys Club in San Francisco (Act Against Violence, 1995), also focuses more frequently on delinquent youth and those at risk for gang involvement.

Self-Enhancement, Inc. in Portland, Oregon, is a grassroots, community-service organization that provides services to at-risk middle- and high school youth. The program works primarily at the individual and interpersonal levels to build resilience and promote the pursuit of healthy, productive lives. Program staff work around the clock to mentor and be available to youth in time of need. The program consists of classroom activities, what is referred to as Exposure Education, and proactive education. Classroom education focuses on anger management, conflict resolution, and problem solving. Exposure education consists of field trips to community agencies. Proactive education includes involving students in assemblies, media productions, and newsletters that are created to promote nonviolence (Gabriel, Hopson, Haskins, & Powell, 1996). Reviews of other programs for older adolescents can be found in Hoffman (1996), Walker et al. (1995), the U.S. Department of Justice (1995), and in Tolan and Guerra (1994), which contains a review of information on program effectiveness.

Community/School Partnerships. One of the most consistent findings from youth violence prevention programs is that parental involvement is extremely important to the success and maintenance of any intervention. Programs with a home/school focus typically include opportunities for parent workshops or training sessions on such topics as monitoring, effective discipline, increasing parental involvement at school, effectively modeling a positive attachment to school, and endorsing positive values related to educational achievement (Steinberg, 1996). Partnerships also stress increased parental awareness and buying into school expectations and consequences for failure to complete school work or for discipline problems. The most effective school programs are the ones that have parental support, with parents backing up school limits and consequences at home. This would also facilitate communication between school staff and parents about which children are experiencing difficulties. It is extremely important that interventions be introduced early, as soon as indicators for significant behavior problems first emerge.

Summary

We have attempted to provide a brief overview of the complex myriad risk factors related to the etiology and onset of youth violent behavior, arguing that effective prevention will emerge only from a developmentally focused perspective on aggression and violence. A developmental framework can illustrate the interdependent nature of the many risk factors related to aggression and violence, as well as the many potential choice points for preventive interventions to occur. We then reviewed the major components of effective prevention efforts, starting with the concepts of violence as learned behavior and aggression as a stable behavior whose early onset predicts future risk for violence. It is helpful to view violence prevention strategies from the perspective of universal and targeted approaches. The most effective strategies are long term, systematic in their treatment of multiple risk factors at multiple levels (individual, family, neighborhood, community), and they are comprehensive in that they include both universal and targeted preventive interventions in a continuum of care for youth and families.

If we are to manage the problem of youth violent behavior effectively, we must be hopeful rather than helpless. We must start early, rather than wait until the window of opportunity has diminished beyond the limits of effecting change. We must be persistent, rather than shortsighted and easily frustrated. We must be proactive, rather than reactive to the winds of political change and social outrage. Violent behavior by youth and against youth will not go away soon, but there are many efforts around the country that hold great promise, both for our present and for our future. The time to act is now, for the waiting and wondering are over.

References

Aber, J. L., Brown, J. L., Chaudry, N., Jones, S., & Samples, F. (1996). The evaluation of the Resolving Conflicts Creatively Program: An overview. *American Journal of Preventive Medicine, 12*(Suppl.), 82-90.

Act Against Violence. (1995). *A guide to action: National Campaign to Reduce Youth Violence*. New York: Educational Resources Center, THIRTEEN WNET.

American Psychological Association. (1993). *Summary report of the American Psychological Association Commission on Violence and Youth* (Vol. 1). Washington, DC: Author.

Boney-McCoy, S., & Finkelhor, D. (1995). Psychosocial sequelae of violence victimization in a national youth sample. *Journal of Consulting and Clinical Psychology, 63,* 726-736.

Botvin, G. L., Batson, H. W., Witss-Vitale, S., Bess, V., Baker, E., & Dusenbury, L. (1989). A psychosocial approach to smoking prevention for urban black youth. *Public Health Reports, 12,* 279-296.

Bower, E. M. (1987). Prevention: A word whose time has come. *American Journal of Orthopsychiatry, 57,* 4-5.

Bretherton, D., Collins, L., & Ferretti, C. (1993). Dealing with conflict: Assessment of a course for secondary school students. *Australian Psychologist, 28,* 105-111.

Brier, N. (1995). Predicting antisocial behavior in youngsters displaying poor academic achievement: A review of risk factors. *Developmental and Behavioral Pediatrics, 16,* 271-276.

Centers for Disease Control. (1995, March). CDC surveillance summaries. *Mortality and Morbidity Weekly Report, 44*(SS-1).

Centerwall, B. S. (1992). Television and violence. *Journal of the American Medical Association, 267,* 3059-3063.

Coie, J. F., Lochman, J. E., Terry, R., & Hymna, C. (1992). Predicting early adolescent disorder from childhood aggression and peer rejection. *Journal of Consulting and Clinical Psychology, 60,* 783-792.

Coulton, C., Korbin, J., & Su, M. (1996). Measuring neighborhood context for young children in an urban area. *American Journal of Community Psychology, 24,* 5-32.

Cohen, P., Velez, C. N., Brook, J., & Smith, J. (1989). Mechanisms of the relation between perinatal problems, early childhood illness, and psychopathology in late childhood and adolescence. *Child Development, 60,* 701-709.

Crawford, D., & Bodine, R. (1996). *Conflict resolution education: A guide to implementing programs in schools, youth-serving organizations, and community and juvenile justice settings.* Washington, DC: National Institute of Justice.

Derksen, D. J., & Strasburger, V. C. (1996). Media and television violence: Effects on violence, aggression, and antisocial behaviors in children. In A. M. Hoffman (Ed.), *Schools, violence, and society.* Westport, CT: Praeger.

Dodge, K. A. (1993, March). *Effects of intervention on children at high risk for conduct problems.* Paper presented at the Biennial Meeting of the Society for Research in Child Development, New Orleans.

Dodge, K. A., Price, J. M., Bachorowski, J. A., & Newman, J. P. (1990). Hostile attributional biases in severely aggressive adolescents. *Journal of Abnormal Psychology, 99,* 385-392.

Durant, R., Cadenhead, C., & Pendergast, R. (1994). Factors associated with the use of violence among urban black adolescents. *American Journal of Public Health, 84,* 612-617.

Earls, F. J. (1994). Violence and today's youth. *Critical Issues for Children and Youth, 4,* 4-23.

Ellickson, P. L., Bell, R. M., & McGuigan, K. (1993). Preventing adolescent drug use: Long-term results of a junior high program. *American Journal of Public Health, 83,* 856-861.

Elliott, D. E. (1994). Serious violent offenders: Onset, developmental course, and termination. *Criminology, 32,* 1-21.

Embry, D. D., & Flannery, D. J. (1999). Two sides of the coin: Multilevel prevention and intervention to reduce youth violent behavior. In D. J. Flannery & C. R. Huff (Eds.), *Youth violence: Prevention, intervention, and social policy* (pp. 53-81). Washington, DC: American Psychiatric Press.

Embry, D. D., Flannery, D. J., Vazsonyi, A. T., Powell, K. E., & Atha, H. (1996). PeaceBuilders: A theoretically driven, school-based model for early violence prevention. *American Journal of Preventive Medicine, 12,* 91-100.

Eron, L. R., Gentry, J. H., & Schlegel, P. (1993). *Reason to hope: A psychosocial perspective on violence and youth.* Washington, DC: American Psychological Association.

Eron, L. D., & Huesmann, R. (1990). The stability of aggressive behavior—Even unto the third generation. In M. Lewis & S. M. Miller (Eds.), *Handbook of developmental psychopathology* (pp. 147-156). New York: Plenum.

Esbensen, F. A., & Osgood, D. W. (1996). *GREAT program effectiveness: Results from the 1995 cross-sectional survey of eighth grade students.* Unpublished technical reprint.

Farrell, A., & Meyer, A. L. (1997). The effectiveness of a school-based curriculum for reducing violence among urban sixth-grade students. *American Journal of Public Health, 87,* 979-984.

Farrell, A., Meyer, A., & Dahlberg, L. (1996). Richmond Youth Against Violence: A school based program for urban adolescents. *American Journal of Preventive Medicine, 12*(Suppl.), 13-21.

Farrington, D. P. (1991). Childhood aggression and adult violence: Early precursors and later life outcomes. In D. J. Peplar & K. Rubin (Eds.), *The development and treatment of childhood aggression* (pp. 5-29). Hillsdale, NJ: Lawrence Erlbaum.

Finkelhor, D., & Dziuba-Leatherman, J. (1994). Victimization of children. *American Psychologist, 49,* 173-183.

Flannery, D. J. (1996). A developmental perspective on the effects of violent environments on children. In W. Reed (Ed.), *Violence and trauma: Understanding and responding to the effects of violence on young children.* Cleveland, OH: Cleveland State University, Urban Child Research Center.

Flannery, D. J. (1997). *School violence: Risk, preventive intervention and policy.* ERIC Clearinghouse on Urban Education, Institute for Urban and Minority Education. Urban Diversity Series No. 109. New York: Columbia University.

Flannery, D. J., Huff, C. R., & Manos, M. J. (1996). Youth gangs: A developmental perspective. In T. Gullotta, G. Adams, & R. Montemayor (Eds.), *Delinquency, juvenile justice, and adolescence* (Advances in Adolescent Development, Vol. 10). Thousand Oaks, CA: Sage.

Flannery, D. J., Singer, M., Williams, L., & Castro, P. (1999). Adolescent violence exposure and victimization at home: Coping and psychological trauma symptoms. *International Review of Victimology, 6,* 63-82.

Flannery, D. J., Vazsonyi, A., Embry, D., Powell, K., Atha, H., & Vesterdal, W. (1997). *Longitudinal evidence of effective violence prevention: A randomized controlled trial of PeaceBuilders elementary school intervention.* Unpublished manuscript. (Available from Institute for the Study and Prevention of Violence, 1305 Terrace Hall, Kent State University, Kent, OH 44242)

Flannery, D. J., & Williams, L. L. (1997). *Final report: Evaluation of the Young Ladies, Young Gentlemen Clubs, Partnership for a Safer Cleveland.* Cleveland, OH. (Available from Institute for the Study and Prevention of Violence, 1305 Terrace Hall, Kent State University, Kent, OH 44242)

Fraser, M. W. (1996). Aggressive behavior in childhood and early adolescence: An ecological-developmental perspective on youth violence. *Social Work, 41,* 347-361.

Gabriel, R. M., Hopson, T., Haskins, M., & Powell, K. (1996). Building competence and resilience in the prevention of youth violence. *American Journal of Preventive Medicine, 12*(Suppl.), 48-55.

Gerbner, G., & Signorielli, N. (1990). *Violence profile, 1967 through 1988-89: Enduring patterns.* Unpublished manuscript, Annenberg School of Communications, University of Pennsylvania.

Goldstein, A. P. (1999). Teaching prosocial behavior to antisocial youth. In D. J. Flannery & C. R. Huff (Eds.), *Youth violence: Prevention, intervention and social policy* (pp. 279-302). Washington, DC: American Psychiatric Press.

Goldstein, A. P., Apter, S. J., & Hartoonian, B. (1984). *School violence.* Engelwood Cliffs, NJ: Prentice Hall.

Goldstein, A. P., & Glick, B. (1987). *Aggression replacement training.* Champaign, IL: Research Press.

Gordon, R. S. (1983). An operational classification of disease prevention. *Public Health Reports, 98,* 107-109.

Gorman-Smith, D., & Avery, L. (1999). Family factors in youth violence. In D. J. Flannery & C. R. Huff (Eds.), *Youth violence: Prevention, intervention, and social policy* (pp. 253-277). Washington, DC: American Psychiatric Press.

Gottfredson, G. D., Gottfredson, D. C., & Cook, M. S. (1983). *The School Action Effectiveness Study: Second interim report* (Report No. 342). Baltimore, MD: Johns Hopkins University, Center for Social Organization of Schools.

Graham, P. (1994). Prevention. In M. Rutter, E. Taylor, & L. Hersov (Eds.), *Child and adolescent psychiatry* (3rd ed., pp. 815-282). Oxford, UK: Blackwell Scientific.

Greenberg, M. T., Kusche, C. A., Cook, E. T., & Quamma, J. P. (1995). Promoting emotional competence in school-aged children: The effects of the PATHS curriculum. *Development and Psychopathology, 7,* 117-136.

Grossman, D. C., Neckerman, H. J., Koepsell, T. D., Liu, P. Y., Asher, K. N., Beland, K., Frey, K., & Rivara, F. P. (1997). Effectiveness of a violence prevention curriculum among children in elementary school. *Journal of the American Medical Association, 277,* 1605-1611.

Hammond, W. R., & Yung, B. R. (1992). *Evaluation and activity report: Positive Adolescent Choices Training (PACT) program* (Grant No. MCJ=393A15-01-1; pp. 75, 77). Ohio Office of Criminal Justice Services. Dayton, OH: Wright State University, School of Professional Psychology.

Hammond, W. R., & Yung, B. (1993). Psychology's role in the public health response to assaultive violence among young African-American men. *American Psychologist, 48,* 142-154.

Hawkins, J. D., Catalano, R. F., Morrison, D. M., O'Donnell, J., Abbott, R. D., & Day, L. E. (1992). The Seattle Social Development Project: Effects of the first four years on protective factors and problem behaviors. In J. McCord & R. Tremblay (Eds.), *The prevention of antisocial behavior in children* (pp. 139-161). New York: Guilford.

Hawkins, J. D., Von Cleve, E., & Catalano, R. F. (1991). Reducing early childhood aggression: Results of a primary prevention program. *American Academy of Child Adolescent Psychiatry, 30,* 208-217.

Hoffman, A. M. (1996). *Schools, violence, and society.* Westport, CT: Praeger.

Huesmann, L. R., Maxwell, C. D., Eron, L., Dahlberg, L., Guerra, N., Tolan, P., VanAcker, R., & Henry, D. (1996). Evaluating a cognitive/ecological program for the prevention of aggression among urban children. *American Journal of Preventive Medicine, 12*(Suppl.), 120-128.

Huesmann, L. R., & Moise, J. F. (1999). The stability and continuity of aggression from early childhood to young adulthood. In D. J. Flannery & C. R. Huff (Eds.), *Youth violence: Prevention, intervention and social policy.* Washington, DC: American Psychiatric Press.

Hughes, J., & Hasbrouk, J. (1996). Television violence: Implications for violence prevention. *School Psychology Review, 25,* 134-152.

Institute of Medicine. (1994). *Reducing risks for mental disorders: Frontiers for preventive intervention research.* Washington, DC: National Academy Press.

Kandel, E., & Mednick, S. A. (1991). Perinatal complications predict violence offending. *Criminology, 29,* 519-529.

Kazdin, A. E. (1994). Interventions for aggressive and antisocial children. In L. D. Eron, J. H. Gentry, & P. Schlegel (Eds.), *Reason to hope: A psychosocial perspective on violence and youth.* Washington, DC: American Psychological Association.

Kelder, S. H., Orpinas, P., McAlister, A., Frankowski, R., Parcel, G. S., & Friday, J. (1996). The Students for Peace Project: A comprehensive violence-prevention program for middle school students. *American Journal of Preventive Medicine, 12*(Suppl.), 22-30.

Kellam, S. G., & Rebok, G. W. (1992). Building developmental and etiological theory through epidemiologically based preventive intervention trials. In J. McCord & R. E. Tremblay (Eds.), *Preventing antisocial behavior: Interventions from birth through adolescence* (pp. 62-195). New York: Guilford.

Krug, E. G., Brener, N. D., Dahlberg, L. L., Ryan, G. W., & Powell, K. E. (1997). A pilot evaluation of a school-based violence prevention program. *American Journal of Preventive Medicine, 13,* 459-463.

Larson, J. F. (1992). Anger and aggression management techniques through the Think First Curriculum. *Journal of Offender Rehabilitation, 18,* 101-117.

Loeber, R., Wung, P., Keenan, K., Giroux, B., Stouthamer-Loeber, M., Van Kammen, W. B., & Maughan, B. (1993). Developmental pathways in disruptive child behavior. *Development and Psychopathology, 5,* 103-133.

Martinez, P., & Richters, J. E. (1993). The NIMH Community Violence Project: II. Children's distress symptoms associated with violence exposure. *Psychiatry, 56,* 22-35.

Moffitt, T. E. (1990). The neuropsychology of juvenile delinquency: A critical review. In M. Tonry & N. Morris (Eds.), *Crime and justice: A review of the literature.* Chicago: University of Chicago Press.

Osofsky, J. D. (1997). *Children in a violent society.* New York: Guilford.

Patterson, G. R., Reid, J. B., & Dishion, T. J. (1992). *Antisocial boys.* Eugene, OR: Castalia.

Perry, B. (1997). Incubated in terror: Neurodevelopmental factors in the "cycle of violence." In J. Osofsky (Ed.), *Children in a violent society* (pp. 124-149). New York: Guilford.

Peters, R. D., & McMahon, R. J. (1996). *Preventing childhood disorders, substance abuse, and delinquency.* Thousand Oaks, CA: Sage.

Powell, K. E., & Hawkins, D. F. (1996). Youth violence prevention. *American Journal of Preventive Medicine, 12*(5), 1-131.

Prothrow-Stith, D. (1987). *Violence prevention curriculum for adolescents.* Newton, MA: Education Development Center.

Raine, A., Brennan, P., & Mednick, S. A. (1994). Birth complications combined with early maternal rejection at age 1 year predispose to violent crime at age 18 years. *Archives of General Psychiatry, 51,* 984-988.

Reiss, A. J., Jr., & Roth, J. (1993). *Understanding and preventing violence.* Washington, DC: National Academy Press.

Resnick, M. D., Bearman, P. S., Blum, R. W., et al. (1997). Protecting adolescents from harm: Findings from the National Longitudinal Study on Adolescent Health. *Journal of the American Medical Association, 278,* 823-832.

Ringwalt, C., Greene, J., Ennett, S., Iachan, R., Clayton, R. R., & Leukfeld, C. G. (1994). *Past and future directions of the DARE program: An evaluation review* (Draft of final report [Award #91-DD-CX-K053]). Washington, DC: National Institute of Justice.

Rivara, F. P., Shapherd, J. P., Farrington, D. P., Richmond, P. W., & Cannon, P. (1995). Victim as offender in youth violence. *Annals of Emergency Medicine, 26,* 609-614.

Rossman, S. B., & Morley, E. (1995). *The National Evaluation of Cities in Schools: Executive summary* (Cooperative agreement #91-JN-CX-K001, Office of Juvenile Justice and Delinquency Prevention). Washington, DC: U.S. Department of Justice.

Sampson, R. J., Raudenbush, S. W., & Earls, F. (1997). Neighborhoods and violent crime: A multilevel study of collective efficacy. *Science, 277,* 918-924.

Singer, M., Anglin, T., Song, L., & Lunghofer, L. (1995). Adolescents' exposure to violence and associated symptoms of psychological trauma. *Journal of the American Medical Association, 273,* 477-482.

Singer, M., & Flannery, D. (1997). *Rates of school violence among children and adolescents in grades 3-12: Psychological trauma symptoms, violent behavior and coping strategies.* Unpublished manuscript. (Available from Institute for the Study and Prevention of Violence, 1305 Terrace Hall, Kent State University, Kent, OH 44242)

Singer, M., Miller, D., Guo, S., Slovak, K., & Frierson, T. (1998). *The mental health consequences of children's exposure to violence.* Cleveland, OH: Case Western University, Mandel School of Applied Social Sciences, Cuyahoga County Mental Health Research Institute.

Steinberg, L. (1996). *Why school reform has failed and what parents need to do.* New York: Simon & Schuster.

Thornberry, T. P. (1994). *Violent families and youth violence.* Washington, DC: U.S. Department of Justice, Office of Justice Programs, National Institute of Justice.

Tolan, P., & Guerra, N. (1994). *What works in reducing adolescent violence: An empirical review of the field.* Boulder, CO: Center for the Study and Prevention of Violence.

Tolan, P. H., Guerra, N. G., & Kendall, P. C. (1995). A developmental perspective on antisocial behavior in children and adolescents: Toward a unified risk and intervention framework. *Journal of Consulting and Clinical Psychology, 63,* 579-584.

Tremblay, R. E., Kurtz, L., Masse, L. C., Vitaro, F., & Phil, R. O. (1995). A bimodal preventive intervention for disruptive kindergarten boys: Its impact through adolescence. *Journal of Consulting and Clinical Psychology, 63,* 560-568.

U.S. Department of Justice. (1995, June). *Guide for implementing the comprehensive strategy for serious, violent, and chronic offenders.* Washington, DC: U.S. Department of Justice, Office of Juvenile Justice on Delinquency Prevention.

Walker, H. M., Colvin, G., & Ramsey, E. (1995). *Anti-social behavior in school: Strategies and best practices.* Pacific Grove, CA: Brooks/Cole.

Webster, D. W. (1993). The unconvincing case for school-based conflict resolution programs for adolescents. *Health Affairs, 4,* 126-141.

Werner, E. E. (1994). Overcoming the odds. *Developmental and Behavioral Pediatrics, 15,* 131-136.

Widom, C. S. (1989). The cycle of violence. *Science, 244,* 160-166.

Yoshikawa, H. (1994). Prevention as cumulative protection: Effects of early family support and education on chronic delinquency and its risks. *Psychological Bulletin, 115,* 28-54.

• *CHAPTER 9*

Consensus and Contradictions in Understanding Domestic Violence: Implications for Policy and Model Programs

PAMELA JENKINS

BARBARA DAVIDSON

In her poetry, Muriel Rukeyser poses the question, "What would happen if one woman told the truth?" (cited in Howe & Bass, 1973, p. 100). She answers, "The world would split open." Over the past two decades, many women have broken their silence to tell their stories of domestic violence. In some ways, shining the light on this once well-guarded secret has split the world open. The movement to end violence against women has grown from a few grassroots organizations to a multilayered, multifaceted network of agencies, groups, and coalitions. Shelters across the world remain as the symbols of the continuing need to protect women and children. Local, state, and national governments have acknowledged the need for laws, policies, and procedures to ensure the safety of women who are victims of domestic violence. Institutions and businesses have begun to design and adopt protocols to respond to domestic violence. Perhaps even more telling is the use of domestic violence as grist for fictive story lines in novels, films, and television, and as topical material for news journalism, news magazines, and talk show programming. Shining the light on this issue in these many venues has also brought to the surface the areas of consensus and contradiction in our understanding of domestic violence.

The Setting

During the Reform Era at the turn of the century, activists documented the brutality that many women suffered in their marriages (Gordon, 1988; Pleck, 1987). The first organized attempts to address the issue about women and violence, however, emerged some 50 years later with the second wave of the women's movement in Western Europe and the United States (Gordon, 1988; Pleck, 1987; Schechter, 1982). The level of interest and involvement has risen since that time, culminating in the adoption of the "cause" at the highest levels of government, the justice system, the medical and mental health institutions, and the business world. During the Clinton presidency, the U.S. government passed the first federal legislation (The Violence Against Women Act as part of the 1994 Crime Act) aimed at supporting victim service programs, strengthening antiviolence laws, promoting effective police and court responses, and establishing links among agencies for developing coordinated responses to domestic violence at the local and state level. The U.S. Surgeon General named domestic violence a leading cause of injury to women, and the American Medical Association proposed medical setting protocols, outlining proper and effective responses to domestic violence victims. Corporations have begun to create safety policies for employees in an effort to address workplace violence resulting from domestic assaults. The problem of domestic violence has rapidly developed from an "unheard of" status in the 1960s to its current status as a major problem facing the country, with attendant concern and funding.

In the rapid evolution of potential solutions, certain assumptions about domestic violence and about battered women became the platform upon which beliefs, practices, policies, and then laws were built. Because the change in the conceptualization of domestic violence, from individual problem to societal concern, occurred so quickly, there has been little time for assessment and evaluation. In this chapter, we examine some of the more commonly held assumptions about domestic violence and their impact on what has been considered the "best practice" policies and programs. We discuss the model programs that embrace, to some degree, some of the commonly held assumptions about domestic violence.

The data for this chapter are derived from a variety of qualitative strategies including interviews with battered women, law enforcement, and shelter workers. Focus groups were conducted with law enforcement, homeless advocates, and battered women's advocates. Field notes from participation observation at law enforcement training and domestic violence coordinating councils were also used.

Assumption One: Everyone defines the problem of domestic violence in the same way. To define and address a social problem, it must first be named (Feagin & Feagin, 1990; Merton & Nisbet, 1971). Abuse that occurs in families has a variety of names, and controversy exists in the literature about the name chosen and its implications (Gelles & Loseke, 1993; Jenkins, 1996; Kurz, 1989). What the problem is named reflects its definition and has far-reaching effects for the development of theory, practice, and treatment. "Family violence" describes a broad range of behaviors whose victim might be anyone in a familial relationship. "Spouse abuse" implies marital violence, abuse committed to or by a spouse. These terms suggest that the theoretical analysis of the problem is gender neutral. For example, some scholars have used these terms to include the possibility that men are as likely victims as women (Gelles, 1993; Gelles & Straus, 1988). In treatment and intervention practice, programs with this analysis attempt to treat families as a whole, encouraging family therapeutic efforts such as couple counseling.

"Domestic violence" has been used to indicate a narrower range of family-based violence—that of intimate partner violence. As the term chosen most often by victim service providers (the national coalition and most state coalitions of victim service providers use this name in their titles), domestic violence implies a gender-specific analysis that is not apparent in its name. Further, "woman abuse," when referring to abuse of an adult woman by her intimate partner, implies a theoretical analysis that is gender specific. Scholars in this area contend that the violence is not only perpetrated more often by men, but is also sanctioned by the patriarchal beliefs of cultures (Dobash & Dobash, 1979, 1992; Yllö, 1993). Treatment and intervention programs with this perspective place priority on services and safety for women victims.

In this chapter, we use the term *domestic violence,* taking the position that women are primarily the victims in domestic violence and that the dynamics of violence are represented best by a gender-specific analysis. While many of the model programs we discuss are gender specific, the issue of who are the victims is far from settled. In the following section, we discuss how the assumption of women as victims is used to develop certain solutions.

Assumption Two: The solution for women who are victims of domestic violence is to leave the situation. By asking, "Why doesn't she leave?" or in advising battered women to leave, it is implied that battered women should disrupt and uproot their lives—leaving jobs and schools and neighborhood networks to be "safe" from an abusive partner. This may seem a small price to pay for the absence of violence in a woman's life, but the act of leaving is much more difficult than it appears. Underlying this assumption is the idea that the subject for change is the battered woman, rather than her abusive partner.

What is often not recognized is that leaving or attempting to leave a violent home is one of the more dangerous times for women in a violent relationship (Hart, 1993). This is so likely an outcome that the term *separation violence* has come into recent usage to describe the escalation of abuse tactics at this point. The abuser's control over his victim's decisions and behavior is challenged by her desire for or actual departure. A variety of behaviors may occur: The frequency and severity of violence may escalate, surveillance and stalking behavior become probable, and the abusive partner may both beg and threaten her to return (Se'ver, 1997).

When a battered woman does leave, she may find safety only temporarily. She has three options: to return to her abuser, to establish independent living near her family and community, or to establish independent living in a new community. Each of these choices holds the possibility of more violence. She may be at more immediate risk in returning to her abuser, but the two other choices may not afford much more safety. If she returns to her family and community in hopes of enjoying their support, she may be accessible to her abuser through either his knowledge or her family's and friends' collusion with the perpetrator. This close bond between the victim, her community, and the perpetrator is described below by a battered woman's advocate.

> This woman came to our shelter from two counties away. She lives way out in the country. One of her nearest neighbors told her about the shelter. The neighbor managed to watch and see when the husband left. She went down the road and told the woman about the services. The battered woman was very reluctant. Her neighbor, however, convinced her to come to the shelter. At the intake, the neighbor was very supportive and the woman remained at the shelter. The woman staying at the shelter gave the accessible shelter phone number to the neighbor. The neighbor turned around and went back to her rural community. When she arrived home, the neighbor found the batterer on her doorstep crying about the woman. The neighbor calls the woman at the shelter. When she gets the woman on the phone, she hands the phone over to the batterer. The victim's whole support for being at the shelter was shattered. She went back. Her neighbor told her that it had never dawned on her that the man would now become her problem.

Even if a woman successfully leaves and relocates to another community and keeps any ties to her old life, she may still be accessible to him through her workplace, her ties with people from her old community, or court-ordered sharing of child custody. In moving to a new community with no support system, she may become more vulnerable, as a woman alone, to stranger violence and crime.

The assumption—that women should leave to be safe—has given rise to the creation of shelters for battered women and their children, perhaps to the exclusion of the development of other solutions that might make battered women safe in their own homes. Shelters for battered women are considered the model of services for battered women. The following sections discuss what arises when shelters are assumed to be the first, and sometimes only, solution for victims of domestic violence.

Assumption Three: Any woman who is battered can go to a shelter. Other explanations underlie this assumption: that all battered women are alike, have similar problems and needs, and that shelters have the resources and capabilities to meet these needs. In this section we examine some of the issues that result in battered women

being unserved or underserved by shelters: class background, im-
migration status, sexual orientation, shelter rules and restrictions,
mental illness, substance abuse, and lack of programs or services.

In the United States, shelters provide emergency housing and
sometimes longer-term ("transitional" or "second-stage") housing
for battered women and their children. Since 1974, approximately
1,500 shelters have opened in the United States (Schechter, 1996;
Sullivan, 1997), operating on a quasi-emergency basis with varying,
but time-limited, stays. Shelters usually provide some form of
counseling, advocacy, and referral to other agencies. Opportunities
are provided for women to learn and to establish safety plans, access
the legal system, and garner group support.

Shelter staff are the first to admit that shelters can solve only part
of the problem. Shelters provide service to those who seek them
out, know how to find them, and are eligible for services. Many
women do not know about shelters, are reluctant to use shelters,
cannot access shelters, or, for various reasons, are not eligible for
services. Many places, particularly rural areas, do not have shelters
or services; many places, particularly large metropolitan areas, do
not have enough services for the demand.

Shelters are often the last resort for many women who have tried
other options. Women with more resources (material, educational,
and social) may have less need for use of the shelter. Consequently,
women with limited incomes are overrepresented in the shelter
population. Shelter workers describe what happens when a middle-
class woman enters a shelter.

> It is hard to tell what class women are at first. But, we have begun to
> see a pattern of behavior with middle class women. They come in,
> look around and then seem a little surprised by the lack of privacy,
> the quality of the shelter, and the number and kinds of people that
> are there. Right after they see all this, they are polite. They then begin
> to think of reasons why they can't stay after all. If they stay and
> participate in shelter activities, they then begin to verbalize reasons
> that make them different from the rest of the women there.

Minority women are also a group that may seek shelter services.
The issue of violence to racial/ethnic minorities is difficult to
unravel (Crenshaw, 1994; Kanuha, 1996; Sullivan, 1997). Because
it is commonly held that violence toward women also knows no

color barriers, the cultural difference between women often goes unrecognized (Crenshaw, 1994), Further, a woman of color is not only a victim of domestic violence, but also a victim of racial discrimination.

In addition, immigrant women find themselves with few options when they are battered. The term *immigrant woman* classifies very different women as the same. Some of the women who come to this country are here illegally. Hence, asking law enforcement to respond to their problems often leaves them at risk for other punitive measures such as incarceration or deportation. Also, the laws concerning marriage of a foreign national to an American citizen require a certain length of time before that person can have rights as a citizen. Such restrictions often prevent women from seeking help from agencies where the consequences may be punitive. These two legal difficulties are often compounded by the shelter staff's inability to understand her language, customs, or religious beliefs (Koss et al., 1994).

Women who are battered by other women find themselves in awkward positions in shelter life. Shelters were created by and for women who are harmed by men. The prevention and treatment of domestic violence assumes that the perpetrator is a man. Women who are abused by their lesbian partners may not find support from the staff or a way to relate to other residents of the shelter. Programs have begun to address the issues of lesbian battering as the literature is growing in the field (Lobel, 1986; Sullivan, 1997).

Shelter policies may also limit who enters or stays at a shelter. Shelters, as they become part of the institutional response, set rules about who can enter the shelters and who cannot. Rules vary from shelter to shelter but they may include not housing male children who are over a certain age (usually because of the facility's physical accommodations rather than philosophical reasons). Some shelters exclude women who have lived in the shelter before, or very recently; women who have previously lived in the shelter then returned to abusive partners; and/or women whose abusive partners have learned of the shelter location.

Battered women who also experience mental health or substance abuse problems are other populations that may be unserved or underserved by shelters. Sometimes shelters exclude or offer minimal services to these women out of concern for the safety of the other shelter residents. Battered women whose problems are compounded by substance abuse, mental health issues, or limited functioning require an enormous expenditure of time and energy by overworked shelter staff. As this quote by a shelter worker illustrates, the complicating factors of mental illness or current/chronic substance abuse strains the services of many shelters and places the shelter staff in the awkward position of refusing services to people who are in need.

> We see a lot of people who are just borderline able to function in the world and not quite ill enough to be continually in an institution but have bouts where they should and sometimes are in an institution. I think there are women who have below average intelligence whether they have been tested and a label has been given to them or not they really have a difficult time functioning independently so they're always living on the edge. And they keep coming around to us.

It seems that as other sources of care are reduced, more and more women whose main problem is not "domestic violence" seek services from battered women's shelters.

> It just seems like more and more homeless women with really serious drug or alcohol problems and mental health problems are coming to the shelter. And, many of them were battered women, but it makes the work a whole lot harder for the people that work with them. I think that when women have both kinds of problems [mental health and substance abuse] that it's harder for our staff to feel connected to them.

Services specifically designed to address mental illness and substance abuse are most often gender neutral at best, or geared more generally for men. This creates a dilemma for shelter staff who feel untrained to handle these issues, yet reluctant to refer to potentially ineffective or harmful treatment programs.

Moreover, many communities in the United States do not have shelters. While there has been a phenomenal growth in shelters, there are still areas unserved or underserved. Women residing in rural and small communities often do not have access to shelters. Programs and services are long distances away, and safety in the community is difficult as the communities are close-knit where a battered woman can be easily tracked. Even in urban areas, some women lead isolated and restricted lives where information about shelters is not readily available (Sullivan, 1997).

Some shelters and services are attempting to modify their programs to meet the needs described in this section. Recently some models have begun to emerge to address the specific needs of battered women. The Minnesota Coalition for Battered Women created a Lesbian Battering Intervention Project, responsible for developing a training manual for battered women's program workers on recognizing and addressing lesbian battering, including guidelines for assessing shelter services for battered lesbians (Elliott, 1990). The Family Violence Prevention Fund, in conjunction with immigrants' rights groups, created an education and training manual, *Domestic Violence in Immigrant and Refugee Communities: Asserting the Rights of Battered Women.* This manual has been made available to the domestic violence service community and seeks to propose solutions to legal hurdles, accessibility problems, and community resources for battered immigrant women (Jang, Mauir, & Pendleton, 1997).

Longtime activists and writers in the field of domestic violence, Susan Schechter (1987) and Edward Gondolf (1998), have designed cross-training curricula for domestic violence workers, substance abuse workers, and mental health practitioners. The Elizabeth Stone House in Jamaica, Massachusetts, houses battered women with mental health issues as dually affected women (Elizabeth Stone House, 1990); the Haven House in Pasadena, California, one of the first shelters for battered women, was created by a substance abuse program to house abused partners of substance abusers, and does so to this day. Other programs have also addressed the issue of chemical dependency and battered women (Wright, 1982).

Given these limitations, it is apparent that not all battered women can or will go to shelters, and that shelters alone cannot provide adequate long-term safety. Although valuable and essential, shelters in and of themselves do not constitute the solution to domestic violence. So, as a model of safety for battered women, shelters represent only part of the answer. Shelters are an important component of providing safety for women and their children. Another avenue that is available for individual women seeking help is through the criminal justice system. In recent years, there has been increased pressure to make the criminal justice system more responsive to victims of domestic violence.

Assumption Four: If the criminal justice system would do its job properly, women would be safe. Prior to the mid-1980s, many police jurisdictions reacted to domestic violence calls from the perspective of order maintenance rather than crime fighting. In that mode, police response was likely separation of the couple at the scene of a domestic violence incident, requiring a "cool off" period, or requiring one party to leave, but rarely writing a report or making an arrest. Since that time, law enforcement has moved toward recognizing and treating domestic violence as a crime (Dickstein & Nadelson, 1989; Fagan, 1996; Hirschel & Hutchinson, 1991). In fact, the entire justice system's response to battered women has changed dramatically in the past 10 years (Berk & Newton, 1985; Ferraro, 1989). Most states and municipalities have adopted proarrest or mandatory arrest policies about domestic violence cases, although the impact of such policies is still under review (see Bachman & Choker, 1995; Buzawa & Buzawa, 1993; Schmidt & Sherman, 1993). Some have contended that proarrest policies create more problems than they solve and should be abandoned. Various studies have shown these new policies to work part of the time, not to work at all, or to work for only certain populations. Others contend that proarrest policies send an important message of support to the victim and of serious and swift consequences to the abuser (Stark, 1993). The common, and perhaps overly simplistic, belief is that if the police and prosecution would do their jobs properly, women would be safe from abuse. Evidence of this belief is that battered women are generally advised by friends and professionals alike to consider the police their first call for help in domestic violence incidents. When battered women seek help elsewhere instead, they are often criticized for not having involved the police.

Yet, an unexpected consequence of the new pro- and mandatory arrest policies is the occurrence of dual arrests in certain jurisdictions. When police officers are mandated to make an arrest, they often react by arresting the woman or arresting both parties. This is especially true when officers have not had adequate training in domestic violence and in determining the primary aggressor in a domestic violence incident, or when policies are written so rigidly that there is little discretion for alternative responses. Further, some law enforcement officers' resistance to the new laws and policies may be the result of their perception of forced compliance and of the loss of officer discretion in arrest decisions.

In police training, one common scenario involves a perpetrator (a man) who has some wounds that are allegedly made in self-defense by the victim (a woman). The scenario usually has the following elements:

> Police arrive at a scene and notice that the man is calm, showing a few bite marks to the inside of his forearm. The woman has a bruised eye and several red marks on face and arms. He claims she hit him; she says that he was going to kill me. The questions officers are asked to answer are: Who goes to jail and for what? (Adapted from Resko, 1989)

Even after a day or half day of training, many officers respond by saying that they both go to jail or he is booked with simple assault and she receives a summons. When asked to identify the primary aggressor, officers may say that it has the appearance that both have committed a crime. In their analysis, they see two people with injury and where before they might not have arrested anyone, with the changes in the law—both parties may go to jail.

Other legal system changes include the expansion of protective remedies such as protective orders, which offer relief to the victim in many ways (see Wallace, 1996). In addition to restraining the abuser, the order may allow the victim access to the shared dwelling, assets, child custody, support, mandated intervention program attendance by the abuser, and other such arrangements. Civil and/or criminal penalties may ensue from violations of such orders. Hart (1993) states that legal and personal safety can be created for women when protective orders provide a wide range of relief and include specificity.

However, enforcement of these orders varies widely. In progressive departments where there is a consensus throughout the justice system from judiciary to police departments, violations of protective orders are taken seriously. Practice has not kept abreast of the rapid and sometimes confusing changes in laws and policies. Many in law enforcement feel the correct action for violations of protective orders should be a return to court instead of an arrest. In police training, officers often state their belief that protective orders are not enforceable if she "violates them" by calling him or inviting him over, sometimes taking only the abuser's word on the alleged call or invitation.

Other elements of the criminal justice system are responding to the new emphasis on safety for women (Wallace, 1996). District Attorneys, city attorneys, and county attorneys are implementing no-drop policies that charge the office with proceeding if the victim is reluctant. Sometimes this prosecution can lead to jail (rather than prison) time, but other times it may lead to alternatives rather than incarceration (Cahn & Lerman, 1991). Also, within many prosecution offices are diversion programs where batterers can, under a variety of conditions (either before or after conviction), be part of a court-ordered counseling program. Judges, in lieu of jail time, can sentence a person convicted of a criminal act related to domestic violence, to counseling (Koss et al., 1994).

While results from no-drop policies and/or mandatory counseling program are encouraging, there are contradictions within these programs. As with the police and with shelter response, what really happens within this structure may not be what advocates for battered women intend. For example, prosecutors and judges now complain of reluctant victims, and some are even calling for sanctions of victims who refuse to testify or who recant on the stand. Judges are teaching about reluctant victims to other judges (Judge J. Giarusso, personal communication, October 1997). Also, as dual arrest occurs, women are also going into diversion programs such as anger management classes and other assignments typical for male batterers.

With the passage of the Violence Against Women Act and the Crime Act of 1994, more funding is now directed toward criminal justice agencies who have pro- and mandatory arrest policies, aggressive prosecution, and proactive judges (Koss et al., 1994). The model programs represent progressive police and judicial systems that are coordinated and respond to the needs of battered women.

The attention of the monies and the interest on the criminal justice system has several outcomes. One is that advocates find themselves in partnership with law enforcement in order to receive funds (Koss et al., 1994). The most recent wave of the federal funding with COPS money was to build partnership between advocate groups and law enforcement (*Community Policing to Combat Do-*

mestic Violence Training Manual, 1997). This partnership, for the most part, can have a beneficial effect in that each set of professionals can learn to trust the other. More important, as many cities have found, is that each can learn that the other is not the "enemy."

Another outcome is that the emphasis on law enforcement often leaves other areas unrecognized. The more progressive law enforcement jurisdictions have accomplished the most basic task for law enforcement agencies and advocacy groups: to unite the system's approach to domestic violence. As part of this basic structural change, the roles of each agency need to be examined and uniform training needs to be provided. Cities such as Quincy, Massachusetts; Duluth, Minnesota; and San Diego, California, offer viable models for such coordination.

Other national models outline training for judges and other law enforcement personnel. In 1992, The National Council of Juvenile and Family Court Judges compiled a listing of model "State of the Art Court Programs" to be used as a guide for developing similar policies and practices around the country (McHardy, 1992). The Council describes 18 programs from around the nation dealing with domestic violence in an effort to provide communities an opportunity to improve their court practices by replicating appropriate and practical policies and procedures. All programs stress the importance of having a coordinated response to domestic violence, one that includes effective law enforcement, prosecution, court policies, and treatment programs. These agencies include counselors, state child protection agencies, hospitals, and private doctors. This medical/social service response to domestic violence is as crucial as that of law enforcement or even of shelters. The following section examines how battered women are viewed and treated by the medical/social service fields.

Assumption Five: Medical, mental health, and social services personnel routinely recognize the signs of abuse, and identify battered women who seek their services. Unlike the police or shelters, a woman does not have to identify herself as a battered woman to seek help from medical or social service agencies. For the medical profession, a woman might try to disguise the actual etiology of her injury for safety, or the medical personnel may not ask about how the injury occurred. When a woman seeks counseling, the counselor may not routinely ask about the presence of domestic violence; if the counselor does ask, the woman may not be forthcoming with this information. When a battered woman seeks social services, she may omit any information about domestic violence out of fear she will be found ineligible for services, or that the services she is receiving will be cut off. As a battered woman seeks help from those around her, their response to her has an impact on how she views herself and what next steps she attempts. It is assumed that personnel in the helping professions know and can act appropriately when confronted with symptoms of domestic violence.

Knowledge about the dynamics of domestic violence is relatively recent in the academy and in the applied world of helping professions. Many professionals still see their patients or clients in the way that they were originally trained, that is, looking for physical symptoms or for particular mental disorders such as depression. Some studies have shown that physicians and nurses are not likely to recognize symptoms of abuse unless they are told so directly (Loring & Smith, 1994; Stark & Flitcraft, 1988; Warshaw, 1993). The emergency room setting as well as private physicians and clinics are among the most important and unrecognized places for intervention. Women who would not seek help from shelters or would not call the police might go to their family physician with a vague complaint. Interview techniques and protocols for identification would aid both physicians and nursing staff in assisting some battered women (Sullivan, 1997). One battered woman, who was later charged in her husband's death, describes her encounter with a physician.

> I went to the same doctor for years. He just kept telling me to leave. Once, he told me—don't come back unless you have left him. I never went back to him, because of the circumstances in my life. I had thought, though, that if I went back to him again, I would ask him for his address. I would tell him that me and my four kids were coming to live with him. I would tell him he would have to watch out for his safety because my husband would try to find me. I never got the chance though.

One of the most controversial areas in professional response to domestic violence is that of therapy. The battered woman's movement has challenged the practices of traditionally trained therapists concerning domestic violence. A critical study showed that when therapists were presented with vignettes of wife battering, only

10% of the therapists addressed the issues of women's safety (Hansen, Harway, & Cervantes, 1991; Whalen, 1996). The critique also discusses what is said to women in therapy about their situation. The critiques of statements in therapy can be categorized broadly as victim blaming, coresponsibility for the battering, and assigning no responsibility for the violence in the home (Hansen, 1993). These areas all fall under the broader category of therapists using a gender-neutral, context-free analysis. Part of this same criticism is the objection to couple counseling by many advocates who believe that women are placed at risk in couple counseling. These issues are important not only to the knowledge base of counseling and therapy, but to the battered woman who seeks help. What can happen when counselors are not educated about domestic violence is illustrated in the following story told by a shelter advocate who attended several of the court hearings.

> A woman left her husband because of his abuse, came to the shelter, and eventually attempted to get a divorce from her husband, a police officer. Prior to leaving, she and her husband had gone for years to couple counseling with a family therapist to work out their problems. At the initial session, each member of the couple was told to write down five things that were most troubling about the marriage. At the top of the list of her five things was her husband's violence. Yet, the issue of the violence was never addressed by the counselor in their years of counseling. During the custody hearing, testimony and notes from the counseling sessions were produced, including the initial lists of problems. However, the counselor testified that the father was the more stable, mature and responsible parent, and he was awarded custody of their two small girls. The counselor's dismissal of the violence as an issue translated into the court's dismissal of the violence as an issue, although the battered woman contended at the hearing, as she had from the beginning, that the violence was indeed the pivotal problem in their relationship.

While is it commonly assumed that women are often the chosen custodial parent, this story illustrates how the courts and other professionals often unwittingly help the perpetrator of domestic violence. Joint custody of children is one of the ways that perpetrators can have access to the victims of domestic violence. The issues of custody for women who are victims of domestic violence is complicated by the violence and the fear for herself and her children (Chesler, 1986; Liss & Stahly, 1993).

Another area where public policy has impacted the lives of victims of domestic violence has been in the area of welfare reform. The recent welfare reform is expected to be a problem for battered women, who represent a sizable proportion of those receiving aid. A variety of studies show that between 30% and 75% of the women enrolled in their programs were victims of past of current domestic violence ("Domestic Violence and Welfare Receipt," 1997). In fact, as a victim of domestic violence, a welfare recipient may have difficulty complying with the new regulations requiring attendance at work training programs and work sites.

Another area of state social service agency involvement is child protection. As Schechter (1996) points out, there would seem to be a natural alliance between the social service agencies and battered woman's programs. Each of these agencies observes a great many women who might be in danger. For the most part, this alliance did not materialize. The paradigms and legal remedies for helping children are often at odds with the needs and safety of battered women. Social service agencies responsible for the safety of children are taught to be on the watch for abusive mothers and caretakers. This charge has often led workers to make mothers responsible for the violence of step-fathers, fathers, and boyfriends (see Bowker, Arbitell, & McFerron, 1988). Schechter (1996) states: "Often in the child welfare community, women's needs and children's needs fail to be seen as complementary and are pitted against each other" (p. 56). An example of this antagonism can be seen in this quote from a battered woman's advocate.

> In our child protection agency, the trend lately has been that the workers see the mothers as the enemy, as the bad guy, as the perpetrator of the crime and they are not really willing to see the father as bad as the mother. Even if the father has committed the violence, the mother is really at fault for not solving the problem.

There is a need for specific training in all these fields about the ways to recognize and identify battered women in these settings, the ways to interview successfully and helpfully, and the ways to connect women with existing resources. In some graduate-level social work curricula, course work in "Family Violence," if offered at all, is offered sporadically, and as an elective.

It is promising that protocols for effective practice have begun to be created and disseminated at the national level. The American

Medical Association has created hospital protocols for medical personnel to aid domestic violence victims, and published *Diagnostic and Treatment Guidelines on Domestic Violence* (1992). The American Medical Association has also produced several other manuals that help medical professionals understand and work with domestic violence victims, such as *Domestic Violence: A Directory of Protocols for Health Care Providers* (Children's Safety Network, 1992). A national network of nurses, Nursing Network on Violence Against Women, has been created and has developed a protocol for the nursing profession. The protocol includes procedures for routinely screening patients for domestic violence. Some states have begun a similar training for welfare eligibility determination as part of the introduction to welfare reform changes.

Schechter (1992) developed a manual describing training for child protection workers, and ways to develop collaborative working arrangements between child protection agencies and battered women's programs. All these changes hinge on established institutions that recognize their own responsibility for helping women find safety. Old fears of legal liability for helping battered women have gradually been replaced by an awareness of the potential for legal liability for NOT helping battered women.

AWAKE, a project operated out of Boston Children's Hospital, brings together domestic violence workers and child protection workers in a medical setting, a model intervention project. The Massachusetts Department of Social Services, the state's child protection agency, has created a separate Domestic Violence Unit to specialize in child abuse cases where domestic violence is involved (Schechter, 1996).

In Cambridge, Massachusetts, the police department, the Cambridge Hospital Network (six neighborhood health centers), and the Cambridge/Somerville Legal Services have created a partnership to work together the better to identify victims and provide coordinated services. This project was funded by the U.S. Department of Justice COPS grant (Paisner, 1997).

Mental health practitioners and advocates are also beginning to work together. Schechter's (1987) manual and protocol for mental health practitioners, *Guidelines for Mental Health Practitioners in Domestic Violence Cases,* and Gondolf's (1998) *Assessing Woman Battering in Mental Health Services* address these issues. Also, the Wellstone/Murray Amendment to the welfare reform bill gives states some authority and flexibility in meeting the needs of people who have been or are currently victims of domestic violence. As experts point out, however, this amendment is optional. So, the safety of battered women who are also receiving welfare will now be decided state by state ("Domestic Violence and Welfare Receipt," 1997).

A Call to Action

Though we have come a long way in a relatively short time, there is still a need to push our understanding farther. It is now generally accepted that woman battering is wrong and that women shouldn't have to live with it. However, it is not enough to provide temporary safety. It is not enough to rely solely on one system or institution within the community to adopt progressive policies to protect battered women. It is not enough to assume that those in helping professions automatically understand domestic violence and can recognize and respond to the needs of victims. Because some women can leave and do leave does not mean all women are now able to find safety on their own. The following example, taken from a parole hearing in 1996, shows how far we have yet to go:

> A woman is at her parole hearing after being in prison close to 20 years for killing her abusive husband. She is asked at the parole hearing by a member of the parole board: "Why didn't you leave?" The woman responded, "I left a number of times." The parole board member asks: "Why didn't you call the police?" She stated, "I did call the police but in those days they didn't have a name for it, they didn't come out and they didn't see it as serious." The parole board member (who was the victim's advocate board member) stated: "When I was a young woman, this guy beat me up once and that was the end of that. I told him I wasn't going to put up with anything like that anymore. If I can do it, anybody can. You are just coming up with an excuse." The member voted against her parole, and the woman is still in prison.

Creating true safety may hinge on our ability to build coalitions and form productive collaborations so that a safety network is created involving the informed participation of the whole community. Many changes have begun, spurred by the recent public attention to domestic violence. When that attention has shifted to a newer pressing issue, will those changes be a lasting effect, will evaluation and evolution of current practice models continue, and will implementation of new policies, procedures, and laws endure?

We are at a strategic moment in the field of domestic violence. For the past 20 years, the knowledge and the programs for domestic violence have expanded enormously. In many ways, as this chapter shows, this success is not complete nor without unintended consequences from the new policy changes. From the judicial system to the medical settings, professionals have begun to respond differently to the problem of domestic violence. In its evolution, the social problem of domestic violence has entered public awareness in unprecedented ways. Solutions and interventions are being proposed and tried in many arenas: victim services, the justice system, the medical and mental health professions, and social services.

Many of the new programs and policies put forth in the past decade show great promise. Much of what has been formulated is based upon common assumptions about battered women that oversimplify the problem and exclude many who need help by assuming that battered women are alike. It is time to move our knowledge forward by examining these underlying assumptions and the role they have played in creating solutions. Current practice should be evaluated for the effectiveness of intended, and unintended, outcomes. Model programs should be replicated in various types of communities to see if their results hold true across variations of demography. We are reminded of the work of Fagan (1996), who stated that, "Without meaningful change in the structure of research and evaluation in domestic violence, a reviewer 5 or 10 years from now will likely reach the same conclusions reached in this review: 'We just don't know, the evaluation data aren't very good' " (p. 48). The need for consistent evaluation as part of any model program, plus the need for methodological tools that can capture the many layers of this problem, is critical to the next wave of programs and policies for domestic violence. Finally, the need for the research findings to have impact on policy in a significant manner should support the collaboration of researchers and advocates (Fagan, 1996). Two areas of future collaboration are the prospects of sustainability of current programs, and the need for expansion of the community that helps battered women.

The issue of sustainability and the type of sustainability across systems is an important area of future analysis for researchers and advocates. When the federal monies are no longer attached to what local municipalities do, it will be important for the partnerships developed to be sustained. The factors that define this sustainability will be negotiated over time. *The other new challenge will be to focus on making communities safe, rather than making individual women safe.* Kelly (1996) points out how the focus of safety for women may need to become one of community organizing around their safety. She argues that the "key resource in establishing safety for women and children," may be found within women's family and friendship networks, neighborhoods, and workplaces (p. 67). It would seem that broadening the safety beyond shelter space may provide one of the avenues to keeping women safe. This is not to diminish the value of shelters and other traditional programming for women, but to say that removing a woman from her community and providing support for her may not be enough to ensure her continued safety.

Obviously, the social and political work is not done (Beasley & Thomas, 1994). It is not the time for the issue of domestic violence to be relegated to a social problem in which we have identified the solution. As our understanding and knowledge have grown, other problems arise. The promise of our work on domestic violence is that it has so successfully challenged much of what was taken for granted about the relations between men and women and the institutional response toward this behavior. It has also triggered resistance in many forms. It is time to ask the larger questions about women in communities. Often when training about domestic violence, we ask the question: "What would happen if the world were safe for women?" The answer is obvious: The community would be safe for everyone.

References

Bachman, R., & Choker, A. L. (1995). Police involvement in domestic violence: The interactive effects of victim injury, offender's history of violence and race. *Violence and Victims, 10*(2), 91-106.

Beasley, M., & Thomas, D. Q. (1994). Domestic violence as a human rights issue. In M. Fineman & R. Mykituk (Eds.), *The public nature of private violence: The discovery of domestic abuse* (pp. 323-349). New York: Routledge.

Berk, R. A., & Newton, P. J. (1985). Does arrest really deter wife battery? An effort to replicate the findings of the Minneapolis Spouse Abuse Experiment. *American Sociological Review, 50*, 252-262.

Bowker, L. H., Arbitell, M., & McFerron, J. R. (1988). On the relationship between wife beating and child abuse. In K. Yllö & M. Bogard (Eds.), *Feminist perspectives on wife abuse*. Newbury Park, CA: Sage.

Buzawa, E. S., & Buzawa, C. G. (1993). The scientific evidence is not conclusive: Arrest is no panacea. In R. J. Gelles & D. R. Loseke (Eds.), *Current controversies on family violence* (pp. 337-356). Newbury Park, CA: Sage.

Cahn, N. R., & Lerman, L. G. (1991). Prosecuting woman abuse. In M. Steinman (Ed.), *Woman battering: Policy responses* (pp. 95-112). Cincinnati, OH: Anderson.

Chesler, P. (1986). *Mothers on trial*. New York: McGraw-Hill.

Children's Safety Network. (1992). *Domestic violence: A directory of protocols for health care providers*. Newton, MA: Education Development Center, Inc.

Community Policing to Combat Domestic Violence Training Conference. (1997, July). Proceedings. Washington, DC: U.S. Department of Justice, COPS Program, Phoenix, AZ.

Crenshaw, K. W. (1994). Mapping the margins: Intersectionality, identity politics and violence against women of color. In M. A. Fineman & B. Mykituk (Eds.), *The public nature of private violence* (pp. 93-120). New York: Routledge.

Diagnostic and treatment guidelines on domestic violence. (1992). Washington, DC: American Medical Association.

Dickstein, L. J., & Nadelson, C. C. (Eds.). (1989). *Family violence: Emerging issues of a national crisis*. Washington, DC: American Psychiatric Press.

Dobash, R. E., & Dobash, R. P. (1979). *Violence against wives: A case against the patriarchy*. New York: Free Press.

Dobash, R. E., & Dobash, R. P. (1992). *Women, violence, and social change*. New York: Routledge.

Domestic violence and welfare receipt. (1997, April 11). *Welfare Reform Network News*, No. 4, pp. 1-6.

Elizabeth Stone House. (1990). Building community skills for staff. Excerpted from *Elizabeth Stone House guide to sheltering people in emotional distress*. Jamaica Plains, MA: Author.

Elliott, P. (Ed.). (1990). *Confronting lesbian battering: A manual for the battered women's movement*. St. Paul: Minnesota Coalition for Battered Women.

Fagan, J. (1996). *The criminalization of domestic violence: Promises and limits*. National Institute of Justice/Research Report presented at the 1995 Conference on Criminal Justice Research and Evaluation (NCJ 157641). Washington, DC: U.S. Department of Justice, Office of Justice Programs.

Feagin, J. R., & Feagin, C. B. (1990). *Social problems: A critical power-conflict perspective*. Englewood Cliffs, NJ: Prentice Hall.

Ferraro, K. J. (1989). Policing woman battering. *Social Problems, 36*, 61-74.

Gelles, R. J. (1993). Through a sociological lens: Social structure and family violence. In R. J. Gelles & D. R. Loseke (Eds.), *Current controversies on family violence* (pp. 31-46). Newbury Park, CA: Sage.

Gelles, R. J., & Loseke, D. R. (1993). *Current controversies on family violence*. Newbury Park, CA: Sage.

Gelles, R. J., & Straus, M. A. (1988). *Intimate violence: The causes and consequences of abuse in the American family*. New York: Simon & Schuster.

Gondolf, E. (1998). *Assessing woman battering in mental health services.* Thousand Oaks, CA: Sage.

Gordon, L. (1988). *Heros of their own lives: The politics and history of family violence, Boston 1880-1960.* New York: Penguin.

Hansen, M. (1993). Feminism and family therapy: A review of feminist critiques of approaches to family violence. In M. Hansen & M. Harway (Eds.), *Battering and family therapy: A feminist perspective* (pp. 69-81). Newbury Park, CA: Sage.

Hansen, M., Harway, M., & Cervantes, N. (1991). Therapists' perceptions of severity in cases of family violence. *Violence and Victims, 6,* 225-235.

Hart, B. J. (1993). The legal road to freedom. In M. Hansen & M. Harway (Eds.), *Battering and family therapy: A feminist perspective* (pp. 13-28). Newbury Park, CA: Sage.

Hirschel, J., & Hutchinson, I. (1991). Police-preferred arrest policies. In M. Steinman (Ed.), *Woman battering* (pp. 49-72). Cincinnati, Oh: Anderson.

Jang, D. L., Mauir, L., & Pendleton, G. (Eds.). (1997). *Domestic violence in immigrant and refugee communities: Assessing the rights of battered women.* Family Violence Prevention Fund; National Immigrant Project of the National Lawyers Guild; and Northern California Coalition for Immigrant Rights. San Francisco: Family Violence Prevention Fund. (Available from publisher at 383 Rhode Island Street, Suite 304, San Francisco, CA 94103-5133)

Jenkins, P. (1996). Contested knowledge: Battered women as agents and victims. In P. Jenkins & S. Kroll-Smith (Eds.), *Witnessing for sociology: Sociologists in the court.* Westport, CT: Praeger.

Kanuha, V. (1996). Domestic violence, racism, and the battered women's movement in the United States. In J. L. Edleson & Z. C. Eisikovits (Eds.), *Future interventions with battered women and their families* (pp. 34-50). Thousand Oaks, CA: Sage.

Kelly, L. (1996). Tensions and possibilities: Enhancing informal responses to domestic violence. In J. L. Edleson & Z. C. Eisikovits (Eds.), *Future interventions with battered women and their families* (pp. 67-86). Thousand Oaks, CA: Sage.

Koss, M. P., Goodman, L. A., Browne, A., Fitzgerald, L. F., Keita, G. P., & Russo, N. F. (1994). *No safe haven: Male violence at home, at work, and in the community.* Washington, DC: American Psychological Association.

Kurz, D. (1989). Social science perspectives on wife abuse: Current debates and future directions. *Gender & Society, 3,* 501-513.

Liss, M. B., & Stahly, G. B. (1993). Domestic violence and child custody. In M. Hansen & M. Harway (Eds.), *Battering and family therapy: A feminist perspective* (pp. 175-187). Newbury Park, CA: Sage.

Lobel, K. (Ed.). (1986). *Naming the violence: Speaking out about lesbian battering.* Seattle: Seal Press.

Loring, M. T., & Smith, R. W. (1994). Health care barriers and interventions for battered women. *Public Health Reports, 109*(May/June), 328-338.

McHardy, L. (1992). *Family violence. State of the art court programs.* Reno, NV: National Council of Juvenile and Family Court Judges.

Merton, R. K., & Nisbet, R. (1971). *Contemporary social problems* (3rd ed.). New York: Harcourt Brace Jovanovich.

Paisner, S. (1997, September). Public health and law enforcement: A new approach to reaching victims. *Domestic Violence Prevention,* pp. 6-7.

Pleck, E. (1987). *Domestic tyranny: The making of American social policy against family violence from colonial times to the present.* New York: Oxford University Press.

Resko, B. (Compiler). (1989). *Training manual for domestic violence counselors/ advocates.* Pennsylvania Coalition Against Domestic Violence, 2505 North Front Street, Harrisburg, PA 17110.

Rukeyser, M. (1973). Kathe Kollwitz. In F. Howe & E. Bass (Eds.), *No more masks! An anthology of poems by women.* Garden City, NY: Anchor/Doubleday.

Schechter, S. (1982). *Women and male violence: The visions and struggles of the battered women's movement.* Boston: South End.

Schechter, S. (1987). *Guidelines for mental health practitioners in domestic violence cases.* Washington, DC: National Coalition Against Domestic Violence.

Schechter, S. (1996). The battered women's movement in the United States: New directions for institutional reform. In J. L. Edleson & Z. C. Eisikovits (Eds.), *Future interventions with battered women and their families* (pp. 53-66). Thousand Oaks, CA: Sage.

Schechter, S., with Gary, L. T. (1992). *Healthcare services for battered women and their children: A manual about AWAKE.* Boston: Children's Hospital.

Schmidt, J. D., & Sherman, L. W. (1993). Does arrest deter domestic violence? *American Behavioral Scientist, 36,* 601-609.

Se'ver, A. (1997). Recent or imminent separation and intimate violence against women: A conceptual overview and some Canadian examples. *Violence Against Women, 3*(6), 566-590.

Stark, E. (1993). Mandatory arrest of batterers: A reply to its critics. *American Behavioral Scientist, 36,* 651-680.

Stark, E., & Flitcraft, A. (1988). Violence among intimates: An epidemiological review. In V. B. VanHasselt & R. L. Morrison *Handbook of family violence* (pp. 293-297). New York: Plenum.

Sullivan, C. (1997). Societal collusion and culpability in intimate male violence: The impact of community response toward women with abusive partners. In A. Cardarelli (Ed.), *Violence between intimate partners: Patterns, causes and effects.* Needham Heights, MA: Allyn & Bacon.

Wallace, H. (1996). *Family violence: Legal, medical, and social perspectives.* Boston: Allyn & Bacon.

Warshaw, C. (1993). Limitations of the medical model in the care of battered women. In P. B. Bart & E. G. Moran (Eds.), *Violence against women: The bloody footprints* (pp. 134-146). Newbury Park, CA: Sage.

Whalen, M. (1996). *Counseling to end violence against women.* Thousand Oaks, CA: Sage.

Wright, J. (1982). *Chemical dependency and violence: Working with dually affected families. A cross training program manual for counselors and advocates.* Madison: Wisconsin Clearinghouse.

Yllö, K. (1993). Through a feminist lens: Gender, power, and violence. In R. J. Gelles & D. R. Loseke (Eds.), *Current controversies on family violence* (pp. 47-62). Newbury Park, CA: Sage.

CHAPTER 10

Community-Based Approaches to Violence Prevention

SANDRA J. MCELHANEY

KATHRYN M. EFFLEY

The Role of Community-Based Violence Prevention Programs

Violence has become one of the nation's most serious public health problems. It affects everyone, regardless of age, race, gender, or ethnicity. The violence can be seen in our schools, neighborhoods, families, and even entertainment activities such as television, movies, and video games. The tragedy is that violence does not have a single impact. Rather, it causes physical pain, mental health problems, community turmoil, and other life difficulties on both personal and environmental levels. Today's violence epidemic requires a strong investment in prevention and the involvement of communities across America.

The purpose of this chapter is to provide a window of knowledge through which professionals can understand community-based violence prevention efforts and the importance of their role in the nation's fight against the violence epidemic. It is designed to motivate individuals to become involved in violence prevention efforts in their own communities. The chapter is divided into five sections. The first section briefly describes community-based violence prevention efforts through a definition of the approach, a review of the advantages, identification of the community risk factors for violence, and a discussion of early intervention by communities. In the next section, the characteristics of effective community-based violence prevention programs are presented. The third section uses the identified characteristics to evaluate promising violence prevention programs. The chapter then overviews the National Mental Health Association's (NMHA) campaign for the prevention of violence. The authors conclude with suggestions for future research and program development.

Violence Prevention and the Community

A community provides a sense of belonging as well as a commitment to meet the basic needs of its members. The importance of safety and the freedom that comes with the feeling of being safe in our community cannot be overstated. Communities are where people live, work, and congregate. Communities can create an atmosphere characterized by happiness, freedom, and safety. When violence imposes itself on the community, it can destroy feelings of security and love for a home environment. At the same time, violence often leads to the mobilization of communitywide coalitions and approaches designed to quell the problem. Such approaches that are supported for over 5 years may theoretically have the strongest impact on reducing violence (Elliott, 1994).

Advantages of a Community-Based Approach

A community-based approach has a unique importance in the overall effort to prevent violence. There are several reasons why this approach is beneficial and should be incorporated into efforts that address the violence problem in America. First, a community-based approach has the ability to impact the entire social environment including individuals, families, and groups. The approach can focus on all aspects of community life including norms, values, and policies. These aspects can be influenced by violence prevention efforts, and in turn have an impact on the community residents. An effort that affects the entire social environment can also eliminate the conditions within the community that place residents at risk. Second, a community-based approach incorporates a broad spectrum of support and teamwork within the community. This prevents any one person, organization, or strategy from solely carrying the

burden of reducing violent crime. By involving the entire community, this approach uses a variety of views on violence prevention.
It brings together children, parents, law enforcement, educators,
religious leaders, policymakers, ethnic groups, and health professions, who can all work together toward the accomplishment of a
common goal: the prevention of violence, and thereby the creation
of a safer community. Third, a community-based approach generally incorporates prevention strategies into the delivery of services
and activities. This process helps to institutionalize violence prevention, thereby allowing prevention efforts to influence the community through a broad spectrum of modalities (Howell, 1995).
Fourth, a community-based violence prevention effort allows residents to have a vested interest in the project. Effective programs
offer buy-in to the community, which instills a sense of ownership
and leadership among community residents and allows them to
develop a sense of proprietorship (Hawkins, 1995). In turn, community residents take responsibility for community activities, and
their desire for and commitment to the program promotes its
continuation and success (Mercy, Rosenberg, Powell, Broome, &
Roper, 1993). Finally, the success of other community-based prevention programs reveals the importance of violence prevention
efforts on the community level. For example, prevention efforts
have influenced the way in which residents of a community view
smoking and high-fat foods. The result is a communitywide effort
that has had an effect on the health of the entire community
(Howell, 1995).

Community Risk and Protective Factors

An effective prevention effort must first identify the risks in a
community that increase the probability that violence will occur, as
well as the protective factors that can buffer residents from these
risks. From there, appropriate interventions can be put into place.
Five risk factors within the community have been identified that
increase the likelihood of violent behavior (Hawkins, 1995). The
first risk factor is the availability of firearms. Research has provided
three key reasons for considering the availability of firearms as a
community risk factor: The presence of guns increases the likelihood that a conflict will result in homicide; there is a strong
association between the availability of guns and homicide rates; and
firearms are known to be lethal. A second community risk factor

involves laws or norms within the community that are favorable to crime. The norms established in a community can be expressed in the form of policies, laws, social practices, and the expectations adults have for young people. A community becomes at high risk for violence when the norms are unclear, conflicting, or favorable to violent behavior. Third, the media play a significant role in the promotion and potentially the minimization of violence. Research has shown that there is a correlation between portrayals of violence in the media and the development of violent behavior. Violence in the media can lead to the development of violent problem-solving strategies. Low neighborhood attachment and community disorganization are identified as a fourth community risk factor. Violence often occurs in communities that lack a sense of attachment; do not have homogeneous characteristics such as race, class, and religion; and that appear to have an indifferent attitude to problems such as disorganization, lack of cleanliness, and vandalism. Finally, a risk factor that arises in communities and increases the occurrence of violence involves a situation of extreme economic deprivation. Violence is more likely to develop in areas with deteriorating neighborhoods and conditions of poverty.

A community should identify and prioritize these risk factors and then incorporate a prevention strategy while keeping the following generalizations in mind. Risk factors can be found in many different domains, and therefore prevention efforts should address risks that are apparent in several areas. As the number of risk factors increases, so does the risk for violence. As a result, the risk of violence developing in a community is significantly decreased by a program that addresses multiple risk factors. Because a risk factor can be associated with various problems, a prevention effort that reduces or eliminates common risk factors may have an affect on a variety of problems in the community. Although the level of risk may vary, research has shown that risk factors are consistent among races, cultures, and classes.

Protective factors can be used to decrease the severity of identified risk factors. The impact that risk factors have on individuals and communities can be reduced by enhancing protective factors. Research has identified three categories of protective factors that provide positive methods for individuals or communities to respond to the identified risks (Hawkins, 1995). These categories include: individual characteristics, bonding, and healthy beliefs and clear standards. Individual characteristics, such as a resilient temperament and positive social orientation, can serve as protection against the risk for dealing with violent situations and developing violent behavior. Bonding refers to positive relationships that exist among family members, teachers, peers, or other adults. The third protective factor includes beliefs such as competency to succeed and to avoid violence, and clear expectations and rules that are established to govern individuals' behavior (Hawkins, 1995).

Early Intervention in Communities

In an effort to understand better the prevention of violence, it is important to be aware of issues around young people. Research has shown that adolescents ages 15 to 16 have the greatest risk of involvement in violent behavior. Similarly, adolescents between the ages of 16 and 17 are reported to have the highest rate of participation in violent acts. In addition, the risk for initiating violence is very low for persons over the age of 20 (Elliott, 1994). Therefore, it is important to recognize the need to incorporate preventive intervention efforts targeting youth. Over the long run, the most effective results may be seen in prevention efforts that are initiated with young children and are focused on shaping knowledge, attitudes, and behavior. The advantages of early intervention are that the effects can be continued throughout the course of a lifetime, and early intervention and the development of nonviolent behavior can be passed down to future generations (Mercy et al., 1993). In addition, a child must eventually expand his or her experiences by attending school, joining clubs or teams, and thereby entering an environment outside of the home and family. It is at this point that the community takes a more active role in childhood development. Therefore, community-based violence prevention programs can have a significant impact on the lives of children, as well as on the reduction of violence (Howell, 1995).

Characteristics of Community-Based
Violence Prevention Programs

Current research on violence and prevention has led professionals to develop numerous community-based violence prevention strategies. There are several dimensions on which effective community-based violence prevention efforts can be distinguished: theoretical foundation, intervention strategy, collaborative approach, baseline data, and evaluation. Each item is a characteristic of an effective program, and together they can be used as a model for the development of a community-based violence prevention program, as well as identifiable criteria for determining the effectiveness of existing programs. The following discussion delineates each dimension and explains the important role each plays in the success of violence prevention efforts.

Theoretical Foundation

A *theory* is a "logical system of concepts that provides a framework for organizing and understanding observations" (Greene & Ephross, 1991, p. 3). Theories provide a knowledge base that can be used to understand the violence phenomenon and guide prevention efforts. Effective community-based violence prevention programs use theories to understand the causal dynamics of violent behavior, as well as to predict future behavior. Theoretical frameworks are essential to community-based violence prevention programs, because they provide a conceptual foundation that is used to shape the direction of prevention efforts and guide specific intervention activities. By providing extensive, simple, and reliable principles that can explain and predict violent behavior, theories can identify factors with explanatory power in prevention (Greene & Ephross, 1991). One theory that may provide some explanatory power for violent behavior is the social learning theory, an examination of which will provide an understanding of the important role theory plays in the prevention of violence.

Bandura's (1977, 1986) social learning theory posits that violence is a learned behavior that results from the observation or imitation of others. Through observation of others, people duplicate a complex array of behaviors, think about what they observe, and make decisions concerning the imitation of others and acquiring those behaviors. According to this theory, learning occurs through cognitive processes, and does not result from punishment or rewards.

In community efforts to prevent violence, the social learning theory can be used to guide programs. For example, a community-based violence prevention effort that is based on the social learning theory would suggest that a prevention program must be designed with the understanding that violent behavior is learned through observing and imitating others, such as family members, peers, television shows, and computer games (Longres, 1995). According to this theory, prevention can be achieved through programs that provide models of alternative, nonviolent behaviors. The knowledge gained from observing positive behaviors can reveal new behavioral options, as well as demonstrate the justification for using these behaviors (Powell et al., 1996).

Prevention Strategies

Effective violence prevention programs can incorporate various strategies in their intervention methods. Tolan and Guerra (1994) have identified strategies according to their level of intervention. These strategies include conducting change on four levels: individual; proximal interpersonal systems; proximal social settings; or societal macrosystems. The distinction between these strategies can been seen in the types of activities associated with each strategy. A strategy that seeks to change the knowledge, skills, or attitudes of individuals is often focused on the delivery of information. Such information is designed to help individuals develop nonviolent attitudes and beliefs; increase their knowledge; impart social, marketable, or professional skills; and deter criminal actions. Community efforts utilizing this strategic approach can involve psychotherapy, behavior modification, social skills training, intensive casework, and mentoring. The second strategy, which involves proximal interpersonal systems, involves activities with family members and peers. Some examples of how this strategy can be used with the family include activities focused on behavior management, family relations, and family problem solving. Activities involving peers may include group interaction, structured interaction, peer mediation, and recruitment of people out of gangs. Strategies focused on proximal social contexts involve activities with schools, neighborhoods, and residential institutions. Examples of activities used with this strategy are teacher practices, motivation, organization, worker practices, positive youth role models, and diversion activities. Efforts with societal macrosystems address issues such as access to guns, violence in the media, educational opportunity, welfare needs, economic opportunity, and police practices (Tolan & Guerra, 1994).

The federal Centers for Disease Control and Prevention (CDC) have proposed a similar framework for prevention strategies. CDC identifies the three general strategies of education, legal and regulatory change, and environmental modification. An education strategy could involve adult mentoring, conflict resolution, social skills training, firearm safety, parenting centers, peer education, or public information and educational campaigns. In addressing legal and regulatory change, the CDC identifies three categories for strategic action: regulating the use of and access to weapons, regulating the use of and access to alcohol, and general regulations. The strategies used to regulate the use of and access to weapons involves approaches such as weaponless schools, control of concealed weapons, and restrictive licensing. Activities that involve regulating the use of and access to alcohol include the appropriate sale of alcohol, prohibition or control of alcohol sales at events, and the training of servers. Additional types of regulations often address appropriate punishment in schools and dress codes (National Center for Injury Prevention and Control, 1993). Tolan and Guerra (1994) and the CDC have proposed viable strategies for preventing violence. While each of the strategies identifies an important aspect of violence prevention programs, the most effective efforts will actually involve a comprehensive strategy that incorporates all areas of prevention. No single strategy will eliminate all forms of violence. The optimal violence prevention effort evaluates various strategies and integrates the strengths of a range of tactics (Roth, 1994).

In designing or choosing preventive strategies, researchers and communities should keep in mind the following key elements. First, all strategies need to focus on known risk factors. Once a community's risk factors are identified, a violence prevention program can be designed that will target the reduction of identified risk factors and enhance protective factors (Hawkins, 1995). Second, it is important for strategies to reach the population at risk and to communicate effectively with those individuals. Effective community-based programs have the ability to empower residents to take ownership of program techniques. A combination of knowledge concerning effective violence prevention programs and local ownership of initiatives will likely result in positive outcomes. Third, the full benefits of a prevention effort are more likely to be recognized with the use of long-term strategies. There is evidence that suggests that norms and behaviors can be changed; but in order to change or shape patterns of behavior, sustained efforts are required. For example, communities across America have changed their views on smoking and high-fat diets. Public health efforts have successfully influenced change on the community level, but for this kind of change to take place, a long-term commitment is required by the entire community. Fourth, violence affects people of all ages, so strategies must be developmentally appropriate. To be effective, a strategy should address the risk and protective factors at all stages of development. In addition, strategies need to address all of the domains that affect the individual, such as family, school, community, individual, and peer group (Howell, 1995).

Collaborative Approach

Comprehensive, community-based violence prevention efforts require collaboration, resource sharing, and integration of multiple disciplines. Collaborations can be formed within agencies, organizations, schools, and other groups that have an interest in violence prevention. These collaborations can include formal and informal relationships among all agencies that can support or improve the violence prevention effort. Another reason to incorporate a collaborative approach is resource sharing (Howell, 1995). Nonprofit organizations often have limited resources, and as these organizations work together, they can share resources to maximize services. In addition, the organizations involved in the prevention effort will have various strengths and can make unified contributions. For example, the involvement of a national organization might increase the marketability of a program through the organization's affiliates, connections, and publications, which are all important resources on the national level. A smaller organization within an individual community might be able to provide a community perspective, as well as important information concerning the target population. Schools can provide a connection with parents, important academic resources, and serve as the facilitator for some programs. In addition, government agencies and police departments can provide financial, legal, and various other critical resources. Another aspect of a comprehensive approach is the incorporation of multiple disciplines. By combining various disciplines, a violence prevention effort will be based on a comprehensive knowledge of the violence epidemic. This will provide a better understanding of diverse disciplines and allow prevention programs to incorporate the most significant information from various fields (Mercy et al., 1993).

Baseline Data

The collection of baseline data is an integral part of community-based violence prevention programs. Baseline data provide a wide range of information concerning the target population. From the collection of data, a profile of the participants can be developed that can identify common elements such as age, gender, and ethnicity. Additional elements of baseline data include: demographics, psychosocial characteristics, and exposure to violence and behavior characteristics (specifically, the frequency of violent behavior). The collection of baseline data can also provide information on outside factors, such as the effect that parental consent has on participation in community-based violence prevention programs for children. The baseline data can allow for a comparison to be made between the participants receiving the intervention and those who are not receiving the intervention. The information that is revealed in the baseline data analysis can allow researchers to identify extraneous variables that influence violent behavior. An example showing the importance of baseline data collection can be seen by verifying the need for a prevention program. Baseline data that reveal a high frequency of violent behavior among participants can be used to confirm the need for a prevention effort as well as to justify the expenditure of resources (Powell et al., 1996).

One method for collecting baseline data is through a needs assessment conducted in the community. The information revealed through a needs assessment will ensure that the most appropriate prevention program is implemented according to a community's individual needs. There are five primary reasons for conducting a needs assessment. First, an assessment of a community's needs has the ability to reveal any violence prevention interventions that currently exist in the community. The process will also serve to justify an effort to implement a new violence prevention program in the community by determining the number of people who are affected by the problem. A third reason to conduct a needs assessment is to determine if existing violence prevention programs are known to or recognized by community residents. In addition, the assessment process can identify barriers that may prevent residents from accessing or benefiting from existing services. Finally, a fifth reason to conduct a needs assessment is to provide documentation of the violence problem in a particular community (Royse & Thyer, 1996).

Evaluation Data

A prevention program must be evaluated in order to know if it is effective. Three primary reasons for conducting evaluations are

> to determine whether the interventions (1) produce desired behavioral changes; (2) produce changes in knowledge or attitudes as indicators of progress toward the behavioral outcomes, and to identify the pathways by which behavioral changes are achieved; and (3) are implemented well enough so that any intermediate and behavioral changes may reasonably be attributed to them. (Powell et al., 1996, p. 6)

A comprehensive evaluation involves two components: a process evaluation and an outcome evaluation. The process evaluation will examine the planning and implementation of the program, as well as any forces that influence the implementation process (Howell, 1995). Rather than looking at the final results, a process evaluation focuses on the intervention and reports the operations of a program. In addition to documenting the activities used and the problems encountered, a process evaluation is also used to explain why expected outcomes of a program were or were not achieved. The data collected in a process evaluation can be used to examine the intensity and reliability of a program's service delivery process. The diverse characteristics of each community make program evaluation essential in order for a program to be implemented in other communities. An outcome evaluation identifies the criteria that are used to differentiate effective and non-effective programs (Royse & Thyer, 1996). The outcome evaluation will measure the success of a program through its ability to prevent violence. An important component of outcome evaluations is an experimental design, which allows for various program components to be compared to a randomly selected control group (Howell, 1995). Experimental designs provide a means for examining the impact that an intervention has on an individual or community. In addition, experimental designs serve as tools for researchers to determine the extent to which a program will be successful the next time it is implemented (Royse & Thyer, 1996).

Tolan and Guerra (1994) present five characteristics of evaluation designs in violence prevention. First, an evaluation needs to include a review of the participants, including demographic characteristics, and the risk of or involvement in violent activity prior to intervention. Second, a comparison group should be part of the evaluation design. The comparison group should be comparable to the group receiving intervention in regards to demographic characteristics as well as risk for or involvement in violent behavior. Ideally, the treatment and control groups should be randomly assigned. Third, it is important to understand the methods of intervention as a measure of program integrity. This information will include: the intervention goals, the method by which they can reduce violence, the method for delivering the intervention, and the level of exposure to the intervention as well as its duration. Fourth, there is a need to measure the program participants' level of violent behavior before and after the intervention. It is also desirable to measure outcomes once the intervention has been put into place. These data will reveal if noted changes are constant, or if behavioral changes occurred once the intervention was completed. A fifth and final characteristic involves the use of quantitative measurements that determine the effects of a program (Tolan & Guerra, 1994).

The five characteristics of community-based violence prevention programs described above will now be used to examine three existing programs. Each program is described in terms of the population served, the various methods used to prevent violence, and the results of evaluations. The three programs that will be discussed include: Richmond Youth Against Violence Project, Violence Prevention Project, and Communities That Care.

Richmond Youth Against Violence Project

The Richmond Youth Against Violence Project is a community-based effort focused on the reduction of violence among urban adolescents. The project targets middle school students and is designed to teach students the knowledge, attitudes, and skills that are needed to reduce their own violent behavior. Through the school environment, the project incorporates a violence prevention curriculum titled "Responding in Peaceful and Positive Ways" (RIPP). The curriculum is designed to be taught in the schools once a week, and consists of sixteen 40-minute workshops (Farrell, Meyer, & Dahlberg, 1996).

Theoretical Foundation

RIPP is grounded in social cognitive learning theory. According to this theory, a violent act is not caused solely by an individual or the environment. Rather, the social cognitive learning theory posits that there are three primary determinants that must be addressed in order to reduce violent behavior. These determinants include the person, the behavior, and the environment. In addition, the social cognitive learning theory suggests that among these three determinants lie reciprocal, interactive relationships. With its basis in the social cognitive learning theory, RIPP addresses the interactive forces that influence behavior, intrapersonal characteristics, and environmental influences.

Intervention Strategy

The program incorporates a variety of strategies in an effort to create a comprehensive approach to the prevention of violence. The strategies attempt to: (a) use conflict resolution and peer mediation as a method for integrating classroom activity with real-life situations; (b) educate others on the important aspects of nonviolent behavior and conflict resolution through staff development efforts and parent training sessions; and (c) provide access to a trained prevention specialist who serves as a model for appropriate, nonviolent behavior and is committed to the school and community violence prevention effort. The RIPP curriculum combines three basic strategies. The first involves repeating behavioral and mentally rehearsing various problem-solving aspects of the social cognitive model, which serves as the basis for the entire curriculum. The model incorporates individual sessions and uses a cumulative method in which each session builds upon past sessions. A second strategy of RIPP is the use of experiential learning techniques. In an effort to obtain full participation in the class, a range of techniques is used to help eliminate gender differences and stereotypes. These techniques include: small group work, role plays, relaxation activities, open discussion, and activities on building trust. The use of didactic learning modalities is a third strategy of the program. RIPP allows students to learn about the nature of violence through didactic modalities, including worksheets, videos, and minilectures that are incorporated into the curriculum (Meyer & Farrell, 1997).

Collaborative Approach

The Richmond Youth Against Violence Project involves a collaborative approach among the Richmond public school system, the Richmond Behavioral Health Authority, and Virginia Commonwealth University. The collaboration was expanded in 1993 to include support from the National Center for Injury Prevention and Control, which is located within the Centers for Disease Control and Prevention (CDC). The groups involved have a common interest in preventing violence. The collaboration permits resource sharing, knowledge building, and a way to integrate local and national expertise. The project combines the local knowledge about the Richmond community and schools with national information on the nature of violence and methods for prevention (Farrell & Meyer, 1997).

Baseline Data

The Richmond Youth Against Violence project has identified the important areas of baseline data that are needed to develop an understanding of the target population. The data were collected through a research study involving 579 participants. A review of the baseline data shows a slight difference in gender participation, with more females identified in the sample. In addition, the data revealed a large difference in ethnicity (94.3% African American, 2.2% Caucasians, and 3.6% other minorities). The project conducted a series of analyses of variance (ANOVA) in an effort to identify differences between the intervention and control groups. No significant baseline differences were found. The baseline data were also used to determine the participants' exposure to violence over their lifetime, involvement in violence over their lifetime, and involvement in violent acts within 30 days before testing. The study found no significant difference between intervention and control groups, but identified significant gender differences. A brief review of the data indicates a higher percentage of boys who reported being assaulted, being threatened by someone with a weapon, carrying a weapon to school, and threatening someone with a weapon (Farrell et al., 1996).

Evaluation

An extensive evaluation of the RIPP curriculum was conducted in three middle schools during the 1995-1996 school year. The evaluation was conducted with approximately half of the sixth graders from each of the three schools. The students were randomly assigned to either an intervention or a control group. The evaluation design included self-report measurements that were conducted at the beginning and end of the school year. In addition, the evaluation design obtained disciplinary code violations at the end of the school year. A summary of the results revealed positive results among RIPP participants. The students who received the intervention were shown to have significantly fewer violations of the disciplinary code regarding fighting and carrying weapons. When compared to the control group, the participants who experienced the curriculum had lower rates of in-school suspension. The self-reported data showed an improvement in RIPP participants' knowledge of the material, increased use of the school's peer mediation program, and decreased injuries related to fighting (Farrell & Meyer, 1997).

Discussion

The Richmond Youth Against Violence Project has been shown to have potential to prevent violence among school-age children. The program's evaluation provides evidence in support of the program's ability to prevent violence through certain strategies incorporated into the program. Because of its recent evaluation, the program is not able to determine if the observed effects from participating in the program will be maintained. A future evaluation that is extended for a longer period of time than the initial one-year evaluation is planned.

Communities That Care

The Communities That Care (CTC) program is a comprehensive, communitywide prevention strategy that is based on research concerning the predictors of health and behavior problems. It is focused on reducing problem behaviors through efforts that reduce risk factors while promoting protective factors. The goal of CTC is to train communities to identify the risk and protective factors that are present in a community and are associated with violent behavior. The strategy mobilizes communities to implement a violence prevention program that is tailored to their prioritized risks (Harachi, Ayers, Hawkins, Catalano, & Cushing, 1996).

Theoretical Foundation

CTC is theoretically grounded in the social development strategy. Employing components of control theory and social learning theory, the social development strategy emphasizes the role of protective factors as protection against the development of conduct problems and misbehavior (Hawkins, Catalano, & Miller, 1992). The goal of the social developmental strategy is to influence the development of healthy behavior. The strategy works toward the accomplishment of this goal through a process that reduces risk factors by enhancing protective factors. Three protective factors are emphasized in the strategy: healthy belief and clear standards; bonding; and individual characteristics. According to the social development model, healthy behavior can be promoted by establishing healthy beliefs and clear standards relating to behavior in the family, school, and community. Clear standards allow people to know what constitutes acceptable, nonviolent behavior. The social developmental strategy suggests bonding that takes place with families, peers, schools, and communities and promotes healthy beliefs and clear standards can serve as a critical protective factor against the risk of developing violent behavior. It is believed that bonding can provide the necessary motivation to protect oneself from being exposed to a risk. A third protective factor identified in the social development strategy involves characteristics of individuals, such as a positive social orientation or intelligence, which affect how a person perceives opportunities, develops skill, and receives recognition. In order to promote bonding, families, schools, and communities must provide opportunities and recognition, especially for those individuals who do not possess these special protective characteristics (Howell, 1995). Research on a comprehensive program utilizing the social development model was shown to reduce the rate of school suspension and expulsion, lower the prevalence of aggressive behavior, and significantly reduce the self-reported rates of delinquency and alcohol use (Hawkins et al., 1992).

Intervention Strategy

In order to reduce risk factors and enhance protective factors, CTC utilizes a community mobilization strategy. The strategy involves four primary phases. The first phase is designed to recruit the involvement of key leaders within the community. Through an orientation, the key leaders develop goals, determine the feasibility of pursuing a risk-focused prevention effort, and determine who will compose a community board or task force. The first phase is the beginning step for mobilization and provides foresight into the community's ability to change. In the second phase, a community board or task force is formed. The board is made up of representatives from diverse groups and areas within the community and is focused on developing a comprehensive, risk-focused prevention program. A risk and resource assessment is conducted during the third phase. This process will result in a comprehensive profile of the community in relation to levels of risk. An "Encyclopedia of Risk Indicators" is included in the CTC training materials and provides board members with the necessary information to identify risk factors in the community. The assessment allows communities to understand research on risk and protective factors, learn how to apply the social development strategy, conduct a risk assessment in the community, and review local existing programs. The final phase of the strategy involves planning the program and deciding on methods for evaluation. A training is held for community board members to develop an action plan. The training assists communities to: utilize the risk assessment data to prioritize risks, select appropriate interventions from a list of programs that have been evaluated for effectiveness, develop an action plan encompassing goals and objectives, identify obstacles and available resources for surpassing those obstacles, and establish a method for evaluating the program (Developmental Research and Programs [DRP], 1993).

The CTC community mobilization strategy requires that intervention take place in at least three domains: family, school, and community. A community empowerment philosophy is incorporated that allows community members to identify risk and protective factors that are present in the community and to select the elements of programs to be implemented within each domain. Within each community, the CTC strategy is expected to vary in relation to the targeted risk factors and the intervention components that are selected (Peterson, Hawkins, & Catalano, 1992).

Collaborative Approach

The CTC model requires a collaborative effort within the community. The success of the program relies on the involvement of diverse groups of people at various intervention levels. The key leaders, who are involved from the beginning, are an essential part of the prevention effort. They have the status, recognition, resources, and authority within the community to initiate change and to launch a prevention effort the magnitude of the CTC model. Through their leadership, approval, and support, these key leaders can strengthen policies and create new directions that lead to a reduction in violence. In addition, the CTC model requires the development of a community board that represents diverse groups in the community. Representatives on the community board will include individuals with various interests in the community, such as the school system, law enforcement, local government, service and civic organizations, human service providers, religious and cultural groups, and parents. The CTC model is a comprehensive effort that empowers communities to take action and creates a sense of ownership among residents. The involvement of diverse groups and individuals within the community is crucial for the success of CTC's communitywide violence prevention effort (DRP, 1993).

Baseline Data

The baseline data for CTC reveal the potential effectiveness of the program. Risk-focused prevention programs can target risk and protective factors at the point that they are malleable. Risk and protective factors are present in both the individual and social environment. As research has shown the effectiveness of risk- and prevention-focused interventions, the elements involved in mobilizing communities to accomplish prevention goals are being widely explored. An approach that mobilizes community residents and leaders may have the greatest potential for health promotion, when compared to approaches such as top-down social planning or conflict-oriented social action. Research has shown that two crucial components of community development efforts are: community ownership and targeting local priorities. CTC is a comprehensive, risk- and protection-focused community mobilization effort.

Evaluation

Evaluated under the program name *Together! Communities for Drug-Free Youth,* the CTC model was initially demonstrated through a project mobilizing 35 Oregon communities. Originally, 40 communities were represented with at least four key leaders present at the orientation, totaling 244 key leaders. A telephone survey was conducted randomly among the participants 4 months after the orientation. The survey revealed that 85% of the participants had plans to carry forward their personal involvement in the project. The key leaders maintained their involvement by recruiting board members. One month following the "Risk and Resource" training, 171 board members were sampled and it was determined that 51% had been recruited by key leaders. Thus, communities were shown to be successful in recruiting diverse board members who represented various sectors within the community such as human service agencies, business, and public and private organizations. Three-hundred-six board members, representing 36 communities, attended the "Risk and Resource" training. A posttest telephone survey was conducted to determine who attended, how information was transferred to those not in attendance, and whether or not the risk assessment process was initiated by their board. Reportedly, 86% of the respondents stated that work had begun. At the second board training, "Promising Approaches," 5 months after the "Risk and Resource" training, 206 members of 35 boards were present. Approximately 1 year later, 31 community boards submitted action plan proposals for funding. During the following year, 28 boards submitted funding plans. One year following the "Promising Approaches" training, before grant money was received, project staff rated the programs that were implemented. Twenty-one boards were shown to have implemented effective risk reduction activities and an additional 4 boards implemented moderately effective activities. In all, some form of prevention program was implemented without external funding from the Oregon State Office of Alcohol and Drug Abuse Programs (OADAP) by 31 of the 35 boards. To summarize, the project demonstrated that multiple communities can be mobilized with the CTC strategy. Volunteer community boards were shown to be both willing and able to determine the level of risk and protective factors present in their community through quantitative assessments (Harachi et al., 1996).

Discussion

Overall, CTC appears to be an effective model for mobilizing communities and implementing an effective violence prevention program. The program utilizes the social development strategy, which has been shown to produce beneficial effects on behavior. CTC has the ability to mobilize communities, and the social development strategy incorporated into CTC increases the ability to prevent violence in a community. However, the program lacks a strong evaluation of its impact on violent behavior. While the evaluation shows that CTC can be used to mobilize communities, further research is needed to determine the impact CTC has on the rates of violence, and to provide evidence that the program has successfully prevented or reduced violence in a community. In order to obtain this evidence, stronger baseline data are needed to determine the level of violence in a community before CTC has been implemented. Sufficient evaluation and baseline data exist for the mobilization process, but there is a need to research and report on the violence conditions that exist in communities before and after CTC is implemented.

Violence Prevention Project

The Violence Prevention Project (VPP) is a community-based violence prevention program that targets youth through outreach and education. The program incorporates an educational curriculum that is designed to improve participants' knowledge about violence. VPP encourages the development of relationships among agencies that can work together for the betterment of society. It is a program that, through education and orientation, can implement a full-scale social change effort that will reduce violence in the community (Hausman, Spivak, Prothrow-Stith, & Roeber, 1992).

Theoretical Foundation

The theoretical basis of VPP incorporates components of both the health belief model (Rosenstock, 1990) and the theory of reasoned action (Hausman, Spivak, & Prothrow-Stith, 1995). The health belief model (HBM) identifies key variables that influence individuals in taking action to prevent, identify, and control poor health conditions. The key variables include an individual's perceived susceptibility, severity, benefits, barriers, and self-efficacy. In the case of violence, perceived susceptibility refers to the risk of becoming involved in violent behavior according to an individual's subjective perception. Perceived severity involves one's concern for developing violent behavior and evaluates the medical, clinical, and social consequences of that behavior. The course of action that is taken to reduce the threat of violence will depend upon the beliefs concerning the effectiveness and feasibility of possible actions, or the perceived benefits of various actions. Aspects that are seen as having negative effects are identified as perceived barriers, and may become obstacles to undertaking a recommended action. Together, the levels of perceived susceptibility and severity create a driving force to take action, and the perception of potential benefits outweighing the perceived barriers identifies the optimal course of action. In an effort to increase the explanatory power of the HBM, the concept of self-efficacy has been incorporated into the original formulations of the theory. The concept of self-efficacy within the HBM suggests that a person taking a particular action to prevent violence will experience a health benefit from the action, and that the person must believe that he or she is capable of taking the specified course of action. Thus, in the prevention of violence, the HBM theorizes that people must believe a threat exists with current behavior patterns and that a recommended course of action will be beneficial through a positive outcome at a cost that is satisfactory to all who are involved. In addition, people must also believe that they are capable and competent of achieving change, as seen in the prevention of violence (Rosenstock, 1990).

The theory of reasoned action attempts to explain violence by predicting the intention that a person has to perform a particular behavior. The theory posits that behavioral intention determines one's behavior and mediates other factors that influence behavior. In order to make an accurate prediction of behavior, the measurements of intention and behavior must closely correspond to each other in relation to influential factors such as time, action, target, and context. Two factors have been identified as affecting the strength of a person's intention to perform a particular behavior. These factors are: the person's attitude toward the behavior, and influences within the social environment or the subjective norms associated with a specific behavior. Each factor is composed of two components. There are two determinants of an individual's attitude toward a behavior: the belief that by performing a specific behavior a given outcome will occur, and an outcome evaluation. Social norm is determined by two additional factors: a person's normative belief concerning what others think should or should not be done, and the motivation of an individual to comply with the wishes and beliefs of others.

Intervention Strategy

VPP is an approach that attempts to achieve social change through two overarching strategies: education and a mass media campaign. The education component of the program involves the incorporation of the *Violence Prevention Curriculum for Adolescents* (Prothrow-Stith, 1987). This strategy is focused on training community service providers from various agencies to administer the curriculum. The curriculum is designed to engage adolescents, encourage them to think about their behavior, help them understand the control they can exert over their behavior, and question the idea that fighting is inevitable (Prothrow-Stith & Weissman, 1991). The 10-session curriculum combines didactic and cognitive activities that provide information about violence and involve adolescents in role plays (Hausman et al., 1992). The first three sessions are focused on providing adolescents with information on violence and homicide. Activities involve discussions of the various types of violence, statistics, and risk factors (Prothrow-Stith, Spivak, & Hausman, 1987). The next set of lessons is concerned with the nature of violence. These classes help students think about their own method for dealing with anger, analyze the costs and benefits of fighting, and understand the steps that lead to violence. The final lessons focus on the different choices for handling conflicts. Role plays are used to enact real-life situations. In a small group process, students create and act out a mock fight. Each role play is videotaped, which provides the opportunity for the students to analyze and discuss how a violent situation is handled. After viewing the videotape, the students can determine the point at which each fight was instigated, the appropriate time to intervene, and how each fight could have been prevented. Through classroom discussions, the curriculum allows adolescents to think of, understand, and incorporate nonviolent strategies for leaving or avoiding violent situations (Prothrow-Stith & Weissman, 1991).

A second strategy of VPP involves a mass media campaign. Designed to raise public awareness of the violence problem, the campaign emphasizes the prominent issues surrounding violence. These issues include the extent to which violence is a problem for adolescents, the risks associated with carrying guns, the serious consequences of fighting, and the role that friends have in defusing or escalating conflicts. The media campaign features the theme, "Fighting is a lousy way to lose a friend. Friends for life, don't let friends fight." A primary component of the campaign is public service announcements that receive citywide television coverage. Two 30-second broadcasts on local stations present facts on the risks of violence. In conjunction with the television announcements, the campaign also created and distributed T-shirts, brochures, and posters advertising the theme. Once implemented across the community, the media component was evaluated along with the rest of the program to determine its effectiveness (Hausman et al., 1995).

Collaborative Approach

A key aspect of VPP is the comprehensive approach within the community and the collaborative approach with community members. The project maintains ongoing communication with community residents and service providers, which represent multiple disciplines and diverse populations. The use of service providers to deliver the educational curriculum ensures ethical and ethnic sensitivity (Prothrow-Stith et al., 1987). VPP is therefore implemented on various levels and in a variety of forms within the community. The program targets various agencies to serve as sites for implementing the program. These agencies include schools, youth organizations, churches, neighborhood health centers, and multiservice centers. The VPP format can be modified to accommodate the setting. The result is the use of one program with a variety of formats that range for the full 10-session format to special activities based on individual lessons (Hausman et al., 1992).

Implemented in Boston, VPP has taken on a comprehensive approach in the community through efforts that link various agencies and integrate multiple disciplines. Partnerships within the community have become an integral part of Boston's VPP. In addition to service providers and educators, health care workers are involved in the program. A multidisciplinary "Victim Care Services" team, which is made up of health care workers, has been created and incorporated into the program. Through the Boston City Hospital, health care workers identify patients who have been injured in an intentional violent act and contact them while they are still receiving treatment. Once this population has been reached, appropriate referrals can be made to community agencies for further services. While in the hospital, the patient can receive education regarding violence (U.S. Department of Justice, 1996).

Baseline Data

In an effort to determine the potential effects of VPP, baseline data were collected on adolescents' knowledge of, attitudes toward, and experience with violence. The data were collected through a random telephone survey of over 400 teens located across neighborhoods within Boston. A professional survey research group conducted the survey in 1987 as part of the VPP evaluation. Results of the survey indicated considerable fighting behavior among girls. While boys were shown to be more often involved in violence, almost one fourth (23%) of the girls reported fighting. The data revealed that fighting is a problem for both sexes. Participation in fights was not shown to be statistically significant between the various races, which is not consistent with other forms of violence.

According to the survey, 69% of the respondents reported witnessing a violent act, and African American teens witnessed more
violence than Caucasian teens. In addition, African American teens
also reported experiencing threats more often, and boys in general
were threatened significantly more often than girls. Despite the
racial differences, African American teens were not shown to be
involved in fighting more often than Caucasians. The results of the
knowledge scores for the overall sample was .67, with 1 being the
total possible score. The score is considered slightly better than a
passing grade, suggesting that there is a need to improve adolescents' knowledge of violence and their understanding of risk factors. The attitudes scores reveal that three quarters of the
participants believe that fights can be avoided. Despite this belief,
the adolescents lack the knowledge of behavioral alternatives. The
regression analysis indicates a positive relationship between adolescents' knowledge and attitudes and their experience with violence.
These results imply knowledge about violence is developed from
experience with violence. The baseline data provide significant
guidance to violence prevention activities by targeting the critical
areas for change (Hausman, Spivak, & Prothrow-Stith, 1994).

Evaluation

A second survey was conducted one year later to determine the
impact of VPP and evaluate the program's effectiveness. Results of
the second survey were compared to the baseline survey that was
conducted before teens had exposure to the prevention program.
The evaluation results indicate that greater knowledge can be
predicted by the exposure to the media campaign. The knowledge
scores from the second survey reveal significantly higher scores for
teens exposed to the campaign than for teens who were not exposed
to the campaign. In addition, the knowledge scores associated with
the exposed teens in the second survey are shown to be somewhat
higher than the knowledge scores found in the original survey. It
was found that the attitude scores revealed in the second survey for
boys not exposed to the media campaign were lower than scores
for girls or exposed boys. The analysis reports that exposure to the
media campaign had the most significant effect on boys among both
races. Overall, high scores in knowledge and attitudes were shown

to be significantly associated with the self-reported measures of exposure to the media campaign (Hausman et al., 1995).

In a separate evaluation, the *Violence Prevention Curriculum for Adolescents* was assessed according to its impact on adolescents' knowledge and attitudes concerning violence, as well as their self-reported behavior. The evaluation was conducted by the Education Development Center during the 1987-1988 school year, and the results were collected from one urban high school in each of the following cities: Compton, California; Houston, Texas; New York; Gary, Indiana; and Philadelphia. The data indicate the 10-session curriculum was found to have a positive effect on the students. More specifically, the data reveal that students who received the curriculum reported being involved in fewer fights throughout the past week as compared with the results found among students in the comparison classes. This result is considered "marginally significant" and is therefore interpreted cautiously. The individual evaluation results among the cities shows that students who experienced the curriculum in Houston received higher scores on the knowledge tests as compared to the comparison classes. The posttest results for students in the Philadelphia class who received the curriculum indicated that the teens were involved in fewer recent arrests. In a measure of self-esteem, the Philadelphia students reported higher scores. When determining who is responsible for preventing fights, students exposed to the curriculum in both cities were less likely to agree that other people bear the responsibility rather than themselves (DeJong, Spiro, Wilson-Brewer, Vince-Whitman, & Prothrow-Stith, n.d.).

Discussion

In conclusion, VPP was shown to have great potential in preventing violence. Together, the media campaign and the curriculum increased the participants' level of knowledge concerning violence, improved their attitudes toward violent behavior, and achieved improved behavior through fewer reports of fighting and arrests. The sustained effects of the program may be more apparent with a longitudinal evaluation. To create a better understanding of the long-range effects of VPP, an evaluation is needed that continues beyond the period of one year. Sufficient time is needed for the program to be implemented and for evaluators to observe the program's effects. In addition, a critical review of VPP has shown it to be grounded in theory. However, a theoretical foundation for the *Violence Prevention Curriculum for Adolescents* was not found in the curriculum materials. As stated earlier in the chapter, a theory provides a knowledge base that guides a program through an understanding of how violence develops, how learning can be used to prevent violence, and valuable information on the etiology of violence. The effects of the curriculum could be better understood with a strong theoretical backing.

Directions for Future Research and Program Development

A review of past and current violence prevention efforts clearly indicates the need for a committed, long-term effort by the community. While the programs described in this chapter are promising, they can benefit from a stronger commitment to research. The following paragraphs offer directions for the success of future community-based violence prevention efforts.

Strong Program Evaluations

There exists a strong need for long-term evaluations of community-based violence prevention programs. Community-based programs are very popular, as can be seen by the large numbers of existing programs appearing all over. Many of these programs, however, lack strong, empirical evaluations. In order to increase the strength of evaluation in prevention efforts, there needs to be support by policymakers and funding sources. In addition, the professionals who are developing and implementing violence prevention programs need to recognize the importance of evaluation and to incorporate the evaluation process into the prevention effort. One possible solution is to make outcome evaluations a requirement for financial support. It is then assumed that ineffective programs would not receive future financial support. In reality, however, evaluations are often not conducted, and programs often receive funding when it has not been determined if they are actually effective. Not only is this a waste of time, but communities are also led to believe they are reducing their violence problem when, in reality, they aren't. Therefore, the potential cost of not evaluating all programs is far too high to avoid investing in evaluations (Tolan & Guerra, 1994).

Use Existing Knowledge in Practice

Another recommendation for community-based violence prevention efforts is to review what we already know and put it to use. Although additional research is needed, there already exists adequate research to impact the violence epidemic effectively. Scientists and practitioners have researched the nature of violence as well as the nature of prevention. Programs have been and are currently being developed and implemented. We have information on which programs are effective, which are not, and what factors play a role in the success or failure of a program. The problem arises when communities and researchers do not implement what prevention experts are telling us. We need to put what we know about violence and community-based prevention efforts into practice. For example, we know that program evaluations can improve the results of a program. Even successful programs can benefit from evaluation efforts in the sense that they can find out how to make the program better. Professionals need to work with communities to understand the current knowledge on community-based violence prevention efforts and implement effective programs (Faenza & McElhaney, 1997).

Policy Initiative

A strong initiative needs to be taken by local, state, and federal governments that addresses the severity of violence and the importance of prevention. Although it is seen as a challenge, it is possible to develop and implement public policies that lead to violence prevention. Just as violence has been a long-standing problem for many years, it will take a long-standing effort to reduce its powerful impact on American communities. Sustained, coordinated efforts will be needed at many levels in the community. Strong polices can help guide this mission of creating safer communities (Mercy et al., 1993). There are many levels on which polices can be implemented. Policies addressing housing can impact violence through deconcentrating the geographic location of low-income families. Through the development of stronger policing policies, the government/ police can respond better to a community's needs (Roth, 1994). On a larger scale, national criminal and juvenile justice policies need to include prevention as a critical element. Policies need to reflect the government's recognition that enforcement alone is not a powerful enough force to reduce violence (Hawkins, 1995). The implementation of policies should increase, strengthen, and support prevention efforts. Policy is needed to provide consistent support to community-based prevention programs, thereby eliminating sporadic funding and inconsistent delivery of program services (Faenza & McElhaney, 1997).

Conclusion

The knowledge that can be gained from this chapter as well as other violence prevention materials identifies the serious nature of violence and the role of community-based prevention strategies. The material in this chapter discusses the tools necessary to implement an effective community-based violence prevention program. By recognizing the power of prevention, it is possible to take an optimist's view in believing that violence can and will be reduced. One reason for this optimism is the fact that we are learning more about violence. Professionals are becoming involved and identifying new solutions. Communities are recognizing their ability to help overcome the violence problem. More and more community residents, leaders, professionals, and advocates are becoming involved and working together as a group united for the accomplishment of a common goal: an end to violence in our communities. We may not see a violence-free America in the near future, but as awareness of the issue increases, as more people become involved, and as additional research is conducted, we are one step closer to reducing violence. Our mission as health professionals, law officers, educators, and community residents is to create a safe and healthy society in which we and our children can maintain peaceful, happy lives. In concluding this chapter, we present you with a challenge: Get involved! Use the information provided in this chapter and take action in your community to implement an effective community-based violence prevention program.

References

Bandura, A. (1977). Self-efficacy: Toward a unifying theory of behavioral change. *Psychological Review, 84*(2), 191-215.

Bandura, A. (1986). *Social foundations of thought and action: A social cognitive theory.* Englewood Cliffs, NJ: Prentice Hall.

DeJong, W., Spiro, A., III, Wilson-Brewer, R., Vince-Whitman, C., & Prothrow-Stith, D. (n.d.). *Evaluation summary: Violence prevention curriculum for adolescents.* Newton, MA: Educational Development Center.

Developmental Research and Programs, Inc. (1993). *Communities that care: Risk and protective factor-focused prevention using the social development strategy.* (Available from author at 130 Nickerson, Suite 107, Seattle, WA 98109)

Elliott, D. S. (1994). *Youth violence: An overview* (Center Paper 008). Boulder, CO: Center for the Study and Prevention of Violence.

Faenza, M. M., & McElhaney, S. J. (1997). Epilogue: Reframing prevention advocacy and looking ahead. In G. W. Albee & T. P. Gullotta (Eds.), *Primary prevention works* (Issues in Children's and Families' Lives, Vol. 6, pp. 401-410). Thousand Oaks, CA: Sage.

Farrell, A. D., & Meyer, A. L. (1997). *Evaluation of Responding in Peaceful and Positive Ways (RIPP): A school-based prevention program for reducing violence among urban adolescents.* Richmond: Virginia Commonwealth University.

Farrell, A. D., Meyer, A. L., & Dahlberg, L. L. (1996). Richmond Youth Against Violence: A school-based program for urban adolescents. *American Journal of Preventive Medicine, 12*(Suppl. 5), 13-21.

Greene, R. R., & Ephross, P. H. (1991). *Human behavior and social work practice.* Hawthorne, NY: Walter de Gruyter.

Harachi, T. W., Ayers, C. D., Hawkins, J. D., Catalano, R. F., & Cushing, J. (1996). Empowering communities to prevent adolescent substance abuse: Process evaluation results from a risk- and protection-focused community mobilization effort. *Journal of Primary Prevention, 16*(3), 233-254.

Hausman, A. J., Spivak, H., & Prothrow-Stith, D. (1994). Adolescents' knowledge and attitudes about and experience with violence. *Journal of Adolescent Health, 15*(5), 400-406.

Hausman, A. J., Spivak, H., & Prothrow-Stith, D. (1995). Evaluation of a community-based youth violence prevention project. *Journal of Adolescent Health, 17*(6), 353-359.

Hausman, A. J., Spivak, H., Prothrow-Stith, D., & Roeber, J. (1992). Patterns of teen exposure to a community-based violence prevention project. *Journal of Adolescent Health, 13*(8), 668-675.

Hawkins, J. D. (1995, August). Controlling crime before it happens: Risk-focused prevention. *National Institute of Justice Journal,* pp. 10-18.

Hawkins, J. D., Catalano, R. F., & Miller, J. Y. (1992). Risk and protective factors for alcohol and other drug problems in adolescence and early adulthood: Implications for substance abuse prevention. *Psychological Bulletin, 112*(1), 64-105.

Howell, J. C. (Ed.). (1995). *Guide for implementing the comprehensive strategy for serious, violent and chronic juvenile offenders* (NCJ Publication No. 153681).

Washington, DC: U.S. Department of Justice, Office of Juvenile Justice and Delinquency Prevention.

Longres, J. F. (1995). *Human behavior in the social environment* (2nd ed.). Itasca, IL: F. E. Peacock.

Mercy, J. A., Rosenberg, M. L., Powell, K. E., Broome, C. V., & Roper, W. L. (1993). Public health policy for preventing violence. *Health Affairs, 12*(4), 7-29.

Meyer, A. L., & Farrell, A. D. (1997). *Social skills training to promote resilience in urban sixth-grade students: One product of an action research strategy to prevention of youth violence in high-risk environments.* Richmond: Virginia Commonwealth University.

National Center for Injury Prevention and Control. (1993). *The prevention of youth violence: A framework for community action.* Atlanta, GA: Centers for Disease Control and Prevention.

Peterson, P. L., Hawkins, J. D., & Catalano, R. F. (1992). Evaluating comprehensive community drug risk reduction interventions. *Evaluation Review, 16*(6), 579-602.

Powell, K. E., Dahlberg, L. L., Friday, J., Mercy, J. A., Thorton, T., & Crawford, S. (1996). Prevention of youth violence: Rationale and characteristics of 15 evaluation projects. *American Journal of Preventive Medicine, 12*(Suppl. 5), 3-12.

Prothrow-Stith, D. (1987). *Violence prevention curriculum for adolescents.* Newton, MA: Education Development Center.

Prothrow-Stith, D., Spivak, H., & Hausman, A. J. (1987). The Violence Prevention Project: A public health approach. *Science, Technology, and Human Values, 12,* 67-69.

Prothrow-Stith, D., & Weissman, M. (1991). *Deadly consequences.* New York: HarperCollins.

Rosenstock, I. M. (1990). The health belief model: Explaining health behavior through expectations. In K. Glanz, F. M. Lewis, & B. K. Rimer (Eds.), *Health behavior and health education* (pp. 39-62). San Francisco: Jossey-Bass.

Roth, J. A. (1994, February). Understanding and preventing violence. *Research in brief* (NCJ Publication No. 145645). Washington, DC: National Institute of Justice.

Royse, D. R., & Thyer, B. A. (1996). *Program evaluation: An introduction.* Chicago: Nelson-Hall.

Tolan, P. H., & Guerra, N. G. (1994). *What works in reducing adolescent violence: An empirical review of the field.* Boulder, CO: Center for the Study and Prevention of Violence.

U.S. Department of Justice. (1996). *Youth violence a community-based response: One city's success story* (NIJ Publication No. 162601). Washington, DC: Author.

Epilogue

MICHAEL M. FAENZA

SANDRA J. McELHANEY

In the time it has taken to write this book, thousands have lost their lives to senseless acts of violence. The dramatic and bloodier acts are familiar to anyone who views television or reads the newspaper. Recently, the school shootings in Jonesboro, Arkansas, and Edinboro, Pennsylvania, captured the nation's attention as reporters rehashed the incidents, interviewed survivors, and speculated about the causes of these tragedies. In short order, the coverage came to a halt as the media turned their attention to covering other events, only to return for the next gruesome killing. One wonders when it might end? We would answer, when the recommendations made by the authors of these chapters are acted upon.

As the nation's oldest and largest grassroots citizen advocacy organization concerned with mental health and mental illness, the National Mental Health Association (NMHA) recognizes the compelling need—indeed the moral imperative—for individuals and organizations representing all facets of society to work actively in states and communities to foster the mind-set necessary to bring an end to violence and to promote peace. As Faenza and his colleagues point out in Chapter 7, NMHA itself was founded in response to violence that was imposed upon the organization's founder, Clifford Beers, a consumer of mental health services nearly 100 years ago. Suffering from manic depression, Beers was hospitalized in the Connecticut State asylum where he was kicked, beaten, and spat upon by the very individuals who were his "caretakers." Despite this treatment, Beers managed to overcome his illness and dedicated the rest of his life to establishing a national organization committed to ensuring social justice for children and adults with mental health needs. Thus, NMHA's very mission of "Working for America's Mental Health and Victory Over Mental Illness" cannot be accomplished without prompt action to quell what public health officials describe as a national epidemic of violence.

Drawing upon the work of the Mental Health Association in Montgomery County, Maryland, whose Voices VS Violence Program has mobilized the community to overcome cultural and other barriers to work to ensure safer lives for children by fostering attitudes and behaviors that prevent and reduce violence in workplaces, communities, schools, and families, NMHA in 1996 developed a position statement on violence in America based on the following two underlying values:

1. We must promote a national mind-set in which violence, be it in the home, on the streets, at work, at school, and as entertainment is simply unacceptable.
2. We must develop social policy, health care, human services, and community supports for children and families that promote individual health, healthy and secure communities, and ultimately prevent violence.

Given NMHA's rich tradition of advocacy for social change, building community coalitions, promoting coordination among health and human service agencies, and investment in prevention, the following strategies are emphasized:

- Development of effective, comprehensive human services systems
- Strengthened, comprehensive community mental health services to all citizens in need
- Coalition building and community problem solving
- Public education about solutions to violence
- Dissemination of the best practices and model programs targeting risk reduction, coping skills, peaceful conflict resolution, and competency development

Drawing from the NMHA position statement and the writings of chapter authors, we further recommend that societal leaders at all levels must make the elimination of violence a top priority. Furthermore, the following specific recommendations are suggested:

1. Regular postpartum home visits by trained professionals to provide health information, teach parenting skills including anger management, and give well-baby care, while taking the opportunity to detect signs of possible child abuse, are encouraged for all high-risk parents. (Chapter 1, Kotch, Muller, & Blakley)

2. The development and dissemination of protocols that would help in the prevention, identification, reporting, treatment, and referral of victims of family violence is encouraged. Such protocols should be age appropriate and emphasize the skills necessary to identify and treat victims of family violence in a sensitive and supportive manner. (Chapter 2, Hampton, Vandergriff-Avery, & Kim)

3. Employers are encouraged to create workplace environments that enhance employee safety. (Chapter 3, McClure)

4. Violence must be addressed from the public health perspective. Accordingly, approaches to end violence must include coalition and collaborative efforts focused on advocacy, public education, and preventive services. (Chapter 4, Potter)

5. The entertainment media must reduce the portrayal of violence in movies, television, music, and video games, and especially avoid presenting violence as an acceptable solution to conflict. (Chapter 5, Jason, Hanaway, & Brackshaw)

6. Policies and sufficiently funded programs are needed to address societal factors (i.e., hatred, prejudice, and racism) that foster violence in our society. (Chapter 6, Winborne & Cohen)

7. The violent victimization of persons with mental illness who are in mental institutions, homeless, or incarcerated in jails and penitentiaries must be stopped. (Chapter 7, Faenza, Glover, Hutchings, & Radack)

8. Programs to teach children social skills for avoiding violence and nonviolent means to express anger and meet other needs are encouraged. Such approaches should incorporate culturally competent and validated approaches to building social competence, problem-solving skills, and instilling a sense of purpose or future. (Chapter 8, Flannery & Williams)

9. Services to victims of domestic violence must expand their coordination across agencies and plan for future sustainability of programs and services. One important focus of service provision must be in

organizing communities so that individuals and families can live in safety. (Chapter 9, Jenkins & Davidson)

10. Available community-based programs to reduce violence must be rigorously evaluated and implemented. Research must be ongoing to determine the most effective means of addressing violence. (Chapter 10, McElhaney & Effley)

Together, these steps will reduce the incidence of violent behavior in our society.

Author Index

Subject Index

About the Editors

Thomas P. Gullotta, M.A., M.S.W., is CEO of the Child and Family Agency. He currently is the editor of the *Journal of Primary Prevention.* For Sage, he serves as a general series book editor for *Advances in Adolescent Development,* and is the senior book series editor for *Issues in Children's and Families' Lives.* He serves as the series editor for *Prevention in Practice.* In addition, he holds editorial appointments on the *Journal of Early Adolescence, Adolescence* and the *Journal of Educational and Psychological Consultation.* He serves on the Board of the National Mental Health Association and is an adjunct faculty member in the psychology department of Eastern Connecticut State University. He has published extensively on adolescents and primary prevention.

Sandra J. McElhaney, M.A., joined the staff of the National Mental Health Association (NMHA) in 1989. Trained as a community counselor, she provides national leadership for all NMHA activities related to the prevention of mental and emotional disorders and the promotion of mental health, including collaborations with other national organizations and provision of information and technical assistance to the Mental Health Association network of 325 affiliates in implementing validated prevention programs. McElhaney is Staff Director to the National Prevention Coalition, a coalition of national organizations that works with Congress and federal agencies to advance prevention concerns. In 1994 McElhaney was appointed as National Director of the NMHA *Voices VS Violence* Campaign, a multiyear initiative to provide communities across the nation with information and resources to form *Voices VS Violence* coalitions that will work to educate the public and implement programs to prevent and reduce the violence that is permeating our nation's streets, homes, playgrounds, workplaces, and media.

About the Contributors

Craig H. Blakely, Ph.D., M.P.H., is the interim head of the Department of Health Policy and Management at the School of Rural Public Health and the Associate Director of the Public Policy Research Institute at Texas A&M University. He has conducted extensive policy work in maternal and child health, including evaluations of several statewide interventions (e.g., Michigan's original Prenatal Care Program and Texas's Maternal and Infant Health Improvement Act). He has evaluated Texas's Medicaid Managed Care Waivers program and the state's Medical Transportation Services program. He conducts Texas's biannual, statewide immunization prevalence studies, and he has been involved in numerous state and national substance abuse prevention efforts. He has published numerous articles in these fields.

Ester Brackshaw received her undergraduate degree from DePaul University, where she majored in psychology. She worked with Leonard A. Jason for several years on a series of evaluations of devices to reduce TV viewing among children who watch an excessive amount of TV.

Renae Cohen is Senior Program and Policy Research Analyst at The National Conference for Community and Justice, a human relations organization founded in 1927 as The National Conference of Christians and Jews dedicated to fighting bias, bigotry, and racism in America. She is responsible for the management and design of its research activities. Before that she was Senior Research Analyst at the American Jewish Committee. She has published in a number of areas, including intergroup relations and anti-Semitism, and has experience in national and international survey research. She is coeditor of *Intergroup Relations in the United States: Research Perspectives.* She received her Ph.D. in psychology from New York University.

321

Barbara Davidson is the Community Education/Training Coordinator for the Battered Women's Program in Baton Rouge, Louisiana. She received an MSW from Louisiana State University, and has been working with battered women for over 15 years. She has written several articles and was commissioned by the Louisiana State Coalition Against Domestic Violence to write the training manual for shelter workers. She also created and has facilitated the Survivors of Domestic Violence Education and Leadership Group in the Louisiana Correctional Institute for Women in St. Gabriel, Louisiana for the past 12 years. She was also named coordinator for the Louisiana Clemency Project, a statewide effort to examine the cases of incarcerated women serving lengthy sentences for the death of an abusive partner. She is presently working on a book, with Pamela Jenkins, concerning the "best practice" models for agencies that encounter victims of domestic violence.

Michael M. Faenza, M.S.S.W., has been the President and CEO of the National Mental Health Association (NMHA) since 1994. Prior to joining NMHA, he directed the Dallas Mental Health Association for 5 years. He has also held clinical and management positions in vocational rehabilitation, child protective services, juvenile justice, and public sector mental health services. He received an M.S.S.W. from the University of Texas in Arlington where he served as an adjunct faculty member.

Daniel J. Flannery is Associate Professor of Criminal Justice Studies and Director of the Institute for the Study and Prevention of Violence at Kent State University, as well as an Associate Professor of Pediatrics at University Hospitals of Cleveland. His research focuses on developmental psychopathology and youth violence. He serves on the editorial board of several adolescent and family journals. He is author of *School Violence: Risk, Preventive Intervention and Policy* (1997) for the ERIC Clearinghouse on Urban Education, and coeditor (with C. R. Huff) of the forthcoming volume *Youth Violence: Prevention, Intervention and Social Policy.* He is principal investigator of a longitudinal study of youth violence prevention funded by the Centers for Disease Control and Prevention.

Robert W. Glover, Ph.D., has been the Executive Director of the National Association of State Mental Health Program Directors (NASMHPD) since 1993. Prior to this position, he served as Commissioner of the Department of Mental Health & Mental Retardation in

Maine for 3 years and also worked in several states' Mental Health Departments, including Colorado, Idaho, Pennsylvania, and Ohio. He is a licensed Psychologist in Ohio and received his Ph.D. in Clinical Psychology from Ohio State University.

Robert L. Hampton, Ph.D., is Associate Provost for Academic Affairs and Dean for Undergraduate Studies, Professor of Family Studies, and Professor of Sociology at the University of Maryland, College Park. He is a Gimbel Mentoring Scholar. He has published extensively in the field of family violence, including five edited books: *Violence in the Black Family: Correlates and Consequences; Black Family Violence: Current Research and Theory; Family Violence: Prevention and Treatment; Preventing Violence in America;* and *Child Welfare: Bridging Perspectives.* He is completing a second edition of *Family Violence: Prevention and Treatment.* He is one of the founders of the Institute on Domestic Violence in the African American Community. His research interests include partner violence, family abuse, community violence, and institutional responses to violence.

Libby Kennedy Hanaway received her master's degree in history from DePaul University. She is coauthor of the book *Remote Control: A Sensible Approach to Kids, TV and the New Electronic Media.* She and Leonard A. Jason have collaborated on several projects involving children and TV over the past 6 years.

Gail P. Hutchings, M.P.A., is Deputy Executive Director of NASMHPD. She was formerly the Assistant Director of the National Technical Assistance Center for State Mental Health Planning, a project sponsored by NASMHPD and the federal Center for Mental Health Services, and Assistant Director of the National Resource Center on Homelessness and Mental Illness. She graduated with honors from the State University of New York at Albany and holds a master's degree in public administration.

Leonard A. Jason, Ph.D., is a Professor of Clinical and Community Psychology at DePaul University. He is a coauthor of the book *Remote Control: A Sensible Approach to Kids, TV and the New Electronic Media.* He has written over 275 research articles and written or edited 10 books. He has received over six and a half million dollars from federal sources to support his research.

Pamela Jenkins is Associate Professor of Sociology at the University of New Orleans. Her work has focused on violence and the institutional response to behavior. She has published numerous articles and book chapters examining the effect of violence on victims and describing the institutional response. She is presently involved in several community efforts to change the norms and values about violence. Also, she has been involved in training law enforcement concerning domestic violence throughout Louisiana. She has developed domestic violence training manuals for law enforcement in Louisiana in partnership with law enforcement agencies. She is currently working on a manuscript with Barbara Davidson that describes the "best practice" models for agencies who encounter victims of domestic violence.

Joan Kim is a medical student at the University of California, Berkeley-UC San Francisco Joint Medical Program, with interests in family, child, and minority health issues. She has previous research experience in homelessness and federally funded services for children, youth, and families.

Jonathan B. Kotch, M.D, M.P.H., is Professor and Associate Chair for Graduate Studies of the Department of Maternal and Child Health, School of Public Health, University of North Carolina at Chapel Hill. Board Certified in both Pediatrics and Preventive Medicine, he has been active in scholarly and policy-oriented activity addressing access to and quality of maternity care, child maltreatment, unintentional child injury, prevention of low-birth weight, and health and safety in child care. Currently, he is undertaking longitudinal research in child abuse and neglect with funding from the Children's Bureau of the Administration for Children and Families, USDHHS. His LONGSCAN project is one of five cooperating longitudinal studies of the etiology and consequences of child maltreatment. He is Chair of the Maternal and Child Health Section of the American Public Health Association.

Lynne F. McClure has been President of McClure Associates Management Consultants, Inc. in Tempe, Arizona, since 1980. She specializes in work relationships and managing conflict, change, and stress. She is the author of *Risky Business: Managing Employee Violence in the Workplace* (1996). She consults for technical and service corporations, government agencies, and small businesses. On a volunteer basis, she gives workshops for social service agencies.

Kathryn M. Effley is a Grant Specialist for Goodwill Industries in Sarasota, Florida. She received her bachelor's degree in family, child, and consumer science from Louisiana State University, and her master's degree in social work from The Catholic University of America. Her work at the National Mental Health Association included research on the issues of mental health needs in the juvenile justice system and community-based violence prevention programs. Her past experience includes providing counseling to children of alcoholics and conducting community needs assessments in Sarasota, Florida.

Greg O. Muller, M.S, A.B.D., is the Director of School-to-Careers at Snow College in Utah and the interim Executive Director of the Center for Community and Family Support. He has completed various studies related to child health issues, including a 3-year national study of adolescent social and religious development, and a 3-year mentor-intervention project that targeted at-risk children within the school and family contexts. He has reviewed proposals for the Department of Education's Safe and Drug-Free Schools Program and for the Substance Abuse and Mental Health Services Administration on a wide range of children's health issues.

Lloyd B. Potter, Ph.D., M.P.H., is the Leader of Youth Violence Prevention in the Division of Violence Prevention, National Center for Injury Prevention and Control, Centers for Disease Control and Prevention (CDC), in Atlanta, Georgia. He is a graduate of Texas A&M University (B.S., sociology), the University of Houston (M.S., education), the University of Texas at Austin (Ph.D., sociology and demography), and Emory University School of Public Health (M.P.H., epidemiology). Before coming to the Centers for Disease Control and Prevention, he worked at Texas A&M University and the University of Texas at Austin as a research associate, at Fordham University as an assistant professor of sociology, and at Emory University School of Public Health as a postdoctoral fellow. Since coming to CDC permanently in 1993, he has been responsible for management of all suicide prevention research and programmatic activities. In 1995, he assumed additional responsibilities for management of all youth violence prevention research and programmatic activities at CDC. His research interests include risk factor identification, and evaluation of prevention programs.

James A. Radack is the NMHA director of media relations. He previously worked as an aide to District of Columbia Mayor Sharon Pratt Kelly. He received a B.A. in history from Georgetown University.

Maria Vandergriff-Avery received her master's degree from the University of Tennessee, Knoxville and is currently a doctoral student in family studies at the University of Maryland, College Park. Her current research interests include marital power, work and family issues, and gender roles.

Laura Williams is a doctoral candidate in the Department of Psychology at Case Western University. Her research interests include adolescent coping and the impact of exposure to violence on television.

Wayne Winborne is Director of Program and Policy Research at The National Conference for Community and Justice, a human relations organization founded in 1927 as The National Conference of Christians and Jews dedicated to fighting bias, bigotry, and racism in America. He is responsible for its research activities, particularly relating to public policy development and programmatic development, implementation, and evaluation; as well as for administrative oversight of the Program and Research Units. He has had numerous publications and presentations on issues of intergroup relations, voting rights and voting behavior, and race and public policy. He is coeditor of *Intergroup Relations in the United States: Research Perspectives*. He holds degrees from Stanford and New York University.